LANGUAGE MINORITY STUDENTS IN AMERICAN SCHOOLS

An Education in English

ESL and Applied Linguistics Professional Series
Eli Hinkel, Series Editor

To order please call our toll free number: 1-800-926-6579,
or visit us online at www.erlbaum.com

LANGUAGE MINORITY STUDENTS IN AMERICAN SCHOOLS

An Education in English

H. D. Adamson
University of Arizona

LEA LAWRENCE ERLBAUM ASSOCIATES, PUBLISHERS
2005 Mahwah, New Jersey   London

Permissions

Grateful acknowledgment is made to the following for permission to reprint previously published material:

Cambridge University Press: Excerpt from *Corpus Linguistics: Investigating Language Structure and Use* by D. Biber, S. Conrad, & R. Reppen. Reprinted with permission of Cambridge University Press.

Georgetown University Press: Excerpt from *Variation and Change in Alabama English* by Crawford Feagin.

Lawrence Erlbaum Associates: Excerpt from *Text-based Learning and Reasoning* by C. A. Perfetti, M. A. Britt, & M. C. Georgi.

Wayne Thomas and Virginia Collier: Excerpt from *School Effectiveness for Language Minority Students* by Wayne Thomas & Virginia Collier.

Lawrence Erlbaum Associates, Inc., Publishers
10 Industrial Avenue
Mahwah, New Jersey 07430

Cover design by Kathryn Houghtaling Lacey

Library of Congress Cataloging-in-Publication Data

Adamson, H. D. (Hugh Douglas)
    Language minority students in American schools : an education in English / H. D. Adamson.
        p.   cm.
    Includes bibliographical references and index.
    ISBN 0-8058-4496-1 (c. : alk. paper) — ISBN 0-8058-4497-X (pbk. : alk. paper)
    1. Bilingual education—United States.   2. Linguistic minorities—Education—United States.   I. Title.

LC3731   2004
428.3′4—dc22
                                                2004040486
                                                CIP

Books published by Lawrence Erlbaum Associates are printed on acid-free paper, and their bindings are chosen for strength and durability.

Printed in the United States of America
10 9 8 7 6 5 4 3 2

This book is dedicated, with love,
to Alice, Marie, and Katie

Contents

List of Figures and Tables

Preface

Language education has been in the news in recent years. California, Arizona, and Massachusetts have passed constitutional amendments prohibiting bilingual education in most circumstances. *Newsweek* has reported that there is a war between the phonics and the whole language methods of teaching reading. The teaching of Black English, or Ebonics, is still controversial following the Oakland School Board's 1996 decision to require the use of this dialect in the schools. And, most recently, foreign language education has taken on new importance following President Bush's declaration of a long-term war against terrorism.

The public discussion of these topics has been characterized by much heat but little light. For example, the fight over California's Proposition 227, the antibilingual education amendment, was waged mainly between two public relations machines, with little input from language education scholars. Leading the charge against bilingual education was Ron Unz, a Silicon Valley millionaire who had been defeated for public office. Unz called his campaign "English for the Children," and built it around slogans and a few anecdotes of bad bilingual education experiences. The pro-bilingual education campaign was run by a public relations firm that decided to focus on the cost of implementing the amendment and the potential for lawsuits, rather than on how best to educate language minority children. Similarly, when the Oakland School Board proclaimed that Ebonics would be used in the schools, political comment drowned out any discussion of research or past experience involving the use of minority dialects in schools. The Reverend Jessie Jackson observed, "In Oakland some madness has erupted over making slang talk a second language. . . . You don't have to go to school to learn to talk garbage" (Fillmore, 1997). Later, Jackson reversed his position and supported the Board. The Linguistics Society of America, which was holding its annual convention in the Bay Area when the Ebonics proclamation was issued, produced a politically correct statement in support of the Oakland School Board that obscured rather than clarified some of the issues. In this book, I hope to shed some light on these controversies by drawing on the large body of research on language acquisition, language education, and my own experiences as an English teacher in Arizona, California, the Washington, D.C. area, Ethiopia, and Spain. In fact, I have not hesitated to inject my own opinions throughout the book, but I have tried to give all sides of the issues a fair hearing.

I have written this book mainly for students who are preparing to become teachers of English as a second language (ESL). Those who are in graduate programs will go far beyond the language acquisition theory and teaching methods introduced here, but often their training does not include a discussion of related educational scholarship, such as the teaching of reading, English as a second dialect, history, and mathematics. These topics are reviewed here and related to second language teaching. I hope that teachers of subjects other than ESL can profit from the book, as well. I am often asked by content area teachers who find themselves facing a class in which the majority of students do not speak English natively where they can learn something about the ESL field. This book, though it emphasizes theories more than classroom techniques, should be a good place to start.

Discussing controversial topics always involves the controversial use of language. Whether you call the creature in a woman's womb an "unborn child" or a "fetus" pretty much determines the outcome of any debate on abortion, and one judge decided to use the alternate terms on alternate days. I have chosen fairly traditional usage throughout the book, for example, *Black English* instead of *Ebonics* or *African American Vernacular English.* The traditional term for students who do not speak English natively is *limited English proficient* (LEP), but *lep* is the Greek root of the words *lepidoptera,* and *leprosy,* and it means "scaly." Perhaps for this reason it has an odd ring to it, and in this case I have chosen to use the more recent terms *language minority student,* and *English language learner* (or *ELL student*).

In chapter 1, I introduce myself and the ESL field by recounting experiences I have had teaching English in the United States and abroad. Teaching English in countries where other languages are dominant is called teaching English as a foreign language (EFL), and it can be quite different from teaching ESL, as I hope the discussion makes clear. Chapter 2 looks at theories of first and second language acquisition. According to Michael Long (1990), there are over 20 theories of second language acquisition alone, so I could not hope to even mention most of them. Rather, I have concentrated on three broad approaches to the study of language and language acquisition that have had a strong influence on the ESL field. Explaining language acquisition theory requires getting a bit technical and drawing a few sentence diagrams. But it is not necessary to follow this explanation to understand the argument I am making, and readers are invited to skip the technical sections of chapter 2 if they wish. Basically, I'm asking you to take my word for how language is acquired anyway.

Chapter 3 considers the relationship between the theories reviewed in chapter 2 and methods of language teaching. I take a historical approach, tracing the development of language acquisition theories and their applications in the classroom. I also attempt to show how the field of language teaching is related to broader research in education, including the fields of teaching reading and mathematics.

The focus of chapter 4 is teaching English as a second dialect, especially to speakers of Black English. In order to understand what a dialect is and how dialects differ, I consider the related topics of language variation, the history of English, grammar gurus, and the Ebonics controversy.

Chapter 5 focuses on the situation of ELL students in mainstream courses, beginning with theories of how content subjects are learned. This discussion continues the theme of chapter 3, pointing out how general theories of learning are related to theories of language learning.

In chapter 6, I attempt to flesh out the largely theoretical argument of the previous chapters by describing the learning experiences of three language minority students in a Tucson middle school.

Finally, chapter 7 discusses bilingual education, the sister discipline of ESL, briefly examining bilingual programs abroad, reviewing the research cited by advocates and opponents, and highlighting the relationship between bilingual teaching and ESL teaching.

ACKNOWLEDGMENTS

Thanks to my students and colleagues in the Interdisciplinary PhD Program in Second Language Acquisition and Teaching (SLAT) at the University of Arizona, especially Rudy Troike and Linda Waugh, for academic, moral, and material support. I owe a special debt to Muriel Saville-Troike for taking over my duties as Director of the SLAT Program so that I could go on sabbatical leave. Thanks also to Carol Evans and Richard Ruiz for insights regarding bilingual education. None of these colleagues is responsible for any of my shortcomings, scholarly or otherwise. I have used some of the material in the book in classes with SLAT students, and their comments have been most helpful, as were the comments of Erlbaum reviewers Mary Jeannot, Gonzaga University, and Duane Roen, Arizona State University.

Thanks especially to Ellen Courtney, the coauthor of chapter 6, and to Caroline Vickers, both of whom provided invaluable help as research assistants. Finally, *gracias de verdad* to the Cortez family and the faculty and students of Cholla Middle School (not their real names), whom we will meet in chapter 6. I would like to think that this book may be of some benefit to them.

A Personal Introduction

INTRODUCTION

My first glimpse of teaching English as a second language (ESL) occurred when, as a college freshman, I read Robert Graves' (1957) autobiography *Goodbye to All That*. Graves had barely survived the trenches of World War I, and after the war had been unable to find a decent job in England, so he applied for the position of Professor of English Literature at the Royal Egyptian University, Cairo. With the help of his friend, T. E. Lawrence (Lawrence of Arabia), Graves got the job, but it did not go as well as he had hoped. Graves taught only one class per week, but he describes it as "pandemonium":

> The students were not hostile, merely excitable and anxious to show their regard for me and liberty and Zaghlul Pasha and the well-being of Egypt—all at the same time. They obliged me to shout at the top of my loudest barracks-square voice, which I had learned to pitch high for greater carrying-power, in order to restore silence (p. 327).

Four years after reading these words, I was facing an equally exuberant group of students at the other end of the Nile River in Debra Marcos, Ethiopia, as a Peace Corps English teacher. And, yes, I took the position because it would delay for 2 years my serving in the trenches in Vietnam. Debra Marcos was a small city with electricity but no paved streets. King Teklehaimanot High School, where I taught, had some fairly nice stone buildings with tin roofs and hard dirt floors, but all of the windows, except those in the principal's office, were broken. One day in class I used a device to get the students' attention that was as desperate as Graves'. I was teaching the English present progressive tense to a ninth-grade class of about 40 students (I had 25 such classes per week). About half of the students wore shoes, and most of them had notebooks and pencils. They sat on benches, some with narrow tables in front of them, facing the blackboard. At the back of the room stood the two tallest boys in the class, who served as monitors. Each monitor carried a walking stick, and if discipline broke down, one of the monitors would come up behind the disturber and knock him on the head with his stick.

I was sick that day, as Peace Corps volunteers often were, but not sick enough to go home, so I decided to work my condition into the lesson.

"I am barfing. . . . Repeat."

"I am barfing," echoed the class.

"He . . . ," I said.

"He is barfing," they chorused, correctly changing the verb to agree with the new subject. I stuck my head out the door and barfed.

"What am I doing?" I asked.

"You are barfing," they answered, again correctly conjugating a new verb that I doubt they ever forgot.

Both Graves and I had mixed feelings about our work. On the one hand, we felt that teaching English was an honorable endeavor. In Graves' case, he had an abiding love of literature and even in those early years must have had some inkling of his theory (spelled out much later in Graves & Hodge, 1943, *The Reader Over Your Shoulder*) that literature, indeed art in all of its forms, has a mystical power to inspire and ennoble. In my case, I thought that reading and talking about literature was great fun, but I believed that a more important reason for teaching English to Ethiopians was that a knowledge of my mother tongue could help them develop their country economically. This was also the official position of the Ministry of Education and the Peace Corps.

At that time, English was taught as a subject in Ethiopian elementary schools, but the language used in all other classes was Amharic, the language spoken by Emperor Haile Selassie and the ruling Amhara tribe. Beginning in the seventh grade, English became the language of instruction, used to teach mathematics, science, European history, and world geography, as well as advanced courses in literature in the upper grades. Beyond elementary school, Amharic was used only to teach the literature and grammar of that language. No regional Ethiopian languages, such as Tigrinya or Arabic, were taught or officially recognized. I should mention that Ethiopia was then, and probably is still, the poorest country in the world. Only about 10% of the population attended public schools; a small number of students attended Coptic schools, training to be priests, and in Moslem areas many children attended Koranic schools. Less than 5% of the population attended high school, and perhaps 1% attended a college or technical training school. These facts suggest why English was the main language of instruction. First, there were few textbooks in Amharic, and even fewer trained Ethiopian teachers. The 15 high school teachers at King Teklehaimanot included about equal numbers of Peace Corp volunteers, Ethiopians (most of whom were university students doing a required year of national service), and East Indians, who had university degrees.

There was also a political reason for the focus on a European curriculum taught in English. Haile Selassie traced his ancestry and authority to the biblical alliance between King Solomon and the Queen of Sheba. According to Ethiopian legend, Solomon tricked Sheba into bed with him, and the result was a son named Menelik I, who, succeeding his mother, ruled Ethiopia from the northern city of Axum. From that time onward, the Emperor wielded both political and religious authority, and that tradition continued after the kingdom converted to Christianity in the 5th century. During the reign of Haile Selassie, power was wielded by a small Christian oligarchy. These traditionalists had no reason to change the country's feudal political system; what they wanted was to modernize certain sectors, especially the military and the police, without spreading dangerous Western ideas like democracy and liberal thought. The ruling class also wanted to educate a small group of technocrats, who could run the modest Western-style enterprises of the country, such as Ethiopian Airlines, maintain the utilities and office buildings in Addis Ababa, and otherwise make the country appear modern without changing the political structure.

As it turned out, the fears of the oligarchy were justified. When Marxist (and American-trained) Air Force officers toppled Haile Selassie in 1975, they arrested the heads of about 60 families and executed them in the basement of the royal palace, thus wiping out the ruling class. The Emperor, by then senile and long removed from real power, was allowed to wander the palace until he died later that year.

After living for a year in Debra Marcos, I moved north to Tigre Province, a non-Amhara area, and it was at this time that the political unrest that foreshadowed Haile Selassie's demise began to spread across the country. My students took advantage of the unstable political situation and voiced their opposition to the status quo. Morning assemblies in the schoolyard were often cut short when rocks thrown by students rained down on tin roofs, and the students and teachers ran for cover. To stop this practice, the Governor stationed troops at the school and, in protest, the Peace Corps volunteers resigned.

We weren't just upset about the troops. After almost 2 years in country, we had come to understand how the system of Western education and the teaching of English were working to preserve the status quo and frustrate the possibility of grassroots change—not just political but economic. Our students and their families didn't need to know new math, European history, and the English present progressive tense. What they needed were classes in basic sanitation, child care, food preservation, animal husbandry, and methods of irrigation that did not depend on outside materials and expertise. These subjects, along with basic literacy, should have been taught in the local languages. Our students needed an education that was relevant to their lives in towns and villages and not just to life in the capital city. Our belief in acting locally and appropriately was bolstered by observing development efforts, some of which became legends.

For example, the Rockefeller Foundation wanted to see what could be done to increase the harvest of *tef*, the local grain, in Tigre Province. The Tigre landscape is dry and rocky, but if the rains don't fail, it is possible to eke out a single *tef* harvest a year. When the rains fail, there is famine, and you have probably seen pictures of the results on television. Over the centuries, Ethiopian farmers had dug a lot of the rocks out of the soil and piled them up in stone fences, but the Rockefeller scientists thought it would be a good idea to dig up more rocks in order to open up more of the soil for planting. This was done at great effort, and the fields were ploughed and planted. But the *tef* harvest failed because the young plants froze. Long ago, the farmers had learned to leave enough rocks in the soil to conserve heat and prevent the ground from freezing. When more rocks were removed, the ground got too cold to grow *tef*.

While the American Peace Corps developed "human capital," the Swedish Peace Corps constructed school buildings using local materials. The Swedes, like most of the Europeans in Ethiopia, thought that the Ethiopian government should contribute something toward development projects, but getting money out of local officials was like getting a carcass away from a hyena. So, the Swedes decided to apply pressure by building schools but not turning them over to the government until some contribution had been received. The schools were attractive stone buildings with tin roofs and concrete floors. After they were completed, the buildings were locked up and guards were posted to protect them from vandals. When the Governor ponied up his 10% or 20% contribution, the locks would come off. Unfortunately, rather than budgeting money for the schools, the Governor sent out his soldiers to shake down the local landlords who, in turn, raised the quota of *tef* that their tenant farmers had to provide. Thus, the new school buildings turned out to be a burden as well as a blessing for the community.

Teaching English in Ethiopia was, by and large, a misguided development project. It was true that the country needed managers and technicians who were literate in English so that they could engage the country with the outside world, and my students were candidates for this elite class. But there just weren't that many Western-style jobs in the country, and many of the students wound up driving taxis or peddling souvenirs in Addis Ababa, frustrated that the promise on which they had based their lives had not been kept.

ORIENTALISM VERSUS ANGLICISM

The question of what should be the focus of education and the role of English in developing countries is an old one and was much debated by the British during the colonial era. Lord Macaulay argued for an education in English, in part because he believed that studying local languages and cultures was worthless. "A single shelf of a good European library [is] worth the whole native literature of India and Arabia," he said (Macaulay, 1835/1972, p. 241).

Linguistic imperialism in the 19th century, which of course involved the teaching of French, German, Dutch, and Italian as well as English, was linked to the moral imperative to spread Christianity and eradicate slavery. This missionary impulse has been called *anglicism*. A competing and historically prior view among the British was *orientalism*, the belief that colonial subjects should be educated in their own languages.[1] One motivation for orientalism was idealistic, the notion of Enlightenment philosophers like Rousseau of the noble savage, whose ways should be valued and preserved. Orientalists urged European administrators to learn local languages and cultures, and in 1800 a college was established in Calcutta to train East India Company bureaucrats from Britain in Indian languages and cultures. This move was opposed by middle-class Indians, who feared that using local languages in government would foster a linguistic ghetto from which they could not move on. They favored the use of English as an official language and the teaching of English to Indians as a way of improving their chances for advancement in the colonial government and throughout the Empire.

Another motivation for orientalism was practical. Some British administrators saw a danger in allowing locals to rise too high in the bureaucracy or to master the laws and customs of the governing country because their loyalty could not be assumed. Gandhi is a perfect example of a colonial subject who used his Western education to work against his Western masters. As one colonial administrator put it, "Whilst we teach children to read and write and count in their own languages . . . we are *safe*" (cited in Pennycook, 1998, p. 86).

---

[1] *Orientalism* has a broader and more sinister meaning that is explained by Edward M. Said (1979) in his book *Orientalism*. Here I use the term in the narrower sense meaning to advocate education in a local language focusing on a local culture.

Anglicism in Bilingual Education

The 19th-century debate about how to educate subjects of the Empire has echoes in the present-day debate about how to educate American citizens and residents who do not speak English proficiently. Some voices in this debate are clear counterparts to Macaulay, whereas their opponents, who advocate teaching minority languages and cultures, are like the orientalists. The two sides can be neatly divided by their position on bilingual education. Modern anglicists argue that minority languages and cultures are fine but that it is not the place of the schools to preserve them. In an early influential book, journalist Noel Epstein (1977), for example, said that sustaining children in an ethnic tradition is the proper duty of parents, churches, and civic associations, but not of public schools:

> Is the *national government* responsible for financing and promoting attachments to ethnic languages and cultures? Would federal intervention result in more harmony or more discord in American society? Would it lead to better or worse relations between groups? . . . Greater separation or integration? What is the federal role? (p. 70).

Epstein's position is echoed by the distinguished essayist and television commentator Richard Rodriguez, who started first grade in Sacramento speaking no English. Rodriguez refers to himself as a "scholarship boy," a term that originally referred to a colonial child chosen by British teachers to attend school in the provincial capital, where he would trade his native language and culture for the language and culture of Britain. Indeed, in his autobiography (Rodriguez, 1982), Rodriguez refers to his movement away from the culture of his family and into the general American culture as a "betrayal" (p. 30). Nevertheless, Rodriguez says that the tradeoff was worth it, and he opposes bilingual education. For Rodriguez, as for the Western-educated Indians of Calcutta, what matters is that children learn the language of public discourse: English. "A primary reason for my success in the classroom," he says, "was that . . . schooling was changing me, and separating me from the life I enjoyed before becoming a student" (Rodriguez, 1982, p. 45). And further, "Bilingual education is weighted at bottom . . . with middle-class romanticism" (1992, p. 352). He fears that the goal of educating children to be bilingual and bicultural is not realistic, and that if the romantics are wrong, language minority students will not learn English. "Dark-eyed children will sit in the classrooms. Mute" (1992, p. 354).

Some working-class Hispanic parents, sharing Rodriguez's beliefs, have opposed bilingual education, as some working-class African-American parents have opposed the teaching of Black English, or Ebonics. A recent poll by Public Agenda, a nonpartisan research organization, found that nationally 75% of recent immigrants oppose bilingual instruction, and as we shall see in chapter 4, when Ebonics readers were introduced in the 1970s, they were opposed by African-American parents and had to be discontinued.

I am in favor of using the mother tongue and mother dialect in education, as I make clear in chapters 4, 6, and 7, though I will try to give both sides a fair hearing. In the rest of this chapter, I describe some of my own experiences teaching language minority students that have convinced me of the value of a modern orientalist approach.

OPERATION SER

I was teaching ESL in an antipoverty program called Operation SER (*ser* means "to be" in Spanish), which took Hispanic kids who were at risk (i.e., they had flunked out of school, been sentenced to probation, or were on parole) and trained them in job skills, including printing press technology, upholstering, auto mechanics, and secretarial skills. The students also took academic classes that would lead to a GED certificate, the equivalent of a high school diploma. The school was residential—it provided full room and board—and the students were paid a good wage as long as they made progress. I taught them reading and Mexican-American history. The school was located in the barrio of San Jose, California, called *Sal Si Puedes*, "Get out if you can," and most of the students were trying hard to get out. I remember one boy in particular, Victor, who told me that he didn't have much interest in the academic aspects of the program, but he could see that Operation SER graduates got decent jobs with good salaries and that getting such a job would allow him to concentrate on things that were more important to him. Victor wanted to take care of business at school. When some students were grumbling about having to watch a filmstrip about migrant workers in California, he said, "We got to understand how the Man is rippin' off our brothers." I doubt that Victor felt much solidarity with migrant workers, but he did want to get the class back on task and to get through the program without any trouble.

All of the teachers and administrators at Operation SER were Hispanic except me, and most of them spoke Spanish. However, many of the students did not. Probably for this reason, there wasn't much Spanish in the official curriculum—only a course in Spanish for native speakers, which taught basic literacy. Nevertheless, the Spanish language was heard everywhere at school. Out-of-class conversations in Spanish were almost as common as those in English, and many of the staff and students code-switched, beginning a sentence in English *y terminando en español*. Most of the teachers used Spanish freely in class on an individual basis when a Spanish-speaking student didn't understand something, and many would address the class in Spanish, though never for long, and always with an English translation. As discussed in chapter 7, this method now has a fancy name: *bilingual structured immersion*.

The English heard at Operation SER was usually Spanish accented, and I believe that this fact was important to the program's success. This variety of English was just one aspect of the Mexican-American culture that permeated the school and eased the transition from home. Victor and the other students struggled with literature, history, and math, but these strange subjects were mediated by the familiar culture and ways of speaking. Operation SER was an Hispanic enterprise that taught academics on its own terms. The goals and methods of the school were set by its Latino administrators, and this fact was apparent to the students. Although English was the language of instruction, it did not threaten the students' home culture and language. Under these circumstances, teaching English literacy, even to some pretty tough kids, was not only possible, but fun.

An important aspect of my reading class at Operation SER was that I had considerable control over the curriculum. Operation SER wanted the students to be able to read well enough to pass the GED exam, but there was no pressure to read Shakespeare, Maya Angelou, or any other specific author. I could choose books my students liked, or better yet, let them choose the books. My first goal was to get the kids reading and enjoying books. With 50 dollars (which went a lot further in those days), I went to a used bookstore and stocked up on popular fiction: romance novels, James Bond, paperbacks with lurid covers. I also bought used magazines: *Real Detective*, *True Romance*, and comic books (I snuck in a few *Classics Illustrated*). When the store owner found out what I was doing, he threw in a revolving stand to display the paperbacks. The books and magazines were a big hit with the kids although they were disappointed to learn that they could only check out three at a time, and even more disappointed to learn that they had to keep a log of everything they read. Victor picked out *Hit Man*, the autobiography of a gunman that had genuine literary merit. I assigned the paperbacks as "extended" or pleasure reading. In class we read books more like regular school texts, including some stories by Steinbeck and *The Plum-plum Pickers* (1971) by Raymond Barrio, which was set in San Jose. Reading as a group, with constant discussion and questioning (*scaffolding* in educational jargon), we got through these more standard readings with understanding and real pleasure. The kids were surprised to see that these qualities could be part of a reading class.

Of course, at Operation SER I was not completely unconstrained. The GED test required my students to answer questions about passages from standard high school texts, so I had to include some of these in my course. I believe that this constraint was good for the class, because the students knew that they were preparing for a real exam, and that passing the exam was an accomplishment that would be recognized outside of Operation SER. I don't think that they would have taken seriously a curriculum entirely devoid of standard academic content.

LANGUAGE MINORITY STUDENTS
IN PUBLIC SCHOOLS

The question of what subjects to teach language minority students is almost as controversial as the question of what language to teach them in. I debated this question with a doctoral student who taught ESL to elementary school children during her comprehensive examination. "In your opinion," I asked, "what is the place of the district curriculum in a bilingual school?" "In my opinion," she answered, "it has no place." She explained that, in her experience, the official curriculum was irrelevant to her students' lives. Subjects like electricity and magnetism, the reproduction of a cell, the ecology of a rain forest, even the Mexican War were so far removed from her students' lives that they were basically nonsense. The students could study these abstract subjects, memorize facts, and pass tests, but all of it meant little to them. Meaning in the lives of her students centered around home, family, and neighborhood. My student advocated building a curriculum in English and Spanish based on local knowledge: What vegetables and medicinal herbs can be grown in Tucson? How does a four-cycle engine work, and how do you fix one that's broken? How do you run an import business? In these areas, some of the students and members of their families were real experts. She said that ecology could be taught in relation to the desert, including the plants in the students' own backyards and gardens. Fixing a broken engine could be an introduction to the study of energy and work. Arithmetic could be taught in connection with running an import business or even measuring ingredients for a recipe. Such a curriculum would reach the students where they lived. Studying what they knew, students would start out as experts instead of bumpkins.

It was a good, orientalist proposal. Such a curriculum would motivate and empower language minority student. Through the rigorous study of their own worlds, students could learn to read and write in two languages; to calculate, to reason, and to create. But I am afraid that it is not enough. Language minority students must also learn about the world beyond their homes and neighborhoods. To participate fully in American society, they must learn some things that are, at first, neither relevant nor interesting. They need to know about rain forests and presidential elections and tectonic plates because as they move up in the educational system this knowledge will be assumed, and they will be competing against students who have mastered it. The official curriculum cannot be bypassed without serious consequences down the line. Nevertheless, I know what my student meant. Teaching abstract and technical material to children and teenagers is difficult, and doubly so if language, school culture, and a lack of background knowledge get in the way. To show what I mean, I introduce three Hispanic students, two of whom, like Victor, were struggling to learn academic subjects and one of whom, like Richard Rodriguez, has succeeded.

Joel

Teachers of language minority students often do not have the time to see their students outside of school. They teach 150 students a week, and after school they must grade papers and prepare lessons. All of this takes from 50 to 60 hours a week, and there is little time for home visits or socializing. A great benefit of teaching at a university is that I have time for research, and over the years I have done what public school teachers wish they could do: visit the students' homes, sit next to them in class, and tutor them in subjects in which they need help. These tutoring sessions, tape-recorded, transcribed, and analyzed, provide a fascinating look into the problems and strengths of language minority students. One student with whom I have worked is Joel.

Joel was a boy who might have attended my doctoral student's ESL class in Tucson. In the sixth grade at the time of this study, Joel was born and schooled in the United States. His father was born in Texas, his mother in Mexico, and they have settled in Tucson. (We will get to know Joel and his family much better in chap. 6.) Spanish is Joel's first language, and his English is not very good. To give a sense of how Joel is struggling with difficult academic material, I will quote from the transcript of a tutoring session in which he is studying for a social studies quiz. His class is taught bilingually, but the English part of the class requires greater linguistic skills and more background knowledge than Joel has.

> Tutor: (Pointing to a world map) Let's look at this first, okay? Now you just
>   read that the Europeans went to live in North America, right?
> Joel: Uh, huh.
> T: Where did they live?
> J: In North America?
> T: Yeah. In what part?
> J: Europe?
> T: Where's Europe?
> J: No response.

T:	(Pointing to a map) Here's the U.S., okay? And here's Mexico down there. South America down here, right? Okay, where's Europe?
J:	No response.
T:	Here you have the Atlantic Ocean, right? Here's the Pacific Ocean. This is Mexico, right here, right? What's this?
J:	Europe.
T:	Well, this is South America. Now Europe is way over here, okay? . . . . You have England, France, Spain—all of those countries are in Europe.

In order to understand the settlement of the West, Joel has to be able to read a map and know something about American and world geography. But as the transcript shows, Joel is unfamiliar with maps and does not have a sense of where the United States is situated in the world. He has, however, developed strategies for dealing with teachers' questions he cannot answer. When the tutor reminds Joel that Europeans went to live in North America and then asks, "Where did they live?" (looking for the answer "in the West"), Joel gives a correct but evasive answer: "North America." When asked what part of North America, he shows that he does not have the background knowledge to fully understand the text he has just read by answering, "Europe."

Marielena

Some students manage to surmount the barriers of language, culture, and irrelevance to achieve academic success. One such student is Marielena, a poet, who made it from a small farming community on the Colorado River to the University of Arizona. Asked to explain her academic success, she wrote:

> My parents drilled it into my child's conscious that we should work our minds hard in school; the body could only last so long. . . . An "A" was rewarded with praise, an ice-cream cone from Dairy Queen, and an occasional smile from my father. "Look at me," he said. "Me only go to fourth grade, but you think I be stupid? You think your father stupid? No, I work hard, I have my house, my car, my job. You do better, next time no gettee B's."
>
> Sometimes we would think this was all exaggeration, but eventually we came to accept the reality of it, especially during the summers when we would work in the fields.

Marielena's father supplied a strong motivation for succeeding at school. But Joel's parents, though very concerned that their children do well in school, are not so involved. Joel's father speaks good English and attended college, but he works two jobs and has little time for anything else.

Joel's mother monitors her children's activities carefully, but she speaks very little English and cannot help them with their schoolwork. Joel takes school seriously and tries hard, but if he is to succeed, the school will have to inspire in him the motivation that his parents cannot by providing a path to success in the form of instruction that is better suited to his linguistic and academic abilities.

George

I was tutoring George in 10th-grade English, and I had asked to visit his home so that I could meet his family and get some sense of his home situation. I hadn't expected to find such an oddly familiar place. The townhouse where George lived was the mirror image of my own. Both were in the same large condominium complex in northern Virginia, just inside the Washington beltway. In fact, from my house you could hear the beltway day and night. Both condos provided six rooms and a tiny back yard for a minimal price. I was paying a mortgage company for my house, but I imagine George's mother was paying a landlord for theirs.

George took me upstairs and introduced me to his mother, Isabel, in her bedroom (just like mine but reversed), where she was watching television. She was a small, enthusiastic woman, who thanked me in English for helping George and spoke proudly about her daughter's graduation from high school. She wished she had more time to talk to me about George's studies, but she had to get ready to go to work (she would be working 60 hours that week, mostly at night), so George and I went downstairs to study at his dining room table. I got the feeling that despite her concern for her son, Isabel did not have the time to help him with his schoolwork.

George's family had come to the Washington area from Colombia 4 years earlier. His father was a businessman; Isabel was a nurse. George (then Jorge) and his older sister were doing well in school. Then came a divorce, and Isabel packed up her kids and moved to the United States. I don't know why she chose Washington, but I imagine that she had relatives or friends there. Nurses were in demand, and Isabel was able to find work and get a green card right away. Now she spoke passable English and had a good job at George Washington University Hospital. (It was there that a crack surgical team saved President Reagan's life. Had Isabel helped?) George's older sister had graduated from Braddock High School and had taken community college classes, aiming to be a nurse. But for now she had temporarily left college and found work as a waitress to help support the family.

George was recommended to me for tutoring because he was having trouble in Sheltered English. A sheltered class enrolls only non-native English speakers, who study the same material as the regular class, though usually covering fewer topics and in greater depth. George's class contained students from Mexico, South America, Ethiopia, Iran, China, Vietnam, and Korea. The last two countries provided the most international students to Braddock High.

George spoke good English with only a slight accent, but the texts he was reading, "The Cask of Amontillado," *The Grapes of Wrath*, and *Romeo and Juliet*, were difficult for any 10th grader. The easiest text for George was the short story, "The Most Dangerous Game," the tale of a madman who hunts human beings for sport. But even this was above George's level. In just one paragraph of the story, George didn't understand the words, *Godforsaken*, *lore*, *jumpy*, and *tough-minded.* He got the general idea of the story, but he could not answer most of the comprehension questions at the end, and he certainly couldn't write the critical interpretation his teacher asked for.

After about 15 minutes of my explaining "The Most Dangerous Game," George was getting bored, so I asked him about his plans for the future. He said he wanted to move back to Colombia and become a businessman like his father. I told him I thought that a bilingual businessman, well-educated in both English and Spanish, ought to have a bright future. I said that he needed to master English reading and writing, that his speaking was fine. He also needed to get good grades so that he could be admitted to a business school, either in Colombia or the United States. But George said that he didn't see the point of studying hard in high school, as the subjects had no relation to a business career. He didn't know exactly what a businessman did, but he was pretty sure it had nothing to do with biology, American History, earth science, and especially, "The Most Dangerous Game." I told him that businessmen had to be broadly educated; they had to know a lot about the world. But George had heard these ideas from teachers before, probably often, and he was ready to finish his worksheet and end our tutoring session. He was in no danger of failing 10th grade—everyone was automatically promoted—and he was rightly confident that he would graduate if he just attended class.

CONCLUSIONS

Let me sum up the lessons I learned at Operation SER, Braddock High, and the schools in Tucson where I have taught and observed. First, the school's curriculum and culture have to be relevant to the students' lives outside of school. I believe it is possible to write a curriculum that interests language minority students and still includes elements of the standard curriculum. To do this, school districts must research the areas of personal knowledge that their students possess, as my doctoral student advocated, and, where it is possible, use this knowledge as a bridge to the traditional subjects. It will also be necessary for the district to allow English language learners to take a modified curriculum, where fewer subjects are studied in greater depth.

Second, the school must come to grips with the problem of discipline. Because of the strong academic orientation of most of the parents, discipline was not a problem at Braddock High, but in chapter 6 we encounter a school where discipline problems seriously interfered with learning. Discipline was a potential problem at Operation SER, but problems didn't get out of hand in part because repeat offenders were dropped from the program. Most of the students, like Victor, considered attending Operation SER a great opportunity, and did not want to mess it up. But the fact that problem students were dropped played a role in allowing learning to take place. I believe that public schools must also find a way to remove undisciplined students from classes where the others want to learn.

Third, minority students' languages must have a respected place in the school. If full-scale bilingual education programs are not possible, as at Braddock High where the students spoke dozens of languages, the school should offer at least some bilingual classes. It should also hire administrators, guards, teachers' aides, and secretaries who represent the students' languages and cultures. These bilingual personnel should be used (and compensated) for helping with informal bilingual counseling and sponsoring bilingual clubs. For example, I believe that Braddock High could have sponsored a thriving Vietnamese literature club, perhaps in cooperation with a local Vietnamese community association, where students would read, discuss, and write literature in Vietnamese and English. In general, it should be understood that throughout the school, languages other than English ought to be used (perhaps on an individual basis) whenever they facilitate learning. These suggestions and other will be developed in chapters 5, 6, and 7, but before we return to a discussion of students and schools, we will take a look at some principles of language acquisition in chapter 2, and their implementation in methods of language teaching in chapter 3.

SUGGESTED READING

For further information on Robert Graves' life, see his autobiography *Goodbye to All That* (Graves, 1957). Graves and Hodge (1943) spell out Graves' literary theory. Pennycook (1994) discusses linguistic imperialism. Epstein (1977) is a mostly negative view of multiculturalism in education. A more balanced view can be found in the articles in Crawford (1992). Baker and Hornberger's (2001) collection of articles by Jim Cummins is an excellent compendium of that writer's influential ideas on questions of minority languages and education. Everybody ought to read Richard Rodriguez's *Hunger of Memory* (1982).

First and Second Language Acquisition

INTRODUCTION: THREE STORIES OF LANGUAGE ACQUISITION

To hear some psycholinguists talk, you would think that we understand practically everything about language acquisition, and all we need to do is fill in a few details. More cautious psycholinguists refer to their theories as "stories," and the term is appropriate because, like stories, theories of language acquisition have grown and changed over the years. In this chapter, we are going to examine three stories of language acquisition. Two of them, or at least the philosophies behind them, have been at odds for centuries. The third story is more recent and is not in direct conflict with the other two, although there are territorial disputes. The first account of language acquisition is no longer current. It is usually related in psychology textbooks to give readers an idea of how the field has developed, but it is of more than historical interest to educators because some of the teaching methods it inspired are still widely practiced. It is called *behaviorism*.

BEHAVIORIST APPROACHES TO LANGUAGE ACQUISITION

Behaviorist psychology began with the work of the Russian Ivan Pavlov, who studied animal behavior. Pavlov noticed that a dog would salivate when it smelled food placed in its dish. He also noticed that after a dog had been fed for several days, the actual smell of food wasn't necessary; the dog would salivate as soon as it heard the door to its room being opened. Similarly, cat owners know that the sound of a can being opened elicits a remarkable response from their pets, even if the can contains tomato soup. Pavlov reasoned that animal behavior could be described as a series of responses to stimuli in the environment. The dog's salivating when the door was opened was a natural response to an unnatural stimulus, which had to be learned. As you may recall from Psych. 101, Pavlov also tried ringing a bell just before he fed his dogs, and before long they had learned to salivate whenever they heard the bell. Such learning, which pairs an unnatural stimulus like a bell with a naturally occurring response like salivation, is called *classical conditioning,* and can be modeled as in Figure 2.1.

In the 1940s and 1950s, the Harvard psychologist B. F. Skinner studied how animals can be trained to do unnatural things, as when a pigeon pecks at a red spot, or a rat presses a bar. He called this kind of learning *operant conditioning.* One kind of experiment took place in an apparatus called a "Skinner box," consisting of a box with a food tray at one end and a bar above the tray. When the bar is pressed, a food pellet drops into the tray. If a hungry rat is placed in the box, it will wander around until it brushes up against the bar, thus releasing a food pellet. After eating the food, the rat will begin wandering again, but this time it will wander more in the vicinity of the tray. Eventually, the rat will brush the bar again, and, after a few more brushes, the rat will just stand at the tray pressing the bar and eating until it is no longer hungry. According to operant conditioning theory, the rat's pressing the bar is the response, and the whole Skinner box apparatus is the stimulus. The food is called *positive reinforcement,* and it must be provided for operant conditioning to occur. In some of Skinner's other experiments, he introduced *negative reinforcement,* in the form of an electric shock. Perhaps Skinner's most important discovery was that animals learn better with positive reinforcement than with negative reinforcement, and he believed that this principle applied to human learning as well. This insight was the guiding principle in the fictional utopian community that Skinner described in his novel *Walden Two* (1948). In this community, everybody lived a happy and productive life and got along with each other because socially desirable behavior was rewarded positively, never negatively. The managers of the community were, of course, psychologists.

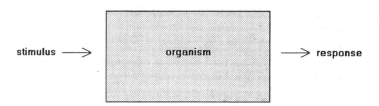

FIG. 2.1.   A model of classical conditioning.

Using a Skinner box, it was possible to investigate various aspects of stimulus–response learning. What would happen if positive reinforcement were discontinued? (Eventually the rat would stop pressing the bar and start wandering around again; in behaviorist jargon, the response would be *extinguished.*) What would happen if the rat got the food every other time it pressed the bar? (It would take a lot longer to extinguish the behavior.)

In his 1957 book *Verbal Behavior*, Skinner claimed that classical and operant conditioning could largely explain language learning. At first, the child would make random sounds, but some of these would resemble words and would be positively reinforced by exclamations and hugs from the parents. The child would also be rewarded for imitating what the parents said. Eventually, the child could be explicitly taught. The parent might say, "Say *bread*," and a child who produced a good imitation of "bread" would be rewarded. The same principle would apply to the learning of grammar. A child who put words together grammatically would probably be understood, and positively reinforced by the parents. Ungrammatical expressions, on the other hand, might be negatively reinforced (verbally not electrically).

Skinner (1957) developed his theory without actually studying many children although he did study his own daughter at length and, yes, he even rigged up a special box-like crib that could provide stimuli and positive reinforcement. But he believed that studying children wasn't necessary because learning mechanisms were essentially the same in animals and human beings.

Child language learning has now been extensively studied, and the facts are quite different from what Skinner supposed. It turns out that young children do not imitate what their parent say, but produce language that is very unlike that of adults, as we will see shortly. Furthermore, teaching young children to improve their grammar is notoriously unsuccessful, as the parents in the following dialogues discovered.

Child: Nobody don't like me.
Mother: No. Say, "Nobody likes me."
Child: Nobody don't like me.
(Eight repetitions of the above)
Mother: Now listen carefully. Say, "Nobody likes me."
Child: Oh! Nobody don't likes me (McNeil, 1966, quoted in Clark and Clark, 1977, p. 336).

Child: Want other one spoon, Daddy.
Father: You mean, you want THE OTHER SPOON.
Child: Yes, I want other one spoon, please, Daddy.
Father: Can you say, "the other spoon?"

Child: Other . . . one . . . spoon.

Father: Say . . . "other."

Child: Other.

Father: "Spoon."

Child: Spoon.

Father: "Other . . . spoon."

Child: Other . . . spoon. Now give me other one spoon (Braine, 1971, quoted in Pinker, 1994, p. 281).

When I took Psych. 101 in the 1960s, behaviorism was the only game in town (at least in Berkeley). The course was very hard, and at the last class meeting, the professor asked us why we were having so much trouble. One student volunteered that because psychology was the study of the mind, it was intrinsically very difficult, a comment that revealed he had missed the most basic point of the course. "We *can't* study the mind," moaned the professor, "we can only study *behavior*." But it seemed like psychology should study the mind, and that is the direction more modern psychology has taken; indeed, it is called *cognitive psychology*, the psychology of knowing.

To compare behaviorism to cognitive psychology, consider again the behaviorist paradigm illustrated in Figure 2.1. A stimulus impinges on the organism represented by a black box and elicits a response. In this model, learning occurs when a particular stimulus (say the presence of a mother) is repeatedly paired with a particular response (the child pronouncing the word *mama*), and the response is reinforced, usually by smiles and hugs. Where are mental processes in all of this? Radical behaviorists claimed that there aren't any. They acknowledged that stimuli are somehow registered in the brain (located in the black box) and that the brain gives appropriate commands to the body. But, they said, this connection is mechanical, like a knee jerk. There is no complicated mental processing, no mind. Most behaviorists, however, conceded that we must have minds, and that they engage in some kind of data processing to mediate between stimulus and response. But, because the black box cannot be opened and its workings observed, we cannot study the mind; we must study things we can observe, namely, behavior and the environment in which it occurs. In this regard, my psychology professor made another memorable remark. "If we could cut up people's brains before they died," he said, "we'd have all the answers in 10 years."

Mainstream behaviorism, then, had two beliefs about mental processes: (1) They cannot be studied, so psychologists must look at external, not internal stimuli, and (2) external phenomena entirely determine the contents of the mind/brain, whatever they are. The infant's mind is like a blank slate to be written on by the hand of experience. There is no innate knowledge. Cognitive psychology assumes the opposite of (1) and vigorously debates (2). The second story of language acquisition we will consider is told by the branch of cognitive psychology that was founded in part by the linguist Noam Chomsky, who believes that children are born with mental slates that contain a great deal of genetically inscribed knowledge.

NATIVIST APPROACHES TO LANGUAGE ACQUISITION

The study of language changed radically in 1957 when Chomsky published a book called *Syntactic Structures*. In it and subsequent books, he argued that mental processes could be studied and that language provided a window on the workings of the mind. Chomsky showed how some mental structures, namely, knowledge of syntax, can be modeled using techniques developed by mathematicians. He also declared that the most interesting question for the field of linguistics was how children learn their native language, thus redefining linguistics as a branch of cognitive psychology. Chomsky claimed that the only way a child could accomplish the formidable task of learning a language was to be guided by innate knowledge—a kind of language instinct.

Plato's Problem

The notion of innate ideas has been debated by philosophers since Plato, who posed the question, "How do we know so much when we experience so little?" His answer was that we are born already knowing many basic concepts, such as TRIANGLE, TABLE, and TREE because we experienced them in a previous life, when we lived in the world of ideal forms. Chomskian linguists reframed Plato's problem (which they call the *logical problem of language acquisition*) as follows: "How do children learn linguistic structures to which they have not been exposed?" The answer is that children are born with specific linguistic knowledge, called *universal grammar* (UG), and the primary goal of Chomskian linguistics is to discover the nature of this knowledge. A secondary goal of Chomskian linguistics is to develop a system of grammatical analysis (called *generative grammar*) that can be used to describe adult language. Such a description amounts to what the child must learn. Thus, in Chomsky's system, grammatical analysis and the study of child language acquisition are inextricably linked. Many UG linguists study child language acquisition not by examining the utterances of children but by working backward from the grammar the adult knows to figure out what the child must have known when starting out. We will adopt this method in the next section, first examining how generative grammar describes the adult linguistic system and then considering how children, guided by UG, can learn it.

Generative Approaches to First Language Acquisition

Generative Grammar

Generative linguists believe that one part of the child's innate grammatical knowledge is a very general design for syntax, that is, a kind of template that works for all languages. To see what this template looks like, consider the structure of this sentence:

(1) The cow jumped over the moon.

Our intuitions tell us that the sentence has two main parts, which your high school English teacher called the *subject* and the *predicate*. The subject is *the cow* and the predicate is *jumped over the moon*. In generative terminology, the predicate is called the *verb phrase*. Our intuitions also tell us that the verb phrase has two main parts: the verb *jumped* (which is called the *head* of the verb phrase) and the prepositional phrase *over the moon* (which is called the *complement* of the verb phrase because it completes the verb, telling where the cow jumped). Similarly, the prepositional phrase *over the moon* has two parts: the preposition *over* (which serves as the head of the phrase) and *the moon* (which serves as the complement). In both the verb phrase and the prepositional phrase, the head comes before its complement. This pattern of a head followed by a complement is maintained in all the major kinds of phrases in English.

Now consider the subject of (1), *the cow*, which is called a *noun phrase*. The head of the phrase is *cow*, but there is no complement. If there were a complement, say a prepositional phrase like *in the rhyme*, the head would come first: *the cow in the rhyme*. All of these facts about English phrase structure can be displayed using a device from mathematics called a *tree diagram* (it is an upside-down tree with the root at the top and the branches spreading downward). The noun phrase structure can be represented like this:

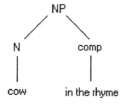

This diagram says that a noun phrase (NP) consists of a noun (N) in the head position followed by a complement (comp). In the example sentence, the complement is a prepositional phrase, but for simplicity we will not include that information in the tree yet.

As you may have noticed, we have not yet dealt with the first word in the phrase: *the.* To do so, we must add another basic component to the list of grammatical constituents that can make up a phrase, namely, the *specifier* (spec). Specifiers of noun phrases include the articles *the, a,* and *an,* the demonstrative adjectives *this, that, these,* and *those,* and quantifiers like *much* and *many,* among other things. Specifiers are added to the noun phrase structure by building on a second story, like this:

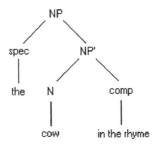

Notice that the lower NP, consisting of just a head and a complement, is distinguished from the upper NP by placing an apostrophe after it. We will discuss this notation later. As mentioned, the basic design for noun phrases also works for the other major phrases in English. This can be seen in the following four diagrams, in which the only difference is the name of the phrase and its head. Thus, if you replace the symbol N in the tree with the symbol V (for verb), you will get a verb phrase tree, and so on for adjective phrases, prepositional phrases, and adverb phrases.

Verb phrase   Adjective phrase

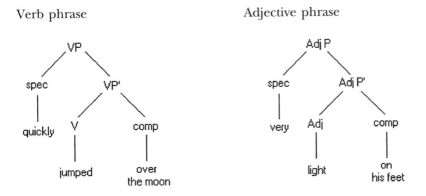

Prepositional phrase

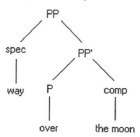

Adverb phrase

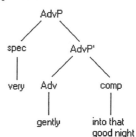

Thus, all the major phrases in English have the same basic structure, and it can be written generally as follows:

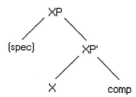

where X can stand for N, V, Adj, or Adv. In fact, this general template, which is called an *X-bar structure*, also works for the sentence as a whole. To show how, I need to introduce a little more grammar. In English, all verbs (at least the kind we have been discussing) have tense; *jumped* is in the past tense, which is marked by the inflection *ed*. Tense can also be marked by means of an *auxiliary verb* (also called a *helping verb*) preceding the main verb. The future tense, for example, is marked with *will* or *shall*: The cow *will* jump over the moon. However, if we wish to include auxiliary verbs in our tree diagrams, we will have to modify them because so far our trees have no branch from which to hang this structure. We will add a branch (and switch metaphors) by building on another story, topped by an S node, which stands for *sentence*. The head position in the new addition can be called AUX for auxiliary verb. The new structure looks like this for now:

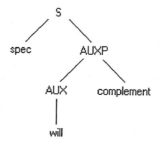

Because this structure is supposed to represent the basic framework of a sentence, we would like to be able to hang the subject in front of *will* and the predicate behind *will*, and there are branches available for doing that. So, we will consider the first NP in the sentence (in our example, *the cow*) to be the specifier of S and hang it from the specifier node, and we will consider the VP (in our example, *jumped over the moon*) to be the complement of AUX and hang it from the complement node.

We ought to make some other changes as well. Notice that the *structure* of the new phrase is exactly the same as that of the other phrases we have looked at, but that the *labels* attached to the branches are not the same. In the other phrase structure trees, all the branches used similar labels; for example, the tree for an NP included NP, NP′ and N. This consistency is lost if S is the label for the highest node in the new tree. One way to solve this problem is to label the top node AUXP and change the AUXP node to AUXP′, and for a while, generative grammars adopted this convention. But it was later decided to use a synonym for AUXP, namely IP, which stands for *inflection phrase*. So, changing the term *AUX* to the term *I* wherever it occurs in the tree, we can finally diagram "The cow jumped over the moon," as follows:

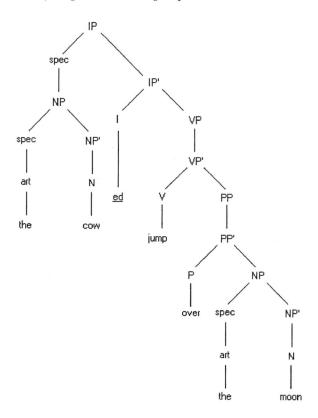

Notice that in this tree, the past tense is marked by the inflection *ed*, which will have to be moved from its position in front of *jump* and attached to the end of *jump*, producing *jumped*. So, the grammar will not only have to specify the structure of basic trees, as we have done so far, but will also have to provide a way to move things around to different parts of a tree. We will discuss how to do that later, but for now notice that we have created a general template (the X-bar structure) that will fit any kind of phrase in English. We are getting closer to describing one kind of innate knowledge children must have to learn English or any language.

I mentioned that Chomsky borrowed the notion of the tree diagram from the field of mathematics, and the term *generative* comes from that field, as well. The mathematical term *generate* doesn't mean to produce something, the way a turbine produces electricity, but rather to define or specify something. For example, the set of even integers (the *integers* are the whole numbers plus their negative counterparts) can be defined, that is, "generated," by this equation:

$$2 \times A = B$$

where A is any integer and B is an even integer. Any integer that can fit into the B slot must be even. Let's test the number 6. Plugging into the formula, we get $2 \times A = 6$. Is there some integer that can be plugged in for A so that the equation will balance? Yes, 3 will work, producing $2 \times 3 = 6$. So, the equation defines 6 as even. Now let's test the number 7. Plugging 7 into the B slot, we get $2 \times A = 7$. Is there an integer that can be plugged in for A? No. The number 3.5 would work, but decimal numbers (and fractions) aren't integers. Therefore, 7 is not defined as even. Because there is an infinite number of integers, we can't possibly test them all, but if we had an infinite amount of time, we could use the equation to test whether every integer was even or not; the equation thus specifies or "generates" all the even integers.

Chomsky pointed out that phrase structure trees can be generated by a mathematical device called a *rewrite rule*. The following rules will generate an NP tree:

(2) XP = spec XP′
(3) XP′ = X complement
(4) X = N

Rule (2) says that an XP has two parts, first a spec and second an XP′. Applying this rule we get the following tree:

We can expand the XP' by applying rule (3), as follows:

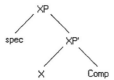

We now have the general structure (the X-bar structure) for any English phrase; to make it a noun phrase, we apply rule (4), which says to substitute N for X wherever X appears, producing

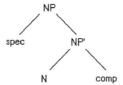

We have now generated an NP tree. If we wanted to, we could generate trees for VP, AdjP, AdvP, or PP just by changing rule (4) to re-write X as V, Adj, Adv, or P instead of N. To add some words to the NP tree, we need some lexical re-write rules, such as these:

(5) spec = the, a, this, that
(6) N = cow, dog, chicken
(7) comp = in the rhyme, that chased the cat, Ø (i.e., nothing)

Rules (5)–(7) work like a Chinese menu: You choose one possibility from rule (5), one from rule (6), and one from rule (7). Let's choose *a, dog,* and Ø. Plugging these choices into the tree produces a good noun phrase, "a dog":

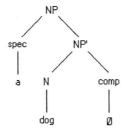

If we made different lexical choices we could generate, "The dog that chased the cat," "The chicken in the rhyme," "A cow that chased the cat," and several other grammatical English NPs. The rules also allow us to test whether a purported NP is grammatical, say, "dog a that chased the cat." Rules (2) and (3) require that the specifier *a* come before a noun, not after, so "dog a" cannot be generated by the rules and is therefore not allowed by the grammar.

It is theoretically possible to write a set of rules, including rewrite rules, lexical rules, and movement rules (like the one needed to attach *ed* to its verb) that will generate all and only the grammatical sentences in a language, thus, in a very abstract way, modeling a speaker's knowledge of that language. In fact, this was the original goal of generative grammar. However, when attempts were made to write a complete set of rules for English, a lot of problems cropped up, especially problems having to do with meaning. For example, what if we add the word *paradigm* to the list of nouns in rule (6). Then the grammar will generate, "The paradigm chased the cat." No paradigm, not even radical behaviorism, can do that. Although it was possible to patch things up for a while, eventually the entire edifice of generative rules became too heavy and threatened to collapse of its own weight. So, generative grammarians modified their goal. The new goal is not to generate all and only the grammatical sentences in a language, but to gain insight into how a language can be learned. Let us now take a look at this more recent program.

Universal Grammar

Generative linguists claim that many aspects of language are known to children at birth in a genetically encoded universal grammar (UG). Several aspects of the grammar trees we have been discussing are believed to be part of UG. One is the hierarchical structure of the trees. As we will see shortly, UG linguists claim that children are programmed to look for hierarchical structures in the speech they hear. A second aspect of UG pertains to the structure of grammatical constituents. Notice that all of the trees we have drawn can be expanded two branches at a time: A node never has more than two nodes directly under it. It is claimed that this binary manner of organization is innate as well. A third UG claim pertains to word order. As we have seen, all English phrases have the same word order—head + complement—but as the reader may be aware, not all languages have this order. Japanese, for example, puts heads at the ends of their phrases. So the UG claim is not that children expect heads to come first, but rather that they expect the heads of all types of phrases in a language to be in the same position, either before the complement or after it. To determine which position is correct, children must receive input from the target language.

Let's look more closely at how children are thought to learn word order. The innate expectation that all types of phrases will have a similar order of head and complement is called the *head direction principle*. Principles of UG often come with associated *parameters*, which the child must set after sampling the target language. In this case, the parameter can be set for head first or head last. English-speaking children choose the head first setting; Japanese-speaking children choose the head last setting. Principles and parameters make learning word order a lot easier because the child can set the parameter (subconsciously, of course) after analyzing only one kind of phrase, and assume that all other phrases will be similar.

The head direction principle and its associated parameter are an example of a UG claim that was arrived at by analyzing the adult linguistic system and working backward toward UG. It seemed logical that the symmetrical structure of phrases would be included in innate knowledge. In fact, in the early days of generative grammar, discussions about language acquisition were carried on in considerable ignorance of what children actually said and understood. It was even argued that speech data should not be used to construct a theory of language acquisition because they are inevitably tainted by psychological processes that are not purely linguistic, such as memory limitations, slips of the tongue, and other inadvertent errors. Linguistics was supposed to be a rational, not an empirical, discipline. However, in recent years a school of generative empiricists has sprung up (e.g., Bloom, 1993; McDaniel, McKee, & Cairns, 1996), and these scholars have examined theoretical claims about language acquisition in light of children's actual speech. Let's look at their work, starting with some sentences spoken by children about 2 years old.

> block broke
> I did it
> Eve find it
> Neil sit
> lie down stool
> man taste it
> doll eat
> doll eat celery (Crain & Lillo-Martin, 1999, p. 105).

Notice that the order of the words in these sentences is far from random; rather it is very much like the most common word order in adult English sentences. As the examples show, early child speech does not contain wildly ungrammatical sentences. Although the child's utterance may not contain all the words in the adult equivalent, those words that do appear are usually in the adult order. For example, to express the notion, "Marie took my dolly," a 20-month-old child might say, "Marie took," or "took dolly," or "Marie dolly," but would not say, "took Marie."

The examples just cited were collected by Harvard psychologist Roger Brown (1973), who recorded three children playing with their mothers for an hour every week over a period of 2½ years. A longitudinal study of this kind is the best way to get information about the nature of children's internal grammars and how they change. Another useful technique is to put children in an experimental situation that will test their knowledge of grammaticality. This technique was used to test for another UG principle, called *binding principle B*, which we will look at next. But first, we need to do some more grammar.

In English, personal pronouns (*I, you, he, she,* etc.) can refer to a noun that has been mentioned previously in the discourse, as in:

(8) Nixon forgot that he was taping.

A second possibility is that the *he* in (8) refers to a person not mentioned in the discourse but understood from the general context. However, if *he* appears first in the sentence, and is meant to refer to Nixon, the sentence is ungrammatical:

(9) *He forgot that Nixon was taping.
    [where *he* refers to Nixon]
    (The * means that the sentence is ungrammatical.)

Why is this so? Perhaps it is because in English a pronoun cannot precede its referent. But this hypothesis is wrong, as shown in (10).

(10) While he was taping, Nixon talked to Haldemann.
     [where *he* refers to Nixon]

In order to state the correct rule for the ordering of pronouns and the nouns they refer to, we must appeal to the hierarchical structure of sentences. Let us examine a diagram of (8).

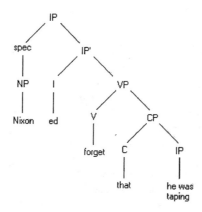

First, notice that this tree diagram is different in two ways from those we have already encountered. For one thing, the sentence contains two clauses (a *clause* is a simple sentence, i.e., an IP). The diagram shows how two clauses can be combined to make a complex sentence. The first clause is *Nixon forgot*. In previous diagrams, what followed the verb was a noun phrase, but here what follows *forgot* is another clause. The second new structure is that the lower clause, *he was taping*, is introduced by the word *that*, which is called a *complementizer* because it introduces a clause that completes the idea introduced by the verb. As the tree diagram shows, complementizers (abbreviated as C) are hung on the left branch of a CP node. The complement of the complementizer (i.e., the IP, or clause) is hung on the right branch of the CP node.

Now consider the structure of the ungrammatical (9), which is diagrammed here.

(9) *He forgot that Nixon was taping.
    [where *he* refers to *Nixon*]

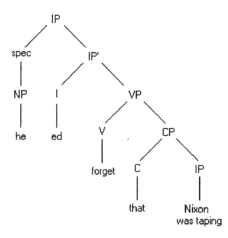

Notice that the structure is exactly the same as in the diagram for (8) except that *he* and *Nixon* have switched places.

Now consider sentence (10).

(10) While he was taping, Nixon talked to Haldemann.

Since (10) is grammatical even though the pronoun precedes its referent, we hope that it will share some feature with (8) that is not shared by (9). Here is the diagram of (10).

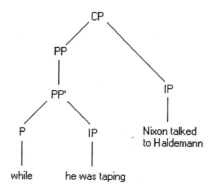

(For simplicity I have considered *while* to be a preposition that introduces the clause *he was taping*. *While* doesn't sound much like a preposition, but some grammarians consider it to be one because it patterns like *before* and *after*, which do sound like prepositions.) Is there a structural feature that allows *he* to precede *Nixon* in (10) but not in (9)? Yes! All three of the sentences we are comparing contain two clauses. In (8), the referent *Nixon* is in a clause above its pronoun *he* in the tree, so that pattern appears to be okay. In (10), *Nixon* is also in a clause above the clause containing *he* (I'm simplifying a lot here). But in (9), *Nixon* is in a clause that is directly below the clause containing *he*. To use the jargon, in (9) *he* c-commands its referent *Nixon*. That pattern is not okay, and is forbidden by a principle of UG called binding principle B, which states that a pronoun cannot refer to a noun phrase that it c-commands.

Crain and McKee (1986) designed an ingenious experiment to see if 3-year-olds knew binding principle B. The experiment involved using puppets to test how children understood sentences like (9) and (10). If children know the principle, they should understand that in a sentence like (11), which has the same structure as (10), *he* can refer to Ninja Turtle.

(11) While he was dancing, the Ninja Turtle ate pizza.

Of course, *he* can also refer to another party that is not mentioned in the discourse but is obvious from the situation. Crain and McKee had Ninja Turtle and Darth Vader puppets act out a story in which Ninja Turtle was dancing and eating a pizza while Vader was just standing around. Then a Kermit the Frog puppet recounted what had happened, and McKee asked the children whether Kermit had told the story correctly. If Kermit said sentence (11) when Ninja Turtle had, in fact, been both eating and dancing, he got the story right and the children gave Kermit a treat. But sometimes when recounting the same story Kermit said:

(12) He was dancing while Ninja Turtle ate pizza.

thus getting the story wrong. Sentence (12) could be true only if Vader (the only grammatical referent of *he*) was dancing. To show Kermit that he had goofed, the children gave him something yucky to eat like a rag or a cockroach (it's not easy being green).

The children's responses showed that they understood that in sentences like (12), *he* cannot refer to the following noun phrase but must refer to someone not mentioned in the sentence. This supports the claim that children have innate knowledge of binding principle B.

Inside the Black Box

Generative linguists and behaviorist psychologists disagreed about what kinds of phenomena language scholars should study. Behaviorists directed their gaze outward to the environment in which speech occurred and examined how environmental factors affected what people said. Radical behaviorists liked to say that studying unobservable mental processes was like studying ghosts or angels. Nativists looked inward, believing that mental processes could be inferred without direct observation. As the use of computers grew, the innatists were provided with a powerful metaphor, in which the brain is compared to a computer's hardware ("wetware"), and the mind is compared to a computer's software. The behaviorist model of the mind/brain was the black box, shown in Figure 2.1, but generative linguists dared to fill in the contents of the box, offering a kind of flow chart of the various mental components believed to be involved in language acquisition. One such chart looks like this:

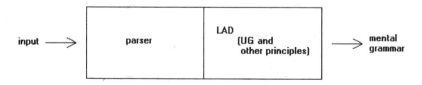

FIG. 2.2. The language module.

The theory of language acquisition represented in Figure 2.2 is that human beings have a language acquisition device (LAD) which contains innate knowledge in the form of UG and other principles, as well as a sentence parser for analyzing the structure of incoming language, possibly producing mental representations that somehow correspond to the trees we have been drawing. These two components work together to construct mental representations of the basic patterns of the target language (a mental grammar), and they form a separate part of the mind, a language faculty or module dedicated to acquiring and using language. The language module interacts with other mental modules like memory, problem-solving abilities, and general learning abilities. The existence of a separate language module containing innate knowledge like binding principle B implies that learning a language is different from learning other subjects, like history or carburetor repair. (Innatist Steven Pinker, 1994, claims that there are separate mental modules, or instincts, for math, mating, parenting, and many other abilities. His critics reply that perhaps there is a module for carburetor repair as well.)

Generative Approaches to Second Language Acquisition

Many studies have investigated to what extent adult second language (L2) acquisition is like child first language (L1) acquisition. Perhaps the most controversial question is whether adults can use UG in the same way as children, or, in the jargon, whether adults have access to UG. There are three positions on this question: (1) Adults have full access (and L2 acquisition is much like L1 acquisition). (2) Adults have no access (and L2 acquisition is essentially different from L1 acquisition). (3) Adults have partial access (and L2 acquisition is an imperfect version of L1 acquisition). Those who argue for the no access position (Bley-Vroman, 1989, 1990) point to the universal success of L1 learning and the very limited success of L2 learning in most circumstances, arguing that something very different must be going on. Those who take the full access position insist that the problem of language acquisition is, as the UG people insist, a logical problem, and that if only a few adults learn an L2 with native-like proficiency, UG must be involved. Partial access advocates say that the limited success of L2 acquisition in most circumstances suggests that adults have limited access to UG. A great deal of research has been undertaken investigating whether adult L2 learners can master the principles and parameters that are postulated by UG.

A considerable hindrance to this work is the fact that UG theory keeps changing radically about every 10 years. Time after time, scholars claimed to have found evidence of a particular UG principle operating in L2 acquisition only to find, sometimes even before they had completed their studies, that theorists now said that the principle did not exist. UG researcher Susan Braidi (1999) observes, "Newcomers to [UG research] may be asking why researchers consider working within a theoretical paradigm that changes so often and has such inconclusive answers." The best reason she can come up with is that, "we may find that future developments in linguistic theory will give a better account of L2 learner data" (p. 76). In other words, empirical investigations guided by UG theory do produce data. Even if the theory changes, the data do not, and any new theory must be able to explain the data somehow.

The Critical Period Hypothesis

Researchers who take the no access position often cite the *critical period hypothesis*, which claims that children go through a period of sensitivity to language learning that ends somewhere around puberty. After this period, languages can still be learned, but by mental mechanisms other than those that children employ. It should be noted that in most discussions comparing L1 and L2 acquisition, the matter of accent is set aside. Everyone agrees that it is extremely difficult for adults to acquire a native-like accent in an L2, but it is believed that this is related to articulation rather than to higher level cognitive processes.

Critical or sensitive periods for learning are found in other species; newborn ducks will follow any suitably sized object that walks past them. This is usually a mother duck, but can be a psychologist in a white coat. However, 24 hours after hatching, the critical period for this imprinting behavior has passed, and the ducklings won't follow even their mother. Similarly, song birds will not learn their species' song unless they are exposed to it during a certain period in life. The structure of the song is largely innate, but this knowledge must be triggered by appropriate experience at the appropriate time.

Critical period advocates often cite a study by Johnson and Newport (1989), who gave a written grammar test to English learners from China and Korea, all of whom had been in the United States for about 10 years. The age at which the subjects had arrived (and thus had first been surrounded by English) varied from 3 to 39 years. A strong version of the critical period hypothesis would predict that the subjects who arrived before the onset of puberty would do much better on the test than those who arrived after that age; in fact, that is the conclusion the authors reached. However, a reanalysis of their data by Bialystok and Hakuta (1994) showed a different pattern. In general, it was true that the earlier the age of arrival, the higher the test scores. However, there was no sharp break in the scores at around age 13. Rather, the scores decreased with age at about the same rate over the entire range of ages. If any sharp break in the scores could be claimed, it was around the age of 20. It was true that there was less variation in the scores of the younger learners. That is, the subjects who arrived before the age of 8 all scored at about the same level—a fact that supports the critical period hypothesis. But it was also true that those who arrived after the age of 20 (and who ought to have been equally unsuccessful at language learning) scored all over the board—a fact that does not support the hypothesis. To further confuse the issue, some subjects in this latter group received scores equal to those of subjects who arrived at age 10.

Bialystok and Hakuta concluded that Johnson and Newport's data are not consistent with a strong critical period hypothesis. Rather, the data suggest that as learners mature, individual and cultural factors become more important in the acquisition process. For example, it is often noticed that when American diplomatic families go abroad, the children come back speaking the local language fluently, but the parents do not. What is sometimes not noticed is that the children's schoolmates and playmates are likely to speak only the local language, whereas the parents' business associates and friends are likely to use English a lot of the time. Also, as any parent of a teenager can attest (as well as many studies, e.g., Eckert, 1991), kids want to talk like their friends. If they live in the United States, they pick up their friends' accent; if they live abroad, they pick up their friends' language.

The debate about whether adults have access to UG is far from resolved, as shown in an issue of the journal *Brain and Behavioral Sciences*. The format of this journal is to publish a "target" article on a controversial subject and then invite 20 or 30 scholars from different fields to take potshots at it. In an article titled, "Second Language Acquisition: Theoretical and Experimental Issues in Contemporary Research," Epstein, Flynn, and Martohardjono (1996) advocate the full UG access position. The critiques of their argument span the spectrum of possible positions. Some reviewers strongly agree with the authors; some support the partial access position; some support the no access position; and some say that the entire UG theory is wrong and should be discarded. What language teachers can take away from the research and debate on UG is that for whatever reason, young children do seem eventually to reach higher levels of proficiency in an L2 than adults, but that adult learners can reach very high levels as well.

Perspectives From Pidgin and Creole Studies

In this section, we will discuss an innatist theory of language acquisition called the *bioprogram*, proposed by University of Hawaii linguist Derek Bickerton, who studies pidgin and creole languages. Before discussing the bioprogram theory, we will take a look at these fascinating language varieties.

Legend has it that in the 7th century B.C., Pharaoh Psamtik I conducted a psycholinguistics experiment. He commanded that two children be taken from their mothers and raised in a remote hut, cared for by a mute shepard. Psamtik believed that the children would invent their own language, which would be the ur-language from which all others are descended. The first word that the children spoke was *bekos*, the word for "bread" in Phrygian, a language spoken in what is now Turkey. There is a similar modern-day academic legend, handed down by generations of linguistics students. They tell of a professor who requested funding for a *Survivor*-type experiment. He wanted to isolate a dozen children on an island, to be cared for by adults who would never speak to them, believing like Psamtik I that the children would invent their own language, which would exhibit the workings of the LAD in pure form. (The proposal was not funded.) The professor was no doubt inspired not only by the ancient legend, but also by a real-life experiment that has occurred naturally many times during human history: the creation of pidgin and creole languages.

Description

A pidgin is a contact language that is created when linguistically diverse populations come together. One circumstance is when the two groups wish to trade, and the word *pidgin* supposedly derives from the English word *business*. A pidgin can also arise when diverse populations are uprooted and mixed together in a foreign place. This occurred in the 19th century when workers from the Philippines, Japan, China, Korea, and other Pacific Rim countries immigrated to Hawaii to find work in the booming sugar industry. It also occurred more catastrophically over a 300-year period when West Africans were forced into slavery and transported to the New World.

Under such circumstances, people invent a system of communication. Readers who have shopped in a foreign market may know how this can be done. Even if the buyer and seller don't share a language, the buyer can just hold something up and say, "How much?" The circumstances make it pretty clear what is being asked. The seller's answer can be communicated by holding up the right number of fingers, and a counteroffer can be made by holding up fewer fingers. Now suppose the buyer is a Japanese immigrant to Hawaii and the seller is a Chinese immigrant, and that they frequently do business. After a while, they will agree on an expression for "How much?" and on words for the numbers and the items in the marketplace. These will probably be English words because that is the common language they are exposed to. As their vocabularies increase, buyer and seller will string words together, but the sentences, like those in early child speech, will lack many grammatical niceties like verb tenses and articles. Also, the order of the words will be influenced by the word order in the speakers' languages, as though they are framing a sentence in those languages but inserting English words. Thus, the Japanese speaker may say, "How much this is?" because in Japanese the verb comes last in the sentence, but the Chinese speaker may say, "How much this?" because in Chinese the verb *be* can be omitted from the sentence. This form of communication is an incipient pidgin language. A pidgin takes vocabulary words from a dominant regional language and strings them together in ways that are simplified and influenced by the speakers' native tongues. Here are some examples spoken by immigrants to Hawaii:

A Japanese: Me capey buy, me check make.
              my coffee bought, to me check made
              "He bought my coffee, he made me a check."

A Filipino: Good, dis one. Kaukau any-kin' dis one.
                          food   of all kinds
              Pilipine islan' no good. No mo money.
              "This place is good. There's all kinds of food. The Philippines
              Islands aren't good. There's no money there" (Pinker, 1994,
              p. 33).

After a pidgin language has been used for years in a community, it becomes more complex and more standard, both because speakers agree to
say things the same way and because they have more contact with speakers
of the language from which the vocabulary was borrowed (called the *lexifier*
language). West African Pidgin English is a good example of a highly developed pidgin. This language is still an L2 to almost all of its speakers, but it
has developed articles, verb tenses, and the other accouterments of an L1,
as can be seen in this folk tale in West African Pidgin English.

Sens-pass-king
Wiser-than-king

There once lived a very clever lad who lived in a beautiful part of Africa,
where he got much wisdom. He was smarter than the king himself, and so his
name was "sens-pass-king" (Wiser-than-king). The king was very annoyed
when he heard that this young boy was outwitting everyone. So, the king sum-
moned the boy and, planning to trick him, demanded that he cut his hair.

Sens-pass-king i bin don gri sey, i gow bap king i het.
Wiser-than-king agreed to cut the king's hair.

i bigin kot-am bot ha i di kot-am, i di sowsow trowwey
He began to cut it, but as he was cutting, he was also throwing down

simol kon fo fawu, we i dey fo king i domot.
a little corn for the chickens in the king's courtyard.

king i aks i sey, hayu di sowsow trow kon?
The king asked him, "Why are you always throwing down corn?"

boi ansa i sey, na lo fo gif chop
The boy answered, "Is there a law against feeding

fo fawu? simol-tam i don finis i wok. king i het don
the chickens?" Soon he finished his work. The king's head looked

nyan'ga bat. king i bigin hala, sey, na wati?
very fine. The king (then) began to shout, "What's going on there?"

simol wowwow pikin klin het fo bik-man?
Can a good-for-nothing child shave the head of an elder?

meyk yu put bak ma biabia wan-tam.
Put back my hair immediately.

a gow kil yu ifi yu now put-am!
I'll kill you if you don't put it back!

sens-pas-king tok sey, now keys. a gri.
Wiser-than-king replied, "No problem. I agree.

i bi dasow se
I will gladly do it

meyk yu gif bak ma kon bifo a gow fiks yu biabia agen.
if you give back my corn before I put it back again."

king i now sabi wati fo tok. i mof don lok.
The king didn't know what to say. His mouth locked up (he was speechless)
(Traugott & Pratt, 1980, p. 368).

A creole language is the child of a pidgin, and the first generation of creole speakers are literally children of pidgin speakers. In Hawaii before the turn of the 20th century, the society of sugarcane workers was extremely diverse, so much so that speakers of different languages often married each other. In these circumstances, native languages gave way to the developing language of the community, Hawaiian Pidgin English. But, when children were born into the pidgin speaking community, a funny thing happened: They invented their own language (Bickerton, 1981, 1984). As we have seen, early pidgin languages do not have many of the features that come as standard equipment with native languages. But the children needed these features in order to communicate efficiently and to express the full range of ideas that the human mind conceives. So, they invented an article system, a system of verb tenses, ways of embedding one sentence within another, and other L1 features that were missing from the pidgin. These new systems were quite different from the equivalent systems in Standard English (although the words used to implement them were English words). Where did these new features come from? According to Bickerton, they sprang full grown from the children's minds. Bickerton (1981, 1984) claims that the LAD can not only abstract linguistic systems from input but, when input is insufficient, it can provide the missing systems, drawing on innate linguistic knowledge.

Bioprogram Theory

Bickerton says that his theory, called the *bioprogram*, is similar in spirit to Chomsky's UG (though the details are completely different). If the bioprogram hypothesis is correct, it predicts that creole languages that have developed independently around the world, such as Hawaiian English Creole and Guyanese English Creole, should have similar systems of articles, negation, tense, embedding, and so on, and, in fact, they do. This structural similarity is also shared by creoles that take their vocabulary from French (e.g., Haitian Creole), Spanish (e.g., Papiamentu, spoken in Colombia), and other languages. When linguists noticed the astonishing similarity of creoles around the world, they assumed that all creole languages must have had a common ancestor, and there was a good candidate: a romance-based pidgin spoken around the Mediterranean that was descended from Sabir, a lingua franca used by the Crusaders. In fact, Portuguese sailors could have spread some features of Atlantic creoles to the Pacific. But the single ancestor theory is not held by most linguists. The range of creole languages around the world and the recency of some shows that some creoles have developed independently, and their similarities must be accounted for by some mechanism like the bioprogram.

Articles in creoles and child language. The article system of creole languages seems to have sprung directly from the bioprogram. English has four articles: *a, an, some,* and *the.* For analysis purposes, we will add one more, Ø, meaning that no article is required. The use of articles in English is complex. They are a perfect example of a linguistic system that has few rules of thumb. After trying for years to teach articles explicitly to English as a second language (ESL) students, I realized that when they consciously tried to figure out which article to use they often got it wrong, but when they just relied on their intuitions they often got it right. So I stopped explaining and just exposed them to the language, letting their LADs do the work.

Articles modify nouns, and four semantic considerations related to the noun determine which article should be used. The first consideration is whether the noun can be counted or not (in the jargon, whether the noun is *countable* or *uncountable*). If it is uncountable, it takes Ø, *some,* or *the*:

I forgot to buy Ø/some/the milk (you can't count milk, although you can count cartons of milk).

If the noun is countable, the second semantic consideration comes into play: Is it singular or plural? If it's plural, it takes Ø, *some,* or *the,* like an uncountable noun.

I forgot to buy Ø/some/the batteries.

If it's singular, it must take *a* or *an.*

I need a/*Ø/*some battery.

The next two semantic considerations are more abstract than countability or plurality. One consideration is whether the noun is specific or nonspecific. If I say, "The dog is man's best friend," I don't have any specific dog in mind, but if I say, "The dog kept me up all night with its barking," I do have a specific dog in mind. The other semantic consideration is whether the noun in question is known or unknown to the listener. Often, the first time a noun is introduced in a discourse it is unknown, but after that it is known. If the noun is countable and singular, *a* is used the first time and *the* is used thereafter:

> In *a* castle there lived *a* beautiful princess. *The* castle was drafty but *the* princess was upbeat.

Here is a simplified chart that shows which articles are used with the various types of nouns.

| | | Specific | |
	Nonspecific	*unknown*	*known*
countable	sg. a book	a castle	the castle
	pl. (some) books	(some) castles	the castles
uncountable	(some) milk	(some) milk	the milk

One of the complexities that the chart leaves out is how to mark generic nouns. Generic nouns are nonspecific and considered known to the hearer based on general knowledge about the world. In the sentence, "The dog is man's best friend," *dog* is generic. But generics can take *a* as well as *the* with no change of meaning: "A dog is man's best friend." And if the generic noun is uncountable, it takes Ø: "Beer is man's best friend." Even rocket scientists can get this mixed up. Neil Armstrong blew perhaps the most famous line in history when he said, "That's one small step for man (–specific, +known, i.e., generic), one giant leap for mankind (–specific, +known, i.e., generic). What he meant to say was, "That's one small step for *a* man [+specific, +known, i.e., me—Armstrong), one giant leap for mankind."

The creole article system, unencumbered by millennia of convention and contamination, is a lot simpler. According to Bickerton, Hawaiian English Creole uses articles only to mark specific nouns. Nonspecific nouns never take articles:

> yang fela [–specific, +known] dei no du dat
> "Young fellows don't do that."
> bat nobadi gon get jab [–specific, –known]
> "But nobody will get a job."

Specific nouns take *wan* or *som* if they are unknown to the hearer, *da* if they are known (kind of like *a*, *some*, and *the*):

> aefta da boi [+specific, +known], da wan wen jink daet milk, awl da maut soa
> "Afterward, the mouth of the boy who had drunk that milk was all sore."

hi get wan blaek buk [+specific, –known]
"He has a black book."

Here is a chart that shows the patterns of article use in Hawaiian English Creole.

		Specific	
	Nonspecific	*unknown*	*known*
countable	sg. buk	wan buk	da buk
	pl. buk(s)	som buk(s)	da buk(s)
uncountable	milk	som milk	da milk

In creole article systems, the specific–nonspecific distinction among nouns is the most important semantic consideration, and it imposes a clean constraint: If a noun is specific, it takes an article; if it is nonspecific, it doesn't. The Standard English system has become mucked up, as we have seen. Bickerton has an intriguing theory about why this is so. The creole system is more basic because the specific–nonspecific distinction reflects a difference between two kinds of cognitive structures: percepts and concepts. A percept is a mental image of a particular entity on a particular occasion, such as my memory of the cat that just walked past my desk; a percept is +specific. A concept is a mental image (*schema* would be a better word, as we will see in chap. 5) of a class of things, such as my mental image of cats in general; concepts are –specific. From an evolutionary standpoint, percepts are more primitive than concepts. The ability to perceive goes pretty far down the phylogenetic ladder—at least as far as frogs, who can perceive flies. The ability to abstract a concept from many percepts is rarer, and it obviously has great survival value. Bickerton suggests that this abstracting ability enables an organism to generalize about its environment, that is, to reason in terms of generics rather than in terms of particulars. He invites us to imagine our ancestors saving their skins by reasoning that, "Wounded boars do such and such, so I can anticipate what will happen and be ready to act appropriately" (1984, p. 277). The concept "wounded boars" is, of course, generic.

The bioprogram has implications for L1 acquisition. Bickerton claims that, like UG, it provides children with a first hypothesis about how articles will work in the language they are exposed to (if that language has an article system). Specifically, Bickerton says,

> Those semantic distinctions whose neural infrastructure was laid down first in the course of mammalian development will be the first to be lexicalized and/ or grammaticized in the course of human language development (1981, p. 242).

In regard to the article system he says,

> When a substantial body of early child language is properly examined, there
> will be found to be a significant skewing in article placement, such that a sig-
> nificantly higher percentage of articles will be assigned to specific reference
> NPs, while zero forms will persist in nonspecific environments longer than
> elsewhere (p. 154).

Thus, the child's first hypothesis about how to use articles will resemble the
creole article system. Child language researcher Gary Cziko (1986) reviewed three studies of child article acquisition that had sufficient data to
test the bioprogram hypothesis; two of the studies were of children learning
English and one was of children learning French. In all three studies, the
bioprogram hypothesis was supported.

To test the bioprogram hypothesis in L2 acquisition, I looked at English
article acquisition by adult speakers of Korean, a language that has no articles (Adamson, 1989). I found that the overwhelming strategy of the lower
proficiency speakers was to omit articles before all noun phrases. But when
they used articles, the speakers used them mostly before specific noun
phrases. The higher proficiency speakers still omitted a lot of articles, but
there was no difference in how often they used them before specific and
nonspecific nouns. It is possible that the lower proficiency speakers were re-
lying, at least in part, on the bioprogram hypothesis as a first guess about
how English articles are used, but the higher proficiency speakers had
abandoned this hypothesis.

PERSPECTIVES FROM COGNITIVE PSYCHOLOGY

I have recounted the behaviorist and innatist stories of language acquisition in some detail because I believe that they have had the greatest effect
on language teaching. But there are other stories as well, and I will briefly
mention two, both of which come more from the field of cognitive psychology than from linguistics.

The Nativization Hypothesis

The discussion of pidgin and creole languages provides a convenient place
to consider the *nativization hypothesis*, proposed by Roger Andersen of
UCLA (1981, 1983). Andersen has pointed out that there are similarities in
pidgins, creoles, the early stages of child language, and the speech of L2
learners (called *interlanguage*). We have already noted that in creoles, child
language, and the interlanguage of Korean speakers, article systems de-

velop in similar ways. Another similarity in these varieties and in pidgins is the strategy of placing negative words before the verb they modify. Standard English puts the negator *not* in the middle of the verb phrase:

> George was *not* planning to recount the ballots.
> Al did*n't* have a chance to recount the ballots.

But a common pidgin strategy is to put *no* in front of the entire verb phrase:

> People no like t'come fo' go wok.
> "People don't want to have him go to work [for them]."
> Yu no go hom pilipin ailen?
> "Didn't you go home to the Philippines?"
> (Bickerton, 1984; quoted in Pinker, 1994, p. 34)

This strategy is found in child language (Brown, 1973), creoles (Bickerton, 1984), and interlanguage (Schumann, 1978), as well.

Andersen (1981, 1983) claims that these and other similarities have the same motivation, namely convergence toward an internal (i.e., innate) norm. He calls this process *nativization*. Nativization, then, is early language acquisition in which the learner employs innate strategies for organizing and processing information. Such strategies were suggested by Berkeley psycholinguist Dan Slobin (1977), who called them *operating principles*. For example, Operating Principle E states, "Underlying semantic relations should be marked overtly and clearly" (p. 110). This principle implies that linguistic systems in which semantic relations are not so marked, such as the English article system, will cause difficulty for learners, and this is indeed the case for learners of both L1 and L2 English. Furthermore, as the studies by Cziko (1986) and Adamson (1989) suggest, learners abide by Principle E when first constructing an article system, using an article to mark only specific NPs. Principle E can also be seen at work in the post-creole continuum (where a creole becomes more like the lexifier language) to be discussed later. We will see that in more nativized English creoles, a single word, *ben, di,* or *did* is always used to mark the notion of past time. But varieties that are closer to Standard English adopt a more complex strategy, where the past tense marker can become part of an irregular verb form, as in *went* and *gave*.

Slobin claims that the operating principles, which now number about 40, comprise a Language Making Capacity (LMC). But the LMC is different from the LAD in at least two respects. First, it is not clear whether the operating principles are devoted only to analyzing language input, like the LAD, or whether they are general ways of organizing any cognitive information. Second, the LMC contains no specific linguistic knowledge, such as the head direction principle.

The nativization hypothesis also addresses the question of how creole languages change and develop in a community. When contact between creole speakers and speakers of a lexifier language increases, the creole becomes more like the lexifier language. This process is called *decreolization.* In communities undergoing decreolization, such as present-day Guyana or Haiti, a continuum of forms develops, ranging from the pure creole used in rural areas to the standard language used in the schools. The pure creole end of the continuum is called the *basilect;* the standard language end is called the *acrolect;* and the varieties in between make up the *mesolect.* The following extract is the complete range of ways to say "I gave him" in Guyana, ranging from basilect to acrolect.

Guyanese Creole (basilect)	mi gii am
	mi bin gii am
	mi bin gii ii
	mi bin gi ii
	mi di gii ii
	mi di gi hii
	a di gii ii
mesolect	a di gi ii
	a did gi ii
	a did giv ii
	a did giv hii
	a giv ii
	a giv im
	a giv him
	a geev ii
	a geev im
	a geev him
English (acrolect)	I gave him
(Romaine, 1994, p. 171)	

In the basilect, the past tense form *gii* is the same as the present tense form, as with Standard English *put.* In the mesolect, past is marked with *bin*, then *di*, then *did*, in accordance with Slobin's Operating Principle E. In the next stage of the mesolect, once again one form, *giv*, serves as both present and past tense. Finally, past is distinguished from present by changing the vowel of the verb, first in *geev* and finally, as in Standard English, *gave.*

Typically, speakers control several of these lects and can shift along the continuum so as to use forms appropriate to their audience. This phenomenon is called *accommodation*, and we all do it. When I was in Ireland, I found myself able to throw in a few "mind you's", "pardon's" and even "Will you be coming, then?" instead of my usual, "Ya comin'?". But I couldn't keep this up for long, and I am told that the same is true of mesolect speakers trying to maintain the acrolect.

The series of forms for *I, gave,* and *him* (Romaine, 1994, p. 171) represents a snapshot of the English used in Guyana today, but it is also a time line showing the development of the language. The basilect forms came first, the mesolect forms came later, and the acrolect, which had served as the lexifier language, gained speakers as education became more widespread. A similar phenomenon occurs when speakers of a pidgin language come into increased contact with the lexifier language. Over time, the speakers may adopt more acrolect features. This process is called *depidginization.* Andersen believes that decreolization and depidginization are similar psycholinguistically. In both cases, a variety that is in some universal sense simple becomes more complex. In other words, speakers accommodate toward an external, more prestigious norm. Andersen calls this process *denativization* and claims that it also operates in both first and second language acquisition.

We will return to the subject of pidgins and creoles in chapter 4, noting their relationship to Black English, but let me briefly preview that discussion here. A particularly interesting form is the word *don,* which is used to indicate completed action, as in *i mof don lock* "his mouth locked" (i.e., he was dumfounded). As we will see, *done* is used in a similar way in present-day Black English, and there are other similarities between pidgins and creoles and modern Black English as well, leading some linguists to suggest that Black English originated as a creole created by slaves, which is now in the very last stages of decreolization. Thus, Black English may be at the upper end of a post-creole continuum—almost completely assimilated to Standard English but still preserving a few markers of its earlier history.

Information Processing Approaches

An information processing model of learning has been developed by the psychologist John Anderson (1980, 1983) and adapted for language learning by the psycholinguist Barry McLaughlin (1980, 1987). Unlike the other accounts of language acquisition reviewed in this chapter, the information processing story is not nativist, and in this sense is a descendant of behaviorism. Information processing models are based on the idea that the mind works a lot like a computer. It is claimed that both mind and computer contain two kinds of knowledge: *declarative* and *procedural.* Declarative knowledge includes facts about the world, such as the fact that the Panama Canal connects the Atlantic and Pacific Oceans or that birds eat worms. Procedural knowledge involves knowing how to do things, like play tennis or speak French. Declarative knowledge is knowing *that*; procedural knowledge is knowing *how.* Declarative knowledge is stored in memory in a network of *schemas*, or mental representations, which we will examine more thoroughly in chapter 5. An example of such a network can be found in Figure 5.1. Another type of schema is called a *script*. Scripts are mental representations of an experience, such as going to a restaurant. The restaurant script includes information about how people usually enter a restaurant, get a table, summon the waiter, order their food, and so on. Not all cultures share the same restaurant script. For example, part of a Spaniard's restaurant script includes the information that to summon the waiter you raise your hand and say "Psst!" in a loud whisper.

Procedural knowledge is stored in a computer program (and by analogy in the mind) in the form of *productions* (also called *demons*), which are sets of rules for performing some action. A skill such as driving a car or spelling the word *retriever* requires activating the appropriate productions. Anderson (1980) gives the following example of a production for shifting from first to second gear in a stick-shift car.

> IF   a car is in first gear
>   and the car is going faster than 10 mph
>   and there is a clutch
>   and there is a stick
>
> THEN   depress the clutch
>   and move the stick to the upper right position
>   and release the clutch (p. 239).

A production, then, consists of one or more conditions and one or more actions, and it requires that the individual or computer have the appropriate declarative knowledge. The Anderson (1980) example requires knowing what a gear, a clutch, and a stick shift are.

The spelling rule "i before e except after c unless sounded as AY as in 'neighbor' or 'way' " could be written as a production like this:

> IF   a word contains an *i, e* combination
>   and a *c* does not precede the *i, e* combination
>   and the *i, e* combination does not represent the AY sound
>
> THEN   write the *i* before the *e*.

Mitchell and Myles (1998) observe that Anderson's mental model has been more successful in describing the learning of content material than in describing language acquisition. For one thing, Anderson originally claimed that procedural knowledge is at first known consciously and later becomes unconscious, or automatic, through practice. This is obviously wrong for language acquisition because, except for a few linguists, speakers have no conscious knowledge of most linguistic rules, such as the rules for making a pronoun agree with its referent (Anderson has since withdrawn this claim). However, the idea that conscious declarative knowledge is stored in memory in a network of schemas is helpful for understanding how content subjects like history are learned, and we will revisit Anderson's information processing model in chapter 5 when we discuss learning in mainstream classes.

SUMMARY: THE COMPUTER METAPHOR

Before considering the third story of language acquisition, which goes off in a very different direction, let me sum up the discussion so far. The behaviorist story descended from the empiricist philosophers like John Locke, who believed that the mind of an infant is a blank slate and that what we eventually know, including language, is learned entirely from experience. This view was disputed by the rationalist philosophers like René Descartes, who said that the infant's mind contains a rich store of knowledge. Lacking a theory of genetics, Descartes thought that innate ideas, such as TRIANGLE, GREATER THAN and, indeed, GOD, were known to the mind by the force of logical necessity. The difference in the two philosophies has narrowed considerably over the years. The behaviorists did not deny that we are up to our ears in genetically controlled behavior. They agreed that our genes determine that we will walk upright, eat with our hands, live in social groups, and that we are capable of learning complex linguistic systems. Since the demise of behaviorism, the difference between the empiricist and rationalist camps has narrowed even more. The descendants of the behaviorists, acknowledge that how we learn is dependent on genetically determined cognitive abilities. One modern school that is distantly related to behaviorism is *connectionism*, which models language learning using computers. Connectionist programs do not use Chomskian rules or anything like principles and parameters, but they require a great deal of initial programming in order to know what to look for in the language input they analyze. This initial programming is very much like some form of innate linguistic knowledge.

Descartes' academic descendants, who include UG grammarians, postulate inborn linguistic knowledge and processing mechanisms, which can also be thought of using the computer metaphor. Like the workings of a computer, the language faculty can be described at different levels of abstraction. At the least abstract level is the "wetware," groups of connected brain cells that are wired to detect specific features in the language input, such as the fact that it will be organized hierarchically and that ways of referring to things in the world may be organized in terms of binding principle

B. These neural networks can be described at a more abstract level using linguistic rules or phrase structure trees, which correspond to the lines of code in a computer program. The rules, like the lines of code, correspond to many individual physical connections that are involved in learning a pattern, such as the fact that the past tense of *go* is *went*. At the highest level of abstraction are Chomsky's principles and parameters. These are like the decision boxes in a flow chart for a computer program, directing the LAD to construct different subprograms (e.g., a subprogram that sets the head direction parameter) depending on what features they detect in the input.

Computer scientists could, if they had to, exactly describe the relationship between a computer's hardware and the software it is running. That is, they could tell what circuits go on and off as the computer is adding 2 + 2 or doing a spell check. To do so, they would have to consult the computer's operating manual. Similarly, it should be theoretically possible for psychologists to describe exactly the relationship between a mental subprogram, like building a noun phrase tree, and the neural circuits that instantiate it. Unfortunately, as my psycholinguistics professor used to say, "We've lost the manual!" Perhaps psycholinguists of the distant future can reconstruct it.

In the view of many psycholinguists, the stories I have told so far sum up what can be said about language acquisition. Radical behaviorists are extinct. Their descendants still argue with the innatists about how much linguistic knowledge is inborn, but both schools agree that the way to study language acquisition is to study the workings of the mind, not the connections between environment and behavior. Cognitive science, and its computer metaphor of the mind, wins the day. And yet, a lot of people are uneasy with the computer analogy. This is partly because people who work with computers know how stupid they are. The machines can do wonders in carefully controlled worlds, like a chess game or an automobile assembly line, but the year 2001 has come and gone, and a computer like Hal in the movie *2001: A Space Odyssey*, who could converse meaningfully, is still science fiction.

Another source of unease with the computer metaphor, one that I hear from my English Department colleagues, is that computers will always be very different from human beings. Computers don't live in societies; they don't bear and raise children; they don't make friends or enemies; they don't get bored or embarrassed; they can turn on, but they can't tune in, or drop out; they aren't pleased, joyous, curious, angry, determined, amused, or inspired. But people do and are these things, and the noncomputational part of being human—the fun part—plays an important role in language acquisition. These noncognitive considerations fall into two categories: affective and social/cultural. We will look at affective factors in our discussion of the acculturation model later in this chapter, and in our discussion of the monitor model in chapter 3. But we now turn to the third major story of language acquisition: the role of social and cultural factors.

SOCIAL/CULTURAL APPROACHES TO LANGUAGE ACQUISITION

Chomsky's theory of language raised concerns of the kind I have just mentioned among scholars of anthropology and sociology who studied language. They believed that his theory was incomplete because it left out the human dimension. These scholars observed that generative grammar was a theory of language *form*, that is, of word order, pronoun reference, subject–verb agreement, and so forth, but that it said nothing about language *use*—how we use grammatical forms to accomplish our human goals. As parents know, children have to learn the social rules of language along with the grammar. Once when my daughter was 3 years old, she was playing dolls on the couch when I sat down. Wishing me to sit somewhere else, she yelled in perfectly correct English, "Get off! Get off! Get off!" This did not accomplish her goal, but got her a lecture on politeness rules. In this section, we will take a look at how speakers learn to use linguistic knowledge appropriately and effectively in their first and second languages.

First Language Acquisition

Communicative Competence

The anthropologist Dell Hymes (1972) used the term *communicative competence* to describe the ability of speakers to use culturally specific rules for language use, without which the speaker would not be able to communicate effectively. For example, in a certain speech community, it may be considered impolite to look the addressee in the eye while speaking, whereas in another speech community, eye contact may be appropriate. All L1 speakers learn such rules as part of becoming competent members of a speech community.

One aspect of communicative competence involves knowing how to do things with words. The British philosopher J. L. Austin (1962) noticed that people can use words to change the state of the world, as when a minister says, "I now pronounce you man and wife," or a judge says, "I sentence you to 30 days in the county jail." Of course, for the couple to actually be married or for the defendant to actually serve time, these words must be uttered in the appropriate circumstances by the appropriate people. Austin called such uses of language *speech acts*, and pointed out that the appropriate circumstances for their use are often spelled out in laws and regulations.

When Richard Nixon resigned the Presidency in 1974, the country became aware that the manner of his resigning was spelled out in Amendment XXV of the Constitution: "[T]he President transmits to the President pro tempore of the Senate and the Speaker of the House of Representatives his written declaration that he is unable to discharge the powers and duties of his office. . . . ."

Austin also noticed that people perform nonlegalistic speech acts everyday. "I compliment you on your presentation," performs the act of complimenting, and "I apologize for calling your presentation preposterous," performs the act of apologizing. For these speech acts to be effective, they too must be performed in the appropriate circumstances. For example, if the person who uttered the apology hadn't criticized the presentation, no true apology would have occurred. The social rules for complimenting and apologizing are not written down, but must be learned along with the linguistic rules of a language.

So far, our examples of speech acts have used the word that names the speech act in the utterance itself: *marry, sentence, compliment,* and *apologize.* Austin calls these kinds of speech acts *performatives.* But one needn't use a performative verb to accomplish a speech act. "That was a great presentation" and "I'm sorry" will accomplish the acts of complimenting and apologizing just as well as the performative versions.

Our examples so far have also involved *direct* speech acts, but *indirect* speech acts are also possible. An indirect speech act occurs when one speech act (a primary act) occurs by means of another speech act (a literal act). For example, "Can you pass the salt?" contains the literal act of asking a question, but the primary act is a request. In other words, the speaker isn't asking whether it is possible for the hearer to pass the salt, but rather requesting that the salt be passed. Further complicating matters for the language user are issues of politeness. For instance, when should you say, "Can you pass the salt, please?" or "Would you mind passing the salt, if it's not too much trouble?" or just "Pass the salt!"?

Understanding a primary speech act concealed within a literal speech act is just one example of the subtleties language learners have to deal with. These subtleties are highlighted in the theory of British philosopher H. P. Grice (1989), who explains how language users cooperate with each other in making meaning. Grice's *cooperative principle* says that a speaker's contribution to a conversation should be no more than is required within the context in which it is uttered. As corollaries to the cooperative principle, Grice proposed four maxims of conversation: (1) the maxim of quality (be truthful); (2) the maxim of quantity (be no more or less informative than necessary); (3) the maxim of relevance (be relevant); and (4) the maxim of manner (be clear). All of this sounds perfectly reasonable and even simple until Grice points out that in actual conversation, these maxims are flouted regularly, and that learners have to understand why. For example, irony often depends on flouting the maxim of quality. Suppose George says, "What if the F.B.I. doesn't catch the terrorist?" Colleen replies, "Oh, come on. The F.B.I. always gets its man." Because Colleen's statement is obviously false, she must be making a point other than her literal meaning. In an attempt to make Colleen's statement make sense, George might take her to mean the opposite of what she said. In that case, Colleen was being ironic and George should be worried.

Learning speech acts. Child language researcher Gordon Wells (1986) has studied how children learn to perform speech acts correctly. Wells directed a massive research project that studied the language development of 32 British children from preschool through elementary school. He and his colleagues observed and recorded the children about once a week and documented the children's developing competence. Listen to 2-year-old Mark's adroit use of language with his mother.

[Mark is in the kitchen with his mother and his sister Helen. He is holding a mirror in which he sees reflected now himself and now his mother]

Mark: Mummy, Mummy.

Mother: What?

Mark: There. There Mark.

Mother: Is that Mark?

Mark: Mark. [pointing to Mother] Mummy.

Mother: [exaggerated rising intonation]: Mm.

[A minute later, looking out of the window at the birds in the garden]

Mark: Look-at-that. Birds, Mummy.

Mother: Mm.

Mark: Jubs [birds].

Mother: What are they doing?

Mark: Jubs bread [Birds eating bread].

Mother: Oh look! They're eating the berries, aren't they?

Mark: Yeh.

Mother: That's their food. They have berries for dinner.

Mark: Oh.

[Some minutes later.]

Mark: Er fwa, Mummy? [Want water.]

Mother: What?

Mark: Er fwa?

Mother: No.

Mark: Fwa?

Mother: No (Wells, 1986, p. 22).

Wells notes that in this passage, Mark performs at least four speech acts, which are among those that all his subjects used: *call, ostention, statement,* and *request.* The function of call is to get someone's attention, and Mark's preferred device here is "Mummy." Having gotten Mummy's attention, Mark directs it to the object of interest, that is, his reflection in the mirror, thus successfully performing the act of ostention. Mark has learned that ostention can precede getting attention (or perhaps serve the two functions at once) when he says, "Look-at-that. Birds, Mummy." Mark performs the act of stating when he says, "Jubs bread," and the act of requesting when he says, "Er fwa, Mummy?"

Learning a Language Variety

The socially appropriate use of language is not restricted to learning how to perform speech acts or flout conversational maxims effectively. Certain socially significant linguistic forms must be learned as well. Here is a personal example. My wife and I speak different dialects of American English: Hers is southern; mine is western. When we met, one obvious difference in our speech was that she used *you all* and I didn't. I made a conscious effort to start using her second-person plural pronoun, partly because the Standard English pronoun system needs beefing up (Amharic has five pronouns that translate as "you"), but mostly because I wanted her family to like me. When our children were born and raised in Northern Virginia, they were exposed to dialects with and without *you all.* Although our children had two parents and plenty of friends and neighbors who said *you all,* they did not say it except at (their mother's) family gatherings. Other southern features were also missing from our children's speech. I suspect that in our Washington, D.C. suburb, southern speech, though abundant, was *marked* (noticeable) and northern speech was *unmarked* (neutral). Children who did not want to proclaim their regional identity chose the unmarked variety. The exception was at my wife's family reunions, where northern speech was as marked as boiled potatoes.

When we were graduate students, Ceil Kovac and I wondered how early children begin to acquire the distinctive patterns of the dialect they are exposed to (Kovac & Adamson, 1981), so we decided to look at one of the most distinctive varieties of American English—that spoken by African Americans. This variety has been called *African American Vernacular English, Ebonics,* and *Black English.* I will use the term *Black English* here because it is the most widespread. As we will see in more detail in chapter 4, Black English and Standard English differ in several respects regarding how they use the verb *be.* One difference is that Black English can delete *be* in the same places that Standard English can contract it. Thus, in Black English the following forms are possible: (1) She is a nurse (full form). (2) She's a nurse (contracted form). (3) She a nurse (omitted form). Standard English has only forms (1) and (2). So, to speak appropriately, children growing up exposed to Black English must learn a more complex system than children exposed to Standard English, and this learning is complicated by a developmental factor: In their earliest utterances, all children omit *be*, as in Mark's speech.

> Mark (looking in the mirror):   Mark there.

Thus, as children learn to use *be*, they must progress along two dimensions: a developmental dimension where they learn to use the various forms of *be* (*am, are, is, was, were*), and a social dimension where they learn to supply, contract, or omit these forms in the same way as other speakers in their speech community.

Ceil and I (okay, just Ceil; Kovac & Adamson, 1981) recorded the speech of 49 children ages 3, 5, and 7, with approximately equal numbers of children from Black English and Standard English backgrounds. We found that the children had indeed progressed along both dimensions. All the children who were exposed to Standard English, including the 3-year-olds, were beyond the stage of omitting *be*, producing it 99% of the time. The children exposed to Black English, which reinforced the pattern of their own early speech, showed more variation. The 3-year-olds omitted *be* 20% of the time, a higher rate than that of the European-American children but lower than that of teenage speakers of Black English (as determined in other studies, e.g., Labov, 1972). The 5- and 7-year-olds increased their *be* omission to 32%, demonstrating that they were acquiring the norm appropriate to their speech community.

Learning to Tell a Story

Almost every time people open their mouths, they perform some speech act. Wells' 2-year-olds stated, requested, and called attention to things, and their parents affirmed, informed, accused, ordered, apologized, and nagged. (Actually, nagging isn't on Wells' list of speech acts, but in a Seinfeld episode, the characters debated whether a fortune cookie contained a fortune or a nag, so there must be constitutive rules for nagging.) The sum of these speech acts comprises the *speech event* of conversing with a child, as it is done in Bristol. Speech events, like speech acts, have rules that must be adhered to in order to get things right. An academic lecture is a speech event in which the professor stands or sits at the front of the class and talks. If students want to talk, they are supposed to raise their hands, and the professor can choose to call on them. When I took a class from a blind professor, this convention was modified so that students who had a question softly called out their names. At Texas A&M University, I am told, professors should not say the words, "University of Texas." If they do, students are allowed to leave the room without penalty. Other examples of speech events include a casual conversation with a friend, a sermon, a job interview, a political debate, a committee meeting, a business lunch, and a story.

For children, learning how to tell a story is part of their enculturation into a community. And, just as language varieties differ from community to community, the rules for successful storytelling differ as well. A classic example comes from Heath's (1983) long-term study of two small communities in North Carolina: one Black and one White. Social values in Roadville, the White community, are traditional, and children are raised to be pious, truthful, and obedient to their parents. When parents correct their children's speech, it seldom involves grammatical lapses, but often involves impolite or untruthful speech.

Storytelling in Roadville also involves strict conventions of accuracy and prohibitions against gossip. It is okay to tell a story about someone else only if that person, or a close friend, is present. Like Bible stories, personal stories usually involve a lesson or moral, often at the storyteller's expense. Roadville children are not allowed to tell stories, unless invited to by an adult, and they are coached in the telling, as seen in the following dialogue, in which 5-year-old Wendy is invited to tell a story by her Aunt Sue.

Sue:	Tell . . . where we went today.
Wendy:	Mamma took me 'n Sally to the Mall. Bugs Bunny was . . .
Sue:	No, who was that, that wasn't Bugs Bunny.
Wendy:	Uh, I mean, Peter, no, uh a big Easter bunny was there, 'n we, he, mamma got us some eggs . . .
Sue:	'n then what happened?
Wendy:	I don't 'member.
Sue:	Yes, you do, what happened on the climbing . . .
Wendy:	. . . Me 'n Sally tried to climb on this thing, 'n we dropped, I dropped, my eggs, some of 'em.
Sue:	Why did you drop your eggs? What did Aunt Sue tell you 'bout climbin' on that thing?
Wendy:	We better be careful.
Sue:	No, 'bout the eggs 'n climbing.
Wendy:	We better not climb with our eggs, else 'n we'd drop em (Heath, 1983, p. 158).

Throughout the story, Aunt Sue insists on strict chronology, truthfulness, and, in the conclusion, an admission of guilt.

In Trackton, the African-American community, children are less engaged by their parents, according to Heath. As infants, they are more spoken about than spoken to by adults. However, they are in constant human company. Community life centers around the plaza, a stretch of dirt road in view of the stoops and porches of the eight or so houses that comprise the center of Trackton. In the plaza and its environs, children can play in groups of relatives, neighbors, and friends that form and reform, watched over by all of the adults in the area.

Boys and girls are enculturated in somewhat different ways. When boys begin to speak, they are taught to defend themselves verbally. One kind of speech event is the verbal accusation (a challenging question) and reply, such as the following exchange between 3-year-old Lem and Lillie Mae, who is exasperated at Lem for taking off his shoes. Lem defends himself by telling an imaginary story in rhyme.

Lillie Mae: You want me ta tie you up, put you on de railroad track?
Lem: Railroad track
Train all big 'n black.
On dat track, on dat track, on dat track
Ain't no way I can't get back
Back from dat track
Back from dat train
Big 'n black, I be back (p. 110).

Heath comments, "Everyone laughed uproariously, and Lillie Mae did not pursue any further the matter of Lem's removing his shoes" (p. 110).

A story in Trackton is very different from a story in Roadville. In Trackton, a good story is modest, didactic, and truthful. In Roadville, a good story is creative, poetic, exuberant, often self-aggrandizing, and not necessarily true. In Roadville, adults turn children's stories into a learning experience; in Trackton, children's stories must stand on their own. The children are not encouraged or questioned during the telling, and the story must be good enough to engage the adults' attention. As we have seen, Lem has the makings of a good storyteller; he is already adept at the use of the poetic devices of alliteration, rhythm, and rhyme.

Second Language Acquisition

Second Language acquisition (SLA) theory recognizes that mastering an L2 involves more than learning grammatical rules if the learner is to communicate effectively with native speakers. In 1980, Canale and Swain developed a model of communicative competence in SLA. As the model developed, four components were included: (1) grammatical competence, (2) sociolinguistic competence, (3) discourse competence, and (4) strategic competence. Grammatical competence involves knowing the grammatical rules of the language; sociolinguistic competence involves knowing how to use the language in the context of the speech community; discourse competence is the speaker's ability to achieve cohesion and coherence; and strategic competence is the learner's ability to use strategies to fill in gaps in the knowledge of the language.

Bachman (1990) also included aspects of communicative competence in his model of language competence. According to Bachman, language competence consists of organizational competence and pragmatic competence. Organizational competence contains grammatical competence and textual competence. Pragmatic competence contains illocutionary competence (the ability to use speech acts appropriately) and sociolinguistic competence (the ability to use linguistic forms appropriate to a particular context, e.g., knowing when to use the full, contracted, and zero forms of *be*). We will now take a closer look at these two components of pragmatic competence.

Illocutionary Competence

Like the children Wells studied, L2 learners must learn how to perform speech acts appropriately. I once asked three of my graduate students to give a brief presentation in class describing their plans for a research project. I chose these particular students because they had all submitted excellent research designs. The first two students, who were Americans, succinctly described how they intended to conduct their studies. The third student, who was Japanese, was reluctant to spell out the details of her project. During her presentation she kept apologizing, as though she thought her design wasn't very good. Everyone in the class had studied interlanguage pragmatics, and we guessed that this mannerism must be transferred from Japanese. Nevertheless, the constant apologizing distracted from her presentation. I later asked a professor of Japanese what was going on, and she said that the student may have been afraid that by assuming the role of teacher, she could be perceived as thinking that her proposal was better than the proposals of the other students (which, of course, it was). Her apologies were meant to say, "I don't take this stuff very seriously; I don't think I'm better than you."

Pragmatic difficulties are often a problem at universities where American freshmen majoring in science and math are taught by professors and teaching assistants (TAs) who come from other countries. A good example is described in a study of a Korean TA conducted by Andrea Tyler (1995) of Georgetown University. Tyler videotaped a tutoring session with the Korean TA and an American undergraduate and then showed the tape to the two participants to get their reactions.

The female American student had been given the assignment of writing a computer program that would score a bowling game. The Korean TA was a computer science major who had lived in the United States for 2 years and whose score on a test of oral English proficiency indicated that he spoke English fluently but with some problems in grammar and pronunciation. The tutoring session did not go well, and later both participants complained to the supervisor about the other's uncooperative attitude.

The basic problem was getting clear which participant had higher status: the tutor, who knew more about programming, or the student, who (she thought) knew more about bowling. The conflict between student and tutor began with this exchange:

Student: Well, do you know how to score [a bowling] game?
Tutor: Yeah, approximately (Tyler, 1995, p. 149).

The student took this answer to mean that the tutor was not very knowledgeable about bowling, which is part of American, not Korean, culture. But in fact, the tutor bowled often and knew very well how to score the game.

The conflict in the rest of the tutoring session revolves around the question of what happens if you bowl a strike. Do you (1) mark a 10 for that frame and move to the next frame, or (2) get another ball and the opportunity to score more than 10 for that frame? The tutor kept telling the student that the correct answer was (1), but she refused to believe him, as the following exchange shows:

Tutor: If it is a strike, that, that, that, will uh comprise one frame. . . . OK?
Student: Hold up, ya know. Let me ask you a question. If that means that's just 1 frame, you get 2 balls per frame, right? So listen. OK you get 2 balls per frame. Let's say you get a strike on the first, you still get to bowl that second ball.
T: Oh no.
S: You don't?
T: You have, you have to move over to next frame.
S: OK.
T: If it is 10, you, you finish one, one frame.
S: Right, OK.
T: OK?
S: So this is an example of strike right here. Right. They finish the . . . And if they finish, they still have that one ball left, right?
T: No, no, no (Tyler, 1995).

The American student is guilty of rudeness toward her tutor, but she has reason to be frustrated since the tutor does not abide by American academic discourse conventions. Why didn't he just say, "Look, I've bowled a lot, and I've scored many games, and this is how you do it"? To understand we need to take a closer look at Korean academic conventions.

In the Confucian tradition, the roles of teacher and student are strictly defined and are not open to negotiation. Each party must show respect toward the other. The student is expected to pay close attention to the teacher's explanations, picking up on subtle assertions and implications. The teacher is expected to devote the time and effort necessary to understand exactly what the student needs to know and to present the information appropriately, taking care not to pressure or embarrass the student, which the TA might do if he baldly stated that he knew more about an American pastime than an American. Students, for their part, are not free to interrupt or even ask questions, as this implies that the teacher has not made everything clear and thus constitutes a challenge to the teacher's status. In American academic culture, on the other hand, teachers and students often negotiate their relative status, and some students feel free to interrupt and even complain that the class isn't very good (one of my favorite complaints: "I had to learn so much for this class that wasn't on the final"). For these reasons, the Korean tutor was reluctant to say directly that he knew more about an American pastime than the student; however, he expected her to understand from his insistence on how to score that this was the case.

Sociolinguistic Competence

In the section on L1 acquisition, we discussed Kovac and Adamson's (1981) study of how young African-American children acquired one of the features of Black English: the variable omission of the verb *be*. L2 learners are also exposed to the distinctive linguistic markers of the target language community in which they live, markers that serve to identify a speaker's region, age, sex, social class, and other characteristics. Whether L2 learners, like children, acquire these sociolinguistic markers is a question addressed in a study conducted by Vera Regan and myself (Adamson & Regan, 1991). We wanted to find out whether Vietnamese and Cambodian immigrants, most of whom were living in Philadelphia, had mastered a very tricky sociolinguistic marker, the pronunciation of *ing*, as in the words *running*, *something*, and *darling*. Sometimes native English speakers pronounce the final syllable of these words EENG and sometimes IN. This latter pronunciation is represented in writing as *runnin'*, *somethin'*, and *darlin'*. Notice that both the vowel and the nasal consonant of the two pronunciations are different. The *i* in *darling* is pronounced EE as in *seat*, whereas the *i* in *darlin'* is pronounced IH as in *sit*. The former vowel is called *tense* because the tongue muscle tenses during pronunciation, and the latter vowel is called *lax* because the tongue muscle relaxes during pronunciation. The second difference between *ing* and *in'* is that the nasal sound in *ing* is formed by pressing the back of the tongue against the velar area at the back of the mouth, producing a *velar nasal*; the nasal sound in *in'* is formed by pressing the tip of the tongue against the alveolar ridge, which is just behind the front teeth, producing an *alveolar nasal*.

As you might suspect, *ing* is more common in formal speech and *in'* is more common in casual speech. In formal speaking situations (e.g., when talking about school or language), people pay more attention to, or *monitor*, the way they speak and aim for the more "correct" pronunciation, even though they occasionally miss the target. In informal speech (e.g., telling a story or a joke), people get more involved in the content of what they are saying and monitor less, so a more natural speaking style emerges containing more *in'*. *Ing* and *in'* usage shows other kinds of patterning as well. *Ing* is used more frequently in all contexts by middle-class speakers than by working-class speakers, and more frequently by women than by men. The frequency at which speakers use the two forms also depends on the grammatical category of the *ing* word. In the examples above, *darling* is a noun, and *running* can be a progressive verb form, as in "They are running." But prior to the 14th century, the progressive form did not take the suffix *ing*, but rather *ind*. Over the years, the final d eroded leaving the last syllable of progressives as *in*. As this sound is very similar to *ing*, the distinction was blurred, and eventually the spelling was changed to *ing* for progressives as well as nouns. But the historical origin of the two forms was preserved because progressives were still more frequently pronounced *in* and nouns were more frequently pronounced *ing*, a pattern that persists to this day.

And it gets even more complicated. Some *ing* words are neither true nouns nor verbs but something in between. For example, a *gerund* is a verbal form used as a noun (The *skiing* was a lot of fun). So gerunds are less "nouny" than nouns. Pronouns, like *something* and *nothing* are more nouny than gerunds but still less nouny than real nouns. A participle is an incomplete verb form that is less verby than a real verb because it cannot be the main verb in a sentence, as illustrated in this sentence: I saw [main verb] Marsha leaving [participle] the party early. It is possible, then, to set up a continuum of *ing* words that range from high nouniness to high verbiness. It looks like this: NOUNS PRONOUNS GERUNDS PARTICIPLES PROGRESSIVES. And, amazingly, in the speech of native English speakers, the pronunciation of *ing* words corresponds to this continuum, with the *in'* pronunciation increasing as you move to the right along the continuum. Taking the factors of speaker's social class, speaker's sex, topic, and grammatical class of *ing* word into account, the percentage of *ing* and *in'* in a stretch of discourse can be predicted fairly accurately (Cofer, 1972).

Vera and I chose to study speakers of Vietnamese and Cambodian because in the early stages of learning English, they use the phonological systems of their native languages, which means that they pronounce all *ing* words as *ing*, not *in'*. The degree to which these speakers learn to supply the informal *in'* appropriately for their demographic group, topic of conversation, and grammatical category of the *ing* word is a measure of how well they have assimilated into the American speech community.

We found that there was little variation in the speech of our low proficiency subjects: They hardly used any *in'*. But in the more advanced speakers, we found some patterning along the appropriate dimensions. Our most interesting finding involved patterning according to gender. For the native English speakers in our study, men of all socioeconomic groups used more *in'* than women in both formal and informal contexts. In fact, some of the working class men we interviewed on south Philadelphia street corners (Rocky's pals) used *in'* almost 100% of the time when telling stories. Our female Asian informants used a bit more *ing* than the American females, but they appropriately "style-shifted" to use more *in'* in informal contexts. However, the Asian males did the opposite. They shifted to more *in'* in formal contexts. This puzzled us at first, but we think we figured out what was going on. As mentioned, in formal contexts native speakers monitor the way they speak, changing to a less natural style in order to sound correct. We think that the Asian men were also monitoring, but in the other direction. They were unconsciously aware that, as men, they should use more *in'*, so in contexts where they were not so involved in the gist of what they were saying, they monitored for *in'*. Our study suggested that, like children, adult L2 learners are sensitive to and can approximate, if not fully acquire, the speech norms of the target language community.

The Acculturation Model

Very few adults completely learn the intricacies of a second culture. An academic legend tells of an American woman who married a Frenchman, moved to France, and learned to speak perfect French without any trace of an accent. Everyone she met thought that she was French, but they also thought that she wasn't very bright because she didn't get some of their jokes, and she didn't know much about the movies and television shows they had all watched as kids. She found that it was a good idea to tell people that she was an American because then they appreciated the extraordinary, though not perfect, degree to which she had mastered a second culture.

Several scholars have suggested that learning a new language is intimately connected with learning a new culture. One of them, John Schumann (1978), proposed the *acculturation model,* which is similar in some ways to the nativization hypothesis discussed earlier except that it considers cultural as well as linguistic factors. The acculturation model claims that second language learners initially develop an interlanguage that, like an incipient pidgin, moves toward an internal norm. The trick for language teachers is to get learners not to stop there, but to move toward an external norm, that is, to acquire the target language. Often students develop some fluency in the language, enough to fulfill basic needs, and then stop, a phenomenon called *fossilization* or *stabilization.* In linguistic systems that are typically learned in stages, such as the system of relative clauses that we will examine in chapter 3, these learners fossilize at one of the stages. In this, they are like speakers in a creole community who have stabilized at a mesolectal stage.

Schumann and his colleagues studied six Spanish-speaking adults who were acquiring English in Cambridge, Massachusetts without formal instruction. They found that over a 9-month period, five of the subjects were making progress, but one of them, Alberto, had fossilized. Schumann believed that this was due to lack of interaction with English speakers. Although Alberto lived in an English-speaking community, Schumann believed that he did not get adequate input for two reasons. The first was social: Alberto had only Spanish-speaking friends, and even at work he associated mostly with Spanish speakers. The second reason was psychological: Alberto distanced himself from the English-speaking community because he felt anxiety and culture shock when dealing with English speakers. Furthermore, his position as a novice in the new society may have threatened his *language ego,* or willingness to risk making mistakes and sounding like a child.

The acculturation model has been tested in several studies that tried to correlate learners' social and psychological distance from the target language group with their degree of language acquisition. The results have been mixed, and it is clear that even learners who are socially and psychologically distant from native speakers can become proficient in an L2. Nevertheless, adult school teachers recognize Alberto as a stereotype; that is, a student who consciously tries to learn English, but is so immersed in his own language and culture that he will never become fluent.

Schumann's claim that a student's attitude toward the target culture is a major factor in L2 learning success is reflected in the studies of Gardner and Lambert (1972), who suggest that the learner may adopt either of two orientations in regard to the target language community, or a position somewhere in between. Learners who adopt an *integrative orientation* wish to become members of the new culture and embrace its beliefs and behaviors. Learners who adopt an *instrumental orientation* wish to use the new language for practical reasons, such as getting a job or a promotion, but they do not wish to change their cultural identity. In their studies of Canadian English speakers learning French, Gardner and Lambert found that an integrative motivation was more strongly associated with successful language learning. An interesting addendum to Gardner and Lambert's theory is provided by Masgoret, Bernaus, and Gardner (2000), who found that a learner's orientation toward the target culture can change over time. Their study of British and Irish ESL teachers in Spain found that as the teachers became more proficient in Spanish, their attitudes toward the Spanish people became less positive and their orientation less integrative.

RECONCILING COGNITIVE AND SOCIAL/CULTURAL
ACCOUNTS OF LANGUAGE ACQUISITION

In this chapter, we have reviewed behaviorist, nativist, and social/cultural approaches to the study of language acquisition, noting that behaviorism is no longer current, although its influence is still felt in certain teaching practices, as we will see in the next chapter. We have also noted some conflicts between the theories. Within nativist theories, UG and the bioprogram theory offer different accounts of what kinds of grammatical knowledge are innate, and information processing theories deny that there is any innate grammatical information. The present position of UG grammarians is that information processing models may be involved in learning "peripheral" aspects of language, such as vocabulary words, idiomatic constructions, and some syntactic patterns. As an example of the latter, Preston (1996) noted that parameter setting cannot determine why embedded questions in English have a different form than regular questions (cf. the embedded question, "I know why George has come," where *George* comes before *has*, with the regular question, "Why has George come?" where *has* comes before *George*). The difference between these two question types must therefore be learned in some way other than UG.

Social/cultural theories generally address aspects of language acquisition that do not involve basic grammar, so there is not overt conflict between these theories and UG or information processing theories. It is possible that both children and adults learn core grammatical structures using UG, that they learn the appropriate frequency for socially significant forms like *in'* using connectionist mechanisms, and that they learn speech acts using other information processing mechanisms, such as productions.

There is, however, a difference between the cognitive approaches (UG and information processing theories) on the one hand and social/cultural approaches on the other, which is more like a cultural divide. The difference has to do with what kinds of questions should be asked and what kinds of research methods should be employed in the study of language acquisi-

tion. As we have noted, sociolinguists look toward the environment surrounding the learner and attempt to ground their research in social facts,
whereas cognitive linguists look inward and attempt to ground their research in biological facts. Frawley (1997), for example, compares parameter setting to the triggering of the immune system by pathogens in the
body. These two approaches are not entirely compatible. Some sociolinguists have viewed the work of their cognitive colleagues as reductionist, focusing on grammatical rules only and ignoring the social rules of language
use. Some cognitive linguistics have viewed social/cultural research (e.g.,
Tyler's study) as representing no more than the impressions of the analyst.

Can these two academic cultures achieve some kind of rapprochement?
One attempt is Vygotskian psychology, a theory that attempts to incorpo-
rate internal and external explanations of language acquisition and, in fact,
all kinds of learning. We will discuss Vygotskian psychology in chapter 5, as
a prelude to taking a look inside a Tucson middle school where Spanish-
speaking students are acquiring English and learning mainstream subjects.

SUGGESTED READING

Ellis (1994) is the canonical 824-page review of theories of SLA. It should
be supplemented with the more recent and shorter Mitchell and Myles
(1998). Crain and Lillo-Martin (1999) provides an introduction to
Chomskian theory applied to L1 acquisition, including a discussion of behaviorism. Cook and Newson (1996) is a readable introduction to UG and
SLA. Epstein et al. (1996) provide a more technical discussion. Johnson
and Newport's (1989) influential article presents research on the critical
period hypothesis in adult SLA. This research is critically reviewed in
Bialystok and Hakuta (1994). Canale and Swain (1980) is the classic statement on the relevance of the theory of communicative competence to SLA.
Bachman (1990) modifies their model. The articles in Kasper and Blum-
Kulka (1993) discuss interlanguage pragmatics. Heath's (1983) book is the
monumental ethnography of language and schooling of Blacks and Whites
in Trackton and Roadville. A discussion of the ethnography of speaking,
with references to L2 situations, can be found in Saville-Troike (2003).
Preston (1989) provides a theoretical rationale for the study of linguistic
variation in interlanguage, which is updated in the more technical articles
in Bayley and Preston (1996).

Language Teaching

INTRODUCTION: THREE APPROACHES
TO LANGUAGE TEACHING

In the last chapter, I told three stories of how language is acquired. One of them, behaviorism, turned out to be false, and the other two, the cognitive approach and the social/cultural approach, seem to be on the right track although there are some conflicts between them. In this chapter, I will describe three approaches to how language can be taught, or, as some scholars would prefer to put it, how teachers can facilitate language acquisition. Throughout the discussion, we will see that theories about language teaching are related to broader educational theories about what constitutes good teaching in general, and we begin with a review of these broader theories.

The *instructional approach* to teaching was nearly universal in the 19th century and is still widespread. The typical instructional classroom features a teacher standing at the front of a class lecturing to students, who are later tested on the material. The Marxist educator Paulo Freire (1970) characterizes this approach with a banking metaphor. The students' minds are like savings accounts in which the teacher makes deposits. The *progressive approach* to teaching was inspired by Rousseau's novel *Emile*, the story of a child who learns in a free and natural way, guided only by her own interests and curiosity. John Dewey was the father of progressive education in the United States, and his ideas have survived remarkably well. One principle of his philosophy is that learners should follow an internal syllabus based on their own interests and developing abilities. A second principle is that learning should be a kind of enculturation into society, achieved through experiences like apprenticeships and internships. The similarity of the first principle to the theory of universal grammar (UG), and the second principle to the theory of communicative competence is obvious. The *behaviorist approach* to teaching has the most straightforward connection between theory and practice. Behaviorism applied to teaching language produced the audio-lingual method, and applied to teaching reading it produced the phonics method, both of which will be discussed in this chapter. Although behaviorist theory is now discredited, these two methods are still very much in use.

I will describe the development of these three approaches to teaching in two historical periods, which I call Before Chomsky and After Chomsky.

LANGUAGE TEACHING BEFORE CHOMSKY

Traditional Education

At the beginning of the 20th century, Americans were proud of their fine public schools. Ninety-five percent of children attended common school (Grades 1 through 8) at least a few months a year, although only 5% went on to high school. Unlike European countries, the United States had no central educational system, but rather thousands of local school boards, as is still the case. Also unlike Europe, there was no national curriculum. Every district wrote its own, but children studied the same subjects pretty much everywhere. The basics were reading, writing, and arithmetic, with attention to penmanship, grammar, spelling, and speaking. Values were also emphasized, including patriotism, honesty, respect, responsibility, and courtesy.

The instructional approach to teaching was fairly standard across the country. Teacher training was not common, and teachers taught the way they had learned, largely by lecture, recitation, and memorization. In learning to write, neatness and penmanship counted, and students spent hours copying cursive script from their Palmer Method lesson books. Everyone, even lefties, had to use the right hand. Arithmetic was taught by adding columns of figures, sometimes mentally with no pencil and paper allowed. It was believed that such mental gymnastics focused the mind and improved the ability to think critically. Getting the right answer was what counted—no partial credit was given for using the right process. Reading instruction began with learning the names of the letters of the alphabet and some of the sounds they made. After the students could sound out some words and recognize a few by sight, they were given simple reading passages including fables, aphorisms, folk tales, stories, and poems, aimed at introducing them to a literary tradition. More advanced reading books, such as the famous McGuffey Readers, included excerpts from writers like Hawthorne, Dickens, and Shakespeare. The upper grades also included lessons in geography and history, taught with a view toward instilling patriotism and good citizenship. The goal of basic education was to strengthen American democracy by producing citizens who were literate, numcrant, and knowledgeable about their country's geography, history, and culture.

There was less agreement about the proper goal of high school instruction. Traditionally, high school students studied a classical curriculum built around Greek, Latin, and mathematics, but also including courses in English literature, rhetoric, history, geography, and physics. The theory that justified spending so much time on dead languages was the theory of mental discipline. It was believed that (like the prospect of being hanged in the morning) studying difficult material focused the mind and improved the powers of concentration and memory. In the saying of the day, it didn't matter what children studied, as long as they didn't like it (Ravitch, 2000, p. 62).

Grammar–Translation Method

The method of teaching languages at the turn of the century was quintessential instructional. It was called the grammar–translation method, and it is still the most widely used method around the world. Because Latin and Classical Greek were no longer spoken, students learned to read and write, not speak these languages. (Of course, some speaking was involved, and there were arguments over how to pronounce the ancient words. Beloved Latin teacher Mr. Chips was urged to adopt the new style of Latin pronunciation, but he resisted, remarking, "A lot of nonsense in my opinion. Making the boys say 'kikero' at school when—umph—for the rest of their lives they'll say 'Cicero' . . ." [Hilton, 1934, p. 77].) The grammar–translation method was also used to teach living languages, and teachers of French, Spanish, and German often spoke English in class more than the target language. At the basic level, the grammar–translation method involves memorizing vocabulary words and grammatical patterns, and often allows students to learn language forms without understanding their meanings. The method also involves, of course, translation, starting with individual sentences or short passages, exercises that are often artificial and boring. But in advanced classes, students translate real literature, like Caesar's *Accounts of the Gallic Wars*, and listen to lectures on literature and history delivered in the target language, thus engaging (if only passively) in meaningful and interesting language use.

Progressive Education

As public education and the taxes to support it increased, the value of the classical curriculum was debated publicly. A strong voice in the discussion was that of Harvard University President Charles W. Eliot. His prescription for improving high schools was to make them preparatory schools for the colleges, and to that end he suggested two main goals. The first was to provide students with a solid background in the arts and sciences, with more emphasis on the latter. Eliot urged that some requirements in grammar, rhetoric, and classical languages give way to the emerging sciences of botany, zoology, and geology. Eliot endorsed the theory of mental discipline, and his second goal was to improve students' mental faculties through the intensive study of rigorous subjects. Unlike the classicists, however, he believed that this could be achieved by studying subjects other than Greek and Latin.

The curriculum of American high schools in the 1880s was eclectic. There was a track for the college bound, which included the study of the classics (though far more often in Latin than in Greek), grammar, literature, mathematics, and the sciences. There was also a vocational track, with courses in mechanical drawing, surveying, woodworking, metalworking, bookkeeping, and secretarial skills. In addition, there were courses for enrichment and enjoyment, such as music, art, and physical education. There was, in fact, so much variety within and among high schools that educators called for a more standard curriculum. This notion was especially important in regard to college admissions. Some colleges had elaborate course work requirements, others gave their own entrance examinations, and still others accepted everyone who graduated from certain high schools. To bring order out of this chaos, the National Education Association formed the Committee of Ten who, in 1893 issued a report on secondary education that included guidelines for curricular offerings. What the Committee recommended was a liberal academic education for all students, similar to what Eliot (who was a member of the Committee) had been advocating (Ravitch, 2000, p. 42). The report immediately came under fire from traditionalists as well as from progressive educators. The classical language professors objected to the notion that just any subject could serve to develop mental discipline and critical thinking. If Greek and Latin alone did not serve this function, who would want to study Greek and Latin? In fact, Greek enrollment had been declining for years and continued to decline in American schools until today, it has virtually disappeared. Latin enrollment, on the other hand, increased so that in 1910, half of all high school students studied the mother of Romance languages. Latin enrollments remained healthy through the 1950s but, perhaps because of federal funding for modern language study that was provided after Sputnik, Latin enrollments have declined so that today, Latin is about as rare in the high schools as Chinese.

The report of the Committee of Ten was attacked from the other side of the education spectrum by a new voice in the debate, the voice of Progressive Education. Not a single movement but a series of overlapping movements, progressive education was tied to progressive political philosophy as embodied in the social work of Jane Addams in Chicago and the muckraking journalism of Jacob Riis and Ida Tarbell. A principal concern of the progressive movement in both its political and educational manifestations was improving the lot of immigrants, who were flooding into American cities in the first decades of the 20th century. In 1908, 71.5% of the children in New York public schools had foreign-born fathers, as did 67.3% of the children in Chicago and 57.8% in San Francisco (Ravitch, 2000, p. 56). The public schools then as now afforded immigrant families a path out of poverty by providing a base for medical and social services and night school courses in English and citizenship, and in many cases serving children the only decent meals they could get.

John Dewey

Progressive educators could see that the existing school curricula, both traditional and eclectic, were not appropriate for immigrant children. The academic track demanded a depth of background knowledge and a level of English proficiency that these children often lacked, and the vocational track was a ticket back to the ghetto. The educational philosophy of John Dewey, however, seemed well-suited for educating both immigrant and mainstream children. Three tenets of Dewey's (1916) philosophy were especially applicable for educating immigrant children: (1) Children should learn practical subjects. (2) Learning should be relevant to the everyday life of the students. (3) Learning should involve hands-on doing. These principles suggested that the curriculum should be built around practical, not academic, courses, but Dewey believed that practical courses could embrace traditional academic study. Mechanical drawing, for example, could be used as an entrée to the study of geometry and mathematics. Horticulture could serve as an introduction to biology and genetics, so that students did not just read about the principles of heredity, but experimented with them. A course in laundering could include not just instruction in how to operate washing machines, but the study of how the machines changed domestic life and affected local businesses. Progressive educators, then, advocated for both immigrant and native children a curriculum rooted in practical study but embracing theoretical and academic subjects. It should be said, however, that some of Dewey's followers did not share his high-minded conception of the practical curriculum. They believed that children from eastern and southern Europe could not succeed in an academic track because they came from backgrounds "where the Anglo-Saxon conception of law, order, and government, and public and private decency do not prevail" (Cubberly, 1919, p. 358).

Progressive educators embraced the doctrine of relevance, and developed curricula that were intended not only to train the mind, but also to improve students' lives: vocational education, health and hygiene, shop for the boys and homemaking for the girls. In my own progressive junior high school, I railed against this requirement, but ended up loving wood shop, where I could lathe down a good piece of mahogany to reveal the table leg within.

Dewey's principle that schooling should be related to everyday life has two corollaries. The first is that instruction should begin with what the child already knows. The second is that lessons ought to be interesting and fun. This latter notion was a reaction to the mental discipline theory, which was widely believed by parents and traditional educators. The third Deweyan tenet is especially relevant to students who have not mastered English. It is that meaning can be conveyed both verbally and experientially. Traditional education focused almost exclusively on the verbal channel in the form of the lecture, or, if students were lucky, the lecture/discussion. But Dewey argued that teachers should not just explain, for example, the theory of static electricity, but should allow students to experience it by placing their hands on a static electricity generator in order to feel their hair stand on end. Providing a hands-on component to learning benefits all students but provides invaluable help to those who have difficulty understanding a lecture or a reading. In Dewey's (1916) words,

> When education . . . fails to recognize that the primary or initial subject matter always exists as matter of an active doing, involving the use of the body and the handling of material, the subject matter of instruction is isolated from the needs and purposes of the learner, and so becomes just something to be memorized and reproduced upon demand (p. 184).

The Direct Method of Berlitz and deSauze

Deweyan principles were embodied, intentionally or coincidentally, in several methods of language teaching that competed with the grammar–translation method. The most famous of these was the direct method of Berlitz and deSauze. The Berlitz schools have been enormously successful around the world teaching languages to adults, especially for business purposes. Berlitz attempted to design a curriculum that would create for adults the conditions under which, he believed, children learn to speak. This meant that the use of the mother tongue was forbidden and vocabulary was taught through context (Diller, 1978). The first Berlitz English lesson teaches the names of 16 common objects, including *pencil, pen, book, paper, key, table,* and *chair.* Students learn these words as Berlitz thought children learned them: The teacher points to a book and says "book." The context makes the meaning clear. Context can also make clear the meaning of simple sentences: "What's this?" "It's a book." "What are these?" "They are books." In understanding and speaking these sentences, the student is not only learning vocabulary, but also getting an unconscious lesson in the present tense forms of the verb *to be*, and in how to form questions.

DeSauze used the direct method to teach American high school students French. His beginning lessons were like those of Berlitz: French was used in a meaningful context. Of course, there comes a time when one must speak of things outside the classroom, where meaningful context is less available. At this stage, deSauze recommended the use of paraphrase, that is, teaching a new word by describing it using known words. For example, one could teach the word *glace* "ice" using this paraphrase:

> "En été l'eau du lac est liquide; en hiver l'eau du lac n'est pas liquide, elle est solide; l'eau solide est de la glace."
>
> "In summer the water in a lake is liquid; in winter the water in a lake is not liquid it is solid; solid water is ice" (deSauze, 1929, p. 16; quoted in Diller, 1978, p. 77).

Teaching language by means of context and paraphrase follows the Deweyan principle of building on what the student already knows. A second Deweyan aspect of deSauze's approach was his emphasis on engaging the students' interest. "The most vital problem in any classroom is how to stimulate and retain the interest of the pupils" (quoted in Diller, 1978, p. 81). One way of maintaining interest was to insist that the language always be used in real communicative situations and that students always understand what was being said. A second way was to emphasize conversation. Most students would rather talk to their friends than read *L'Etranger*, and deSauze tried to choose vocabulary that would enable students to talk about their own lives and interests. Reading and writing were allowed only after the students could discuss a topic competently.

Behaviorism

The theory of mental discipline was challenged in the early decades of the 20th century by the emerging field of behavioral psychology. We saw in chapter 2 that later, during the 1940s and 1950s, B. F. Skinner and his colleagues conducted experiments to determine how rats, pigeons, and other animals learned, and extrapolated their findings to human beings. But Skinner's behaviorist predecessors, particularly Edward Thorndike, studied human subjects. One question that Thorndike addressed involved "transfer of training," which directly tested the mental discipline theory. Thorndike questioned whether the study of Latin or mathematics improved the general capacities of the mind, and many experiments supported his skepticism. The most famous of these had been conducted by William James himself. James (1890, pp. 666–667) memorized passages of *Paradise Lost*, but found that this experience was no help at all in his subsequent efforts to memorize French poetry. Thorndike concluded that the only benefit of learning Greek, for example, was actually knowing Greek, and that had never been a strong reason for including it in the school curriculum.

The Audio-Lingual Method

Behaviorism applied to language teaching produced the audio-lingual method (ALM), which was developed in a hurry out of wartime necessity. During World War II, the Allies sent troops to all corners of the world, where they had to work with people who spoke little-known languages. In the movie, *The Bridge Over the River Kwai*, a British linguistics professor who speaks the local language leads a guerrilla mission into Japanese-held Burma. In reality, however, when the U.S. Army set out to recruit university experts in exotic languages, they often found that the professors, who had learned using the grammar–translation method, couldn't speak the languages they taught, though they were very good at reading and writing them. So, the Army had to train its own interpreters, and it turned for advice to two linguists at the University of Michigan. Professor Charles Fries was the foremost descriptive linguist of the time, and his colleague Robert Lado was a highly regarded expert in language teaching. Both scholars had strong and radical ideas about language teaching, which they were eager to implement in the service of their country.

The ALM was the method I was using in the Ethiopian classroom I described in chapter 1. As readers may have noticed, the ALM method was similar in some ways to Skinner's method for training rats. Here's what a typical ALM lesson looked like:

Teacher: I walk to school every day. Repeat.
Student: I walk to school every day.
Teacher: Run.
Student: I run to school every day.
Teacher: Skip.
Student: I skip to school every day.

Recall from chapter 2 that behavioral psychology claimed that language, like all behavior, is a set of habits. Therefore, the students shouldn't be allowed to make mistakes, as these would lead to bad habits. As Brooks (1960) put it, "Error, like sin, is to be avoided at all costs" (quoted in Hinkel & Fotos, 2002, p. 22). However, the teacher should avoid correcting errors as that was a form of negative reinforcement. So, the language the students were asked to produce had to be very carefully controlled, as in the previous example, where the only part of the pattern the student is allowed to change is the verb. What the example is teaching is subject–verb agreement: When the subject of a sentence is *I* and the tense is present, the verb takes its base form. Behaviorists believed that the more times a student repeated sentences pairing *I* with the base forms of verbs, the better this pattern would be learned, like practicing scales on a piano. A second behaviorist principle illustrated in the example is that the meaning of what you are saying isn't very important. Notice that the students don't have to know the meaning of *walk*, *run*, or *skip* to get the pattern right, and, in fact, they could easily substitute a nonsense word into the pattern, say *galumph* (I galumph to school every day).

I have discussed an extreme version of the ALM, which not all of its practitioners subscribed to. Many teachers and textbooks included a lot of meaningful activities, but behaviorist theory held that understanding what you are saying isn't that important, and some teachers took this belief seriously. The first two weeks I studied Amharic using the ALM, all we did was repeat sentences we didn't understand in order to learn correct habits of pronunciation. I sometimes wonder what our Ethiopian teachers had us saying.

The ALM had elements of both the instructional and the progressive approaches. The tightly controlled exposure to the target language, the teacher-centered classroom, and the emphasis on correctness were all very instructional. However, the idea that second language (L2) acquisition is a lot like first language (L1) acquisition (even though the behaviorist theory of L1 acquisition was completely wrong), as well as the practice of immersing the student in the target language (no native language was allowed), were elements of progressive pedagogy.

LANGUAGE TEACHING AFTER CHOMSKY

During the 1950s and 1960s, the ALM was the method of choice in teacher training programs in the United States. In my program at UCLA, it was characterized as "the best game in town" as late as 1969. However, as cognitive psychology and generative linguistics eclipsed behaviorism, the ALM came under a cloud, and progressive methods, which emphasized meaning, communication, and student motivation, received new life. The progressive approach also received a new name, communicative language teaching (CLT), and it is fair to say that CLT is now the best game in town.

Cook (2001) notes that, "There is surprisingly little connection between the communicative style [of language teaching] and SLA [second language acquisition] research" (p. 214). Nevertheless, CLT is compatible with the two theoretical approaches to language acquisition that emerged in the second half of the 20th century: the innatist approach and the sociocultural approach. The innatist approach especially resonates with CLT because most L2 specialists subscribe to the full access or partial access position described in chapter 2 and believe that under the right conditions, L2 acquisition can occur naturally in adults, as L1 acquisition occurs naturally in children. The scholar who is best known for developing an innatist rationale for CLT is Professor Stephen Krashen, whose influential theory we now review.

The Monitor Model

Krashen's theory of L2 acquisition was much influenced by Chomsky's theory of L1 acquisition. Krashen adopted Chomsky's idea of the Language Acquisition Device (LAD), which he incorporated into his *monitor model*, a simplified version of which is shown in Figure 3.1. According to the monitor model, in order to analyze a language, the LAD must receive samples of the target language, called *input*. But not every sample of the target language that a learner hears will be useful to the LAD, only those which are understood. For example, a person forced to listen to Radio Beijing all day will not learn Chinese because the input is meaningless. However, when learners interact with target language speakers or receive contextualized instruction, as in the Total Physical Response Method described later in this chapter, context makes the meaning clear, and language acquisition can occur.

According to Krashen, even meaningful input may not be of use to the LAD, which can do its work only when affective conditions are right. Thus, if input is to result in acquisition, it must pass through an *affective filter*. *Affect* refers to the emotional and motivational circumstances of the learner. Children usually learn their L1 under perfect affective conditions: They are in a loving and supportive environment, their happiness and that of their parents depends on communicating with each other, and both parties work hard to create a dialogue that is meaningful and fun. In addition, children are usually surrounded by older children whom they wish to please and emulate.

The affective circumstances in a French 101 classroom can be very different. Here, the student may have no particular desire to communicate with anybody in French, and the relationship between teacher and student is often not one of love and support. The teacher is the taskmaster who dishes

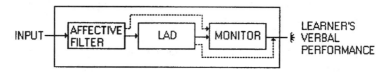

FIG. 3.1. The monitor model.

out punishment in the form of C grades when tasks are not performed correctly. Furthermore, students may be put on the spot and forced to display their ignorance in front of the whole class, resulting in an emotion unknown to very young children: embarrassment. According to Krashen, under such conditions, the affective filter is raised and input does not get through to the LAD. A third important feature of input concerns its grammatical content. Krashen subscribes to the idea that some grammatical structures are, in a universal sense, easier to learn than others and that learners progress from easy structures to more difficult ones. Thus, if the student is using a particular structure, call it structure i, the ideal input will contain structure i+1. Later in the chapter, I will discuss a study of relative clause learning that investigated precisely this prediction.

In the monitor model, shown in Figure 3.1, the LAD unconsciously constructs the rules constituting an individual's basic linguistic system, and this system serves as the basis for language production. The model also posits a second mental mechanism for internalizing knowledge of language called the *monitor*. The monitor is a general learning device, not dedicated to language learning. Using the monitor, adults can learn about language in the same way we learn about physics and history: We consciously learn facts and the connections between them. An example is the spelling rule, "*i* before *e* except after *c*, unless sounded like EY as in *neighbor* or *sleigh*," or something like that. In a typical language class that uses the grammar–translation method, most of the learning is conscious, via the monitor. The students learn grammar rules and vocabulary words by drill, memorization, and error correction. This kind of learning is represented in Figure 3.1 by the dotted line connecting the affective filter to the monitor. The dotted line from the LAD that bypasses the monitor represents the fact that it is possible to learn an L2 entirely by means of the LAD with no conscious knowledge of grammatical rules, as children learn their L1. The ideal situation is represented by the solid line from the affective filter to the LAD to the monitor to output. In this case, speech is initiated by the subconscious rules of the LAD, but can be monitored for formal correctness, especially when writing, by conscious rules in the monitor.

Learning a language by means of the LAD is obviously very different from learning a language by means of the monitor, so different that Krashen gives the two cognitive processes different names. He calls the unconscious process involving the LAD *acquisition* and the conscious process involving the monitor *learning*. He believes that learning is of very limited value and that only acquisition leads to fluent language use.

The monitor model has come in for some heavy criticism, and during the 1980s, "Krashen bashin' " was a standard feature of applied linguistics conferences. In this spirit, Gregg (1996) characterizes Krashen's work as, "Fairly superficial, if not naive, in its treatment of linguistic theory" (p. 49).

One problem with monitor theory is that the evidence Krashen cites for the two internalization mechanisms is based on studies of questionable research design. It is true that the notion of conscious and unconscious learning is generally accepted in the field of cognitive psychology, but in psychological theory, no sharp line is drawn between the two kinds of knowledge; rather, they form the two endpoints on a continuum of "attention" so that well-learned tasks require less attention than new tasks. A second controversial claim of the monitor model is that only simple "rules of thumb" can be used for conscious monitoring. An example is the rule that plural nouns end in *s*. The rules for English article use, on the other hand, are too complex to be remembered and consistently applied, as the discussion in chapter 2 implied. A third problem with the monitor model is Krashen's claim that learning can never become acquisition. Conventional wisdom in psychology specifically denies this.

A study that helps to clarify these issues was conducted by Green and Hecht (1993). Three hundred German speakers who had been taught English formally for 3 to 12 years were shown sentences containing grammatical errors and asked to correct them. They were also asked to state the rule that the error had broken. Overall, the subjects were able to correct 76% of the errors. But the rate of correction was much higher when the subjects consciously knew the rule involved. When the rule was known, the correction rate was 85%, but when the rule was not known, the correction rate was only 43%. This result is compatible with the monitor model in the respect that it shows that conscious knowledge can be involved in a task that requires editing and for which learners have sufficient time. However, the study is incompatible with the monitor model's claim that the monitor contains only a few simple rules of thumb. We will discuss more research relevant to the monitor model after we have looked at Krashen's program for language teaching.

The Natural Way

The major claim of the monitor model is that two conditions are necessary and sufficient for successful L2 acquisition: lots of meaningful input and good affective conditions. This means that instructional language teaching, including the grammar–translation method, is not the best language teaching. Instructional teaching, according to Krashen, mostly involves the monitor, not the LAD. Effective lessons immerse the students in meaningful input, letting the LAD do its work, as it does for children. Lead your students to interesting and meaningful language, and they will acquire.

Krashen does not recommend a single method of language teaching, but an approach embracing several compatible methods, which he calls "the natural way." One method for beginners sanctioned by the natural way is

Total Physical Response (TPR), where students are not asked to say or write anything, just respond to commands from the teacher. For example, the teacher might say to the class:

Stand up!

and motion for the class to stand up, thereby making the meaning of the command clear. Any student who doesn't understand what "stand up" means can just observe what the other students are doing. The next command might be:

Turn around!

and the instructor should turn around several times to demonstrate the meaning, repeating the command. Other commands used in the first lesson might include:

Go to the board!
Write your name!
Erase your name!
Go to your seat!
Sit down!

All of these commands are modeled by the instructor so that no one can fail to understand their meaning.

An activity that Krashen (Krashen & Terrell, 1983) recommends for low-intermediate students involves an exchange of information about course schedules. In an English as a second language (ESL) class at the middle school level, the teacher distributes the actual schedules of four of the students in the class. The teacher then asks the class questions about information in the schedules. After the teacher is sure the students understand how to read the schedule, the class breaks up into small groups and the students ask each other questions about their own class schedules. As a final activity, the teacher hands out blank schedules and divides the class into groups of two. Each student has to fill out the schedule for the other student by asking appropriate questions.

These two lessons meet Krashen's two conditions for language acquisition. First, the language used in the lessons is meaningful. The meaning of the commands is obvious because everyone performs them. In the schedules lesson, the vocabulary of courses and schedules should be well-known to intermediate-level students because they have to fill out and follow such schedules every semester. Second, both lessons should foster good affective conditions because, if well-taught, the lessons are interesting and engaging.

Students who have to sit at desks all day welcome the chance to get up and move around. If interest lags, the teacher can drum up more enthusiasm by putting on some music and teaching commands like:

Twist!

OK, now moon walk!

Moon walk to the board and write, "Michael Jackson."

The class schedules lesson is of interest because students are usually curious to know what classes and teachers their friends have during the day.

Community Language Learning

During the 1970s, a number of progressive methods emerged that were associated with powerful individuals who had creative ideas about language teaching. Richards and Rodgers (2001) characterize these as the "guru-led" methods, and they included TPR, which was associated with Professor John Asher at San Jose State University. Perhaps the most communicative of the new methods was community language learning (CLL), developed by Father Charles A. Curran (1976) (a student and colleague of counseling psychologist Carl Rogers), who had no background in linguistics or language teaching. When language teachers discover the CLL method, they tend to get excited. Pedagogy specialist Robert Blair (1982) confessed that when he encountered CLL, "I was not just excited, I was moved" (p. 10). My own opinion is that I would rather begin a new language using CLL than any other way.

CLL can be implemented in various ways, but here is how it worked in a class in Arabic that I attended. I should mention that originally Curran called his method "counseling–learning" and the reason for this will become clear. Eight adult students (Curran used the word *clients*) who did not know any Arabic sat in chairs placed in a circle. Our teacher (Curran used the word *counselor*) stood outside the circle. We were told to start a conversation in English, and one of the students said something like, "Hi, my name's Marsha." The teacher moved around behind the speaker, placed her hand on the speaker's shoulder, and translated the sentence into Arabic. Marsha then repeated the phrase in Arabic, speaking to the group and also into a tape recorder. Another student then said something like, "Hi Marsha, my name's John," and Marsha passed the microphone to him. The teacher moved around behind John, placed her hand on his shoulder and translated the phrase, which John repeated. This procedure was continued around the circle until everyone had been introduced. Toward the end of the introductions, we had learned how to say "Hi" and "My name is . . ."

After the introductions, someone changed the subject to families. Questions were asked and answers were given, all translated and repeated into the microphone. Again we found that certain words and phrases tended to reoccur: "Are you married?" "Do you have any children?" "I'm not married." "I have one/two/three children." We found that we could sometimes make a contribution to the conversation directly in Arabic using these phrases, but if we got stuck, our teacher was right behind us to help out. It was okay for us to ask her for vocabulary words ("How do you say *five?*") and then put the word into our emerging Arabic, "I have five children."

After 30 minutes, the teacher made us stop although we wanted to continue. The conversation had been enjoyable, interesting, and not in any way stressful. The teacher then played the tape we had made. It was a 10-minute conversation in Arabic (none of the English was recorded), spoken and completely understood by students who hadn't known any Arabic half an hour earlier. I could see why Blair was moved! Then, using phonetic characters, the teacher wrote on the board some of the phrases we had been able to say without her help, pointing out a few grammatical patterns, like the fact that the verb usually comes last in the sentence.

After several weeks of such lessons, I am told, students are able to carry on simple conversations largely without translations from the teacher, although she is always present to provide vocabulary and help out if someone gets stuck. In intermediate-level courses, the students are speaking fairly freely and, of course, making lots of errors, which the teacher can selectively correct. In advanced courses, the teacher need not be present in the room, but should be accessible by telephone in case the group needs help.

It should be said that CLL has not enjoyed wide success since it became well-known in the 1980s. The reason is probably economic: To work well, CLL classes must be small and must meet 10 or so hours per week. Foreign language classes in public schools and colleges usually have 20 to 30 students per class and meet only 3 or 4 hours per week. This is because it is more economical to place much of the learning burden on students in the form of homework rather than to pay teachers to meet just a few students for many hours each week. Nevertheless, teachers might want to use CLL occasionally in large classes, actively teaching six or eight students and letting the rest of the class observe, in order to provide a glimpse of what a very communicative language teaching method is like.

Content-Based Instruction

Content-based instruction (CBI) is a communicative method par excellence and the one most relevant to teaching English to language minority students in American schools. The idea of CBI is to teach an academic subject in the target language with only occasional reference to the language itself, thus immersing students in authentic input. In addition, academic skills such as notetaking, library use, and testtaking can be taught in connection with academic material. For English language learner (ELL) students in public schools or colleges, the value of learning material that is related to what they will be studying when they join regular classes is obvious.

There are many permutations of CBI, but they can be divided into three basic types: theme-based courses, sheltered courses, and adjunct courses. Theme-based courses are most common at the college level. Textbooks for such courses contain chapters on a wide range of subjects: ecology, evolution, computers in society, money and finance, civil rights, and so on. The materials on these topics are also various, including newspaper articles, op-ed essays, interviews with experts, and even poems and short stories. The goal of the course is to give students a taste of what an academic curriculum is like in order to prepare them for mainstream classes. A disadvantage of the theme-based course is that it often contains popular rather than academic readings, such as articles from *Newsweek* and *People* magazines. Also, the topics do not necessarily relate to what the students in mainstream classes are studying, and thus, the course does not directly prepare students to join the mainstream. An even bigger disadvantage of theme-based courses is that none of the subjects is studied in depth. The units do not build on each other the way chapters in a real textbook do. As we will see in chapters 5 and 6, a great deal of the difficulty that ELL students have in mainstream classes is studying a subject in depth, which requires them to construct and relate knowledge over weeks and months.

Sheltered courses are content courses that enroll only ELL students. They are popular in Grades 6 through 12, where they are used to teach mainstream academic subjects to students who are not yet ready to compete with native speakers. Sheltered courses can be taught by a content instructor, who modifies the difficulty of the material, by an ESL teacher who has expertise in the subject matter, or by both. Typical accommodations for the ELL students include additional demonstrations and explanations, vocabulary exercises, study questions, and shorter-than-usual writing assignments. Sheltered courses often cover fewer topics than comparable mainstream courses so that more time can be devoted to each topic, but sometimes this is not the case. Unfortunately, some districts will give graduation credit only for sheltered courses that cover the same material as the equivalent mainstream courses, so teachers have to speed through the book leaving many of their students behind, as was the case with George, whom we met in chapter 1.

Sheltered courses have many advantages: They are directly relevant to the students' academic goals; at the more advanced levels, they provide authentic academic texts; and they provide background knowledge that the students will need when they join the mainstream. But studying academic subjects in a sheltered environment does have a disadvantage. Preparing ELL students to compete with native speakers cannot be fully accomplished in an environment without native speakers. The third type of CBI course, which could be taken after a sheltered course, solves this problem.

Adjunct courses, sometimes called *bridge courses,* enroll ELL students, either for credit or audit, in a course with native speakers and in a related ESL course, where the ESL teacher reviews the content material and teaches related language forms and study skills. Adjunct course students who are taking a real academic course for the first time can be overwhelmed by the difficulty of the material (Ghawi, 1995). They must read a whole chapter in a psychology textbook in one night, when the most they could manage in their sheltered course was a few pages. They must take notes on a lecture delivered at regular speed, by a professor who may have a strange accent, and who does not explain idioms or cultural peculiarities. The ESL teacher often finds that most of the time in the language-oriented part of the course is taken up just explaining the meaning of the content material to the students, leaving little time for work on study skills and language forms. Furthermore, students may find that the study skills that worked for them in a sheltered course do not work well in the more authentic environment of the adjunct course. For example, students may have been able to take notes in English in sheltered courses, where instructors modified their speech to accommodate learners, but in a mainstream course, this may not be possible—the information just comes too fast. Many ELL students develop a hybrid notetaking style, writing in English when the material is well understood and switching to the native language when they cannot both understand and write in English at the same time.

The adjunct course provides the most authentic setting for preparing ELL students for mainstream courses and has been highly successful in colleges (Adamson, 1993; Brinton, Snow, & Wesche, 1989), but unfortunately it is less often found in the public schools, where students must move directly from sheltered courses to mainstream courses. In chapter 5, we will take a closer look at an adjunct course taught at the college level.

Teaching Communicative Competence

Earlier I mentioned that although there is no strong research base for the effectiveness of CLT, sociocultural theories of language, such as those of Austin (1963), Grice (1978), and Bachman (1990), reviewed in chapter 2, resonate strongly with the CLT philosophy. Students need to learn not only correct forms but also how to use these forms appropriately to ask a question, order a meal, request a meeting with a teacher, accept a compliment, demand an explanation, make a date, and so on. ESL lore is full of anecdotes about students who have said things grammatically but inappropriately. For example:

> Student to teacher: "Please come to my house for dinner on Saturday. Don't bring your children."
>
> Ethiopian student complimenting my wife: "Madam, you are looking very fat."

Teaching speech acts in low-level ESL courses lends itself to lessons that involve the practical side of surviving in a new country. Some popular topics include dinner at a friend's house (with attention to how to decline food that violates your religion and/or common sense); a conference with a teacher, a doctor, or an employer; how to shop for food, furniture, a car, a house; how to read a bus schedule, a menu, a catalog, or a tax form.

Following Bachman's (1990) reappraisal of Canale and Swain's (1980) model of communicative competence, L2 acquisition theorists have discussed if and how pragmatic competence can be taught in L2 classes. Those who are skeptical about the value of explicitly teaching pragmatics point out that Grice's cooperative principle and conversational maxims (see chap. 2) are thought to be universal, and should transfer from the L1. Also, Blum-Kulka (1991) pointed out that the main problem learners in her study faced in framing appropriate utterances was not a lack of pragmatic knowledge but a lack of the necessary L2 linguistic knowledge. One approach to pragmatics instruction is to raise learners' awareness of differences in how to perform speech acts in the native and target language communities. Advocates point out that although many speech acts are found in all cultures, they may be performed very differently in the L1 and L2 communities. For example, here is my translation of how two Amharic speakers who have not seen each other for several weeks, might greet each other. (Indented lines are uttered simultaneously with the preceding line.)

> Tesfaye: Hello, hello.   How are you? How are you?
> Abebe: Hello, hello. How are you?
> Tesfaye: Are you fine?   How are you? Are you fine?
> Abebe: I am fine. Are you fine?

These greetings are accompanied with polite handshakes and bows. A much looser translation of this greeting would be, "I am very glad to see you, my friend." Obviously, greetings take a very different form in English.

A popular awareness-raising activity is viewing videotapes of target language interaction, such as greeting people at a party, followed by a discussion of how greetings are similar and different in the native and target language speech communities. This activity might be followed by the real-world assignment of reporting to the class how greetings were done at a party the students attended. It is believed that such activities can alert students to pragmatic differences not just in greetings but in other areas of interaction, as well.

A second, and compatible, approach to pragmatics teaching is direct instruction. One popular type of lesson is role playing, where students are given a situation and must come up with what to say, as in the following exercise:

> Stanley is shopping at the supermarket on Saturday morning when the store is crowded. Reaching for a jumbo bottle of maple syrup, he accidently knocks it over, and it falls on the floor, breaking and splashing syrup all over him and another shopper.
>
> Role Assignments:
>
> 1. Stanley—a college student who is upset and in no mood for comments from anyone.
> 2. Mr. Prickly—a middle-aged man whose shoes were ruined and feels that Stanley should buy him a new pair.
> 3. Ms. LaRue—the store manager, who wants Stanley to pay for the broken bottle of syrup.

After the students have acted out the role play in groups, one group might perform in front of the class, after which the audience would comment on the appropriateness and effectiveness of their complaining, placating, demanding, denying, and other speech acts. Other kinds of pragmatic instruction include watching and discussing portions of movies, or putting on a play. Advocates of pragmatics teaching point out that such activities can provide a needed supplement to textbooks, which often present target language interactions in stilted and unrealistic ways.

Historically, the notion of teaching language functions has been taken more seriously in Britain than in the United States. The British believed that using language for different purposes entailed learning different kinds of communicative competence, so they organized their courses around these purposes rather than around grammar patterns. Different learners needed to know different kinds of speech acts. Waiters had to know formal greetings, requests, complaints, apologies, and small talk. Pilots had to be able to understand instructions, give orders and warnings, and ask for clarifications. Accordingly, British language programs were organized around specific purposes: English for waiters, English for pilots, and (the most common) English for academic purposes, which was a precursor of content-based language instruction.

RESEARCH ON LANGUAGE TEACHING—
FOCUS ON FORM

"When we entered the field of second language acquisition in 1980," remark two well-known scholars (Doughty & Williams, 1998), "some influential researchers [they mean Krashen's followers] were claiming that instruction made no difference because natural language acquisition processes are all-powerful" (p. 1). Things certainly had changed from the time when I had entered the field a decade earlier. Then, behaviorism and the ALM were the best games in town and influential researchers believed that instruction made all the difference. I did, too. When my wife and I spent a summer traveling around Mexico in a Volkswagen camper, I brought along a tape recorder and some tapes of audio-lingual drills. While the people of Mexico passed by talking, joking, arguing, and singing in Spanish, I was sitting inside the camper repeating:

> Rosa, i qué bonita es tu casa! carro
> (Rosa, how beautiful is your house! car)
> Rosa, i qué bonito es tu carro!
> (Rosa, how beautiful is your car!)

As we have seen, after the demise of the ALM, CLT took center stage and attention to language form, including grammar instruction, error correction, and the grammar-based syllabus, fell out of favor. The monitor model claimed that conscious knowledge of grammar rules was not very useful, and this principle was reflected in the communicative methods we have discussed. The pendulum has now swung again, and a focus on form is back in fashion, although as always in the thesis, antithesis, synthesis cycle, the new grammar focus is very different from the old. We will now look at two studies that support the claim that teachers should pay attention to grammatical form. But keep in mind that those who take this position still believe that meaningful and communicative language use is of first importance.

Swain and Lapkin's Study

The question of whether to just expose students to the language or to draw their attention to specific forms is still controversial, and recently there has been a considerable amount of research on the topic. Important counter-evidence to Krashen's claim that comprehensible input and good affect are enough to insure acquisition comes from French immersion programs in Canada. As discussed at greater length in chapter 7, these programs take English-speaking children and immerse them entirely in French for the first three years of school. After that, instruction in English is introduced and gradually increased until, by the end of high school, English predominates. This system produces students who score higher on academic achievement tests given in English than comparable students educated entirely in English. The schooling of the immersion students is similar to the schooling of native French-speaking children. Teaching is mostly meaning based, though traditional French grammar is also taught (in the same way that it is taught to French-speaking children). In short, the method is compatible with the natural way.

The French immersion program is generally considered successful (see chap. 7 for a dissenting opinion), but it does not produce native-like French speakers. The students understand French very well and have good communicative competence, but their French is simplified and contains typical learner errors. In fact, in some ways it resembles pidgin French. Canadian researchers Merrill Swain and Sharon Lapkin (1989) believe that this is due, at least in part, to a lack of focus on form. In studying a sixth-grade immersion class, Swain and Lapkin were surprised to find that although the students were exposed to a lot of comprehensible input in French, they didn't talk much. Most of their utterances consisted of single sentences or parts of sentences. The researchers also noted that there was little systematic attention to the students' errors. The teachers did make corrections, but they were haphazard and did not focus on particular problem forms. As the immersion class complies with Krashenite orthodoxy, the students' lack of oral proficiency poses a problem for monitor theory.

Swain and Lapkin believe that speaking and focusing on form are related, and they have proposed the *output hypothesis* to explain why. They claim that for acquisition to take place, speakers must "notice" that there is a discrepancy between their speech and that of native speakers. For such noticing to occur, learners must actually speak and write the language, not just hear and read it. Furthermore, contra Krashen, Swain and Lapkin claim that it is helpful for the teacher to call the students' attention to their errors, either by correcting them or by asking for a clarification. The output hypothesis, then, claims that conscious knowledge is important in the psycholinguistic process of acquisition.

To investigate how French immersion students made use of conscious knowledge of language forms when writing, Swain and Lapkin asked eighth-grade students to "think aloud" as they were writing in French. What the students said showed that their French did not flow smoothly from mind to pen but was analyzed and puzzled over based on ideas they had about grammar. Some of these ideas were well formed and concrete. For example, one student, wanting to write "to wear some clothes," said, "*Port du . . .* (to wear some . . .) no, not *du*, it's *des*. It's plural. *Des vestments* (some clothes)" (Swain & Lapkin, 1989, p. 155). This student consciously knew the rule for article–noun agreement. On the other hand, some of the students' ideas about grammar were pretty fuzzy, amounting to little more than intuitions. One student said, "I was going to write *les droits d'animaux* (the rights of animals), but it doesn't sound right, so I said *les droits des animaux*" (p. 155). This student apparently did not consciously know the article–noun agreement rule.

Doughty's Study

Swain and Lapkin's research suggests that it is helpful for teachers to point out errors and provide explanations about how to avoid them—in other words, that teaching grammar is good. However, the study does not directly address this question. To directly examine the value of grammar teaching, the researcher should teach an explicit grammar lesson to one group of students and teach a lesson containing the same grammatical structure (but no explicit grammar lesson) to a control group. Then the researcher should test the two groups to see if the instructed group learned more than the control group. Such a study was conducted by L2 acquisition scholar Catherine Doughty (1991), whose experiment involved teaching English relative clauses to university students. Before describing the study, I must describe the relative clause and the intriguing Noun Phrase Accessibility Hierarchy.

Relative clauses are sometimes called adjective clauses because they provide additional information about a noun phrase. Unlike single-word adjectives, they come after the noun they modify:

The balloon *which I found*
The forest *which burned down*

You may remember from high school English that there are two kinds of relative clauses and that you are supposed to know the difference because one of them is offset by commas. *Restrictive* relative clauses give essential information about the noun phrases they modify:

You should bet on the horse *which is nearest to the rail* (no comma).

Nonrestrictive relative clauses give additional but not essential information about the noun phrases they modify:

You should bet on horse number 3, *which is nearest to the rail* (comma required).

Doughty's experiment dealt only with restrictive relative clauses.

Notice that the relative clauses in these examples begin with the relative pronoun *which*. Other relative pronouns include *who, whom, where,* and *that.* Notice also that the relative clauses in the examples (like all clauses) have a subject and a verb, and that some of the relative clauses have a direct object, a prepositional phrase, or both. Here is a grammatical analysis of the restrictive relative clauses we have encountered so far:

		Relative Clause			
	Modified NP	*Subject*	*Verb*	*D. O.*	*Prep. P.*
(1)	the forest	which	burned down		
(2)	the horse	which	is nearest		to the post
(3)	the balloon	I	found	which	

In these examples, the relative pronouns refer to a noun phrase that precedes them. In (1), *which* refers to *the forest*; in (2), *which* refers to *the horse*; and in (3), *which* refers to *the balloon*. In (1) and (2), *which* is the subject of the relative clause and (like other subjects) comes before the verb. But in (3), *which* is logically the object of *found*. So why doesn't it come after the verb like other direct objects? The answer is that there is a rule of English relative clause formation that says that a relative pronoun must come at the beginning of its clause regardless of how it functions in the sentence; thus, in (3), *which* gets moved to the front of the clause to produce *the balloon which I found.*

Relative pronouns can also serve as indirect objects (as in *the man who(m) I gave the ticket to*) and as objects of prepositions (as in *the people with whom you talked*). A clause that has a relative pronoun as its subject is called a *subject focus* relative clause; a clause that has a relative pronoun as its direct object is called a *direct object focus* relative clause; and, as you have guessed, clauses that have a relative pronoun as an indirect object or the object of a preposition are called *indirect object focus* and *object of preposition focus* clauses, respectively.

To summarize, a relative pronoun can function within a relative clause as subject, direct object, indirect object, or object of preposition. Now here's a remarkable fact: The order of relative clauses that I just mentioned is the order of frequency with which relative clauses appear in the languages of the world (Keenan & Comrie, 1977). That is, languages with subject focus clauses are more common than languages with direct object focus clauses, and languages with direct object focus clauses are more common than languages with indirect object focus clauses, and so forth. Here's an even more remarkable fact: The above order of relative clauses is also an *implicational hierarchy*, which means that if we know that a language has object of preposition focus clauses, we can be sure that it has all of the kinds of relative clauses that come before it in the hierarchy; similarly, if we know that a language has indirect object focus clauses, we can be sure that it has all of the kinds before it in the hierarchy (but we can't say anything about whether it has object of preposition focus relative clauses; Keenan & Comrie, 1977).

The ordering of relative clauses according to their focus is called the Noun Phrase Accessibility Hierarchy (NPAH), and it implies that in some universal sense, subject focus clauses are somehow simpler than the other kinds and are acquired first by learners, followed by direct object focus clauses, followed by indirect object focus clauses, and so on. Studies of L1 acquisition (Adamson, 1992; Romaine, 1984) and L2 acquisition (Pavisi, 1984) suggest that this is so.

In an article titled "Second Language Instruction Does Make a Difference," Doughty (1991) describes an experiment that involved teaching relative clauses to 20 international university students from different language backgrounds who were not using relative clauses in their speech. The students were divided into three groups: (1) a meaning-oriented group, (2) a rule-oriented group, and (3) a control group. All three groups read a number of short stories presented one sentence at a time on a computer screen. At the end of each story, they answered questions to check for understanding. The meaning-oriented group also viewed material in a second window on the screen that enhanced their understanding of the stories, such as definitions of keywords and rephrasings of the relative clause sentences. The rule-oriented group viewed in a second window a program called "animated grammar," which explained the structure of the relative clauses encountered in the story. The control group did not get a second window on their screens.

All of the students were tested for their knowledge of relative clauses before and after the 10-day instruction period, and the gains in scores were compared. Doughty's hypothesis prior to the study reflected the conventional wisdom. She predicted that the meaning-oriented group would make the greatest gains, the rule-oriented group would be next, and the control group would be last. But she found that the meaning-oriented group and the rule-oriented group made about equal gains and, as expected, both of them outperformed the control group.

Doughty's study supports Krashen's claim that comprehensible input aids acquisition, at least in the short term. The meaning-oriented group understood the stories better than the other two groups, and they learned relative clauses without explicit instruction on how they are formed. However, the performance of the rule-oriented group contradicts Krashen's claim that explicit grammar instruction does not aid acquisition. This group did not fully understand the stories, yet they learned relative clauses partly on the basis of grammar instruction.

There is more to the story. Doughty did not teach her subjects all four types of relative clauses: She taught only object of preposition clauses. But the students learned all four types anyway. Apparently, if students know that object of preposition clauses are grammatical, they assume that those clause types further up in the NPAH are grammatical too. This finding is relevant to Krashen's i+1 hypothesis, discussed earlier. In regard to relative clauses, the students were at level i (no use of relative clauses). But instead of teaching them the i+1 structure (subject focus clauses), Doughty taught them the i+4 structure (object of preposition focus clauses), and they learned the other structures automatically. Thus, it may be possible in some circumstances to "beat the natural order" of acquisition by teaching harder structures before teaching easier ones. Nevertheless, this strategy should be used sparingly. Doughty's subjects were highly motivated students at an Ivy League university, who received high quality individual instruction. In more common circumstances, it still makes sense to start with what is easiest and then move on to what is harder. Children don't usually learn to walk by starting out on icy sidewalks.

Summary

Nowadays, L2 acquisition scholars agree that meaning-based instruction is more important than form-based instruction, but that the ideal lesson will contain some attention to forms that are embedded in meaningful language. Nevertheless, the form versus meaning debate continues for two reasons. First, there is disagreement about exactly how to focus on form. Should teachers call attention only to forms that their students are using but having trouble with (the reactive approach), or should they anticipate the forms that their students need but are not yet using (the proactive approach)? Second, it takes a long time for the conventional wisdom of researchers to spread to the schools, and many ESL teachers who were trained during the Krashen era have an aversion to teaching grammar. Others, who were trained before the Krashen era, or in foreign language departments (where monitor theory hasn't had a large impact) or who were never trained but became ESL teachers out of necessity, believe that teaching a language means teaching its grammar, and their students and the students' parents are likely to agree.

TEACHING OTHER SUBJECTS

Sociolinguist J. P. Gee (1996) has pointed out that Krashen's learning/ acquisition distinction provides a helpful framework for viewing the teaching of subjects other than language. Instructional methods of teaching reading, writing, and arithmetic are very much like Krashen's notion of learning. Gee puts it this way:

Learning is a process that involves conscious knowledge gained through teaching . . . or through certain life-experiences that trigger conscious reflection. This teaching or reflection involves explanation and analysis, that is, breaking down the thing to be learned into its analytic parts. It inherently involves attaining, along with the matter being taught, some degree of metaknowledge about the matter (p. 138).

Methods in the tradition of progressive education, on the other hand, are very much like Krashen's notion of acquisition, where teaching is more like an apprenticeship, with students and teachers engaging subject matter together. In Gee's words:

Acquisition is a process of acquiring something (usually subconsciously) by exposure to models, a process of trial and error, and practice within social groups, without formal teaching. It happens in natural settings which are meaningful and functional in the sense that acquirers know that they need to acquire the thing they are exposed to in order to function and they in fact want to so function. This is how people come to control their first language (p. 138).

As we have seen, the debate about which of these two approaches is best is at least as old as the turn of the last century, when progressive education came on the scene, and the debate still rages, with "back to basics" advocates urging a return to instructional methods. We now take a brief look at controversies in the teaching of reading and mathematics that mirror the learning versus acquisition controversy in language teaching.

Reading

The Reading Wars

In 1987, California adopted a progressive approach to teaching reading called *whole language*. Coincidentally, in the same year, the state stopped administering tests of reading proficiency that could be compared with those of other states. When California re-instated the national tests in 1994, it found that it had the lowest reading scores in the country, tied with Louisiana (Saunders, 1996). Although there could be many reasons for this decline, including an influx of ELL students, many blamed the whole language approach. In response, the California State Legislature passed a bill banning the use of whole language and requiring that reading be taught by the rival phonics method.

The phonics versus whole language debate is now national. In October 1997, an article in *Time* (Collins, 1997) described "a war . . . between supporters of phonics and those who believe in the whole language method of learning to read." Similar articles appeared in *Newsweek* and *U.S. News and*

World Report. Phonics appears to be winning the war. In 1998, President Clinton signed the Reading Excellence Act, which provides funds to states for training reading teachers and tutoring children from poor families. This law defines reading instruction in terms compatible only with the phonics method (Coles, 2000, p. xv). The war between whole language and phonics is a classic case of conflict between an acquisition/progressive approach and a learning/instructional approach to teaching. Let us look more closely at these two ways of teaching reading.

The Whole Language Approach

The whole language approach has been influenced by the ideas about language acquisition discussed in chapter 2, which were in the air during the 1960s and 1970s. As you might expect, Krashen is a whole language advocate (Krashen, 1999). He believes that learning to read can be as natural to a child as learning to speak. What is required in both cases is that students be exposed to the target language (written language in the case of reading), that the language be understandable and interesting, and that the affective circumstances be positive.

Teach your baby to read. Whereas whole language advocates have not claimed that children can learn to read at the same time they learn to talk, this claim was made in the 1960s by rehabilitational therapist Glenn Doman (1964), who developed a program called "Teach Your Baby to Read," which anticipated some of the whole language philosophy. Doman's method, and his confidence in the linguistic abilities of very young children, were developed in the course of his work with brain-damaged children. He believed that the neurological processes involved in learning written language were essentially the same as those involved in learning spoken language and that the main reason children didn't learn to read at the same time they learned to talk was that their visual abilities were not sufficiently developed to see the small black letters on a page. So, Doman advised parents to write their children's first words, or any words they could understand, in red letters at least four inches high on white flash cards. Anticipating Krashen, Doman believed that the two important factors in teaching a 2-year-old to read were exposure to meaningful written language and good affective circumstances. In a word, the reading experience should be "joyful." Doman also believed in a critical period for learning to read: "Two years of age is the best time to begin" (p. 21). After 2 years old, it gets harder.

A typical lesson might go as follows. The mother touches the baby's foot and says, "This is your foot." Then she touches her own foot and says, "This is my foot." Then she shows the baby a card with *foot* written on it and says, "This says *foot*." This game should be played several times a day. After learning to read several cards, the child can be given a testing game, where the cards are placed on the floor and the child is asked, "Which one says *foot*? Which one says *Daddy*?" Right answers should be rewarded with exclamations and hugs, as parents hardly need to be told.

There is no systematic research on whether you really can teach your baby to read. Robert Lado, father of the ALM, and his students (I was one of them) tried out Doman's method and reported mixed results. Lado had considerable success with his grandson, which he documented on a videotape that showed 2-year-old Tony reading sentences written in red on large cards. My wife and I (okay, mainly Alice) gave lessons to our daughter for about 5 months when she was 2 years old. Marie did learn to read several words, including *bow*, her word for any animal, and *whee*, her word for swing, see-saw, and other things you ride on. In the end, however, we stopped the reading lessons because of the pressure of time and our desire to just play with Marie instead of teach her. This was not the first nor the last time that a progressive teaching method has failed because of practical considerations.

Whole language theory. The whole language approach was developed by reading researchers Kenneth and Yetta Goodman, and stems from Kenneth Goodman's groundbreaking theory of the reading process. Before Goodman (1968), researchers thought that reading was a decoding or "bottom-up" process, where people mentally translated letters into sounds, groups of sounds into words, and groups of words into sentences. This psychological model assumes that readers have no preliminary ideas of what a text will be about. But this is obviously wrong. We can often guess what a text will say before we have read it. For example, the reader is invited to match the following summaries of opinion pieces with their authors without benefit of reading the actual articles. The possible choices are Molly Ivins, Bill O'Reilly, and George Will.

Progressive education

The process approach to teaching writing is rooted in the excesses of the 1960s and has resulted in illiterate and unemployable students.

Parenting

My parents raised me in a rigid but caring regime which instilled the discipline and motivation that have led to my success.

Clinton versus Republicans

Faced with a hostile and partisan Republican Congress, President Clinton acted professionally and in the best interests of the country.[1]

---

[1]George Will (1997) decried the process approach to teaching writing; Bill O'Reilly (2000) praised tough parenting; and Molly Ivins (1998) stood up for Bill Clinton.

I'll bet you got them right. In fact, I'll bet you could write your own summaries just by knowing the writer and the topic. Confronted with an article by these writers, readers can just skim the text to confirm that their preconceptions are correct (or, skip the articles altogether and read something less predictable).

Goodman (1968) suggested that readers make use of the predictability of a text by guessing the meanings it contains and then engaging in selective decoding to confirm or disconfirm their guesses, a process he called a "psycholinguistic guessing game." Because meaning is central to this understanding of the reading process, the whole language approach endorses teaching methods that emphasize meaningful language rather than the regularity of the letter–sound correspondences, and recommends that beginning students read about familiar, predictable topics.

The language experience method. One method compatible with the whole language approach is the language experience method. A language experience lesson begins with the students doing some activity, such as a trip to the zoo, a visit to the school cafeteria, or just playing in the classroom. In one language experience lesson, four-year-olds Sheona and Sara were playing at a sand table pretending to be witches making a cake. Both girls talked in scary witch voices.

Sheona: When he licks his fingers, he'll say "Thick! Yuk!" We'll put syrup on it. He hates syrup!

Sara: We should put popcorn on, right? Because we want him to get sick. And he hates sprinkles so we put on sprinkles . . . (normal voice) I wish we was bakin' a real cake (from Roskos 1999, p. 73).

While the children were playing, the teacher roamed around the classroom writing down some of the vocabulary they were using. For Sheona and Sara, she wrote *syrup*, *popcorn*, and *yukky cake*, among other words. Each word was accompanied by a simple picture to make the meaning clear. Then, using the list of words and pictures as a guide, Sheona and Sara told the story of what they were playing to the teacher, who wrote it down:

We made a icky, picky, yukky cake. First we put syrup on because he hates syrup . . . Then we put popcorn on . . . etc. (p. 74).

After reading the story several times to themselves, the girls were able to read it (with some errors) to their classmates. Other children who liked the story copied it down in a book with a sentence and a picture on each page. The book was added to the class library of dictated stories available for anyone to read.

Exposed to words in this manner, children eventually learn to associate letters with their sounds unconsciously, as in the "whole word method," which was used in the United States during the 1940s and 1950s in the Dick and Jane readers. However, it should be emphasized that whole language also teaches children to consciously sound out words, but only as a backup tool, after they have a good idea of what a passage is about.

In the language experience approach, after children have read a number of dictated stories, they are encouraged to write a few sentences on their own. Their writing will, of course, contain many errors: backward letters, random capital letters, misspelled words. To the horror of traditionalists, these are not corrected. The teacher responds only to the meaning of the story, mostly with praise. If an idea isn't clear, the teacher may suggest adding a word or changing a spelling that will make it clear. Errors are allowed during the beginning stages of writing in order to engage the child immediately in meaningful language use. Errors are not seen as bad habits but as the natural products of learning, just as in the case of learning to talk. It is thought that errors in writing, as in speech, will mostly disappear as proficiency increases, and that any remaining errors can be dealt with at a more advanced stage.

The Phonics Method

Phonics refers to teaching the relationship between letters and sounds and encouraging children to sound out words. The McGuffey Readers used a partial phonics method, teaching the principal sounds of the letters and some additional phonics information. But complete phonics programs that taught all of the complex sound–symbol correspondences in English were not developed until the 1930s (Aukerman, 1971).

The problem with using phonics to teach reading in English is that the relationship between letters and sounds is far from simple. Despite the urging of George Bernard Shaw, Mark Twain, and others, English has not undergone spelling reform. As this verse warns:

Beware of *heard*, a dreadful word
That looks like *beard* and sounds like *bird*,
And *dead*: It's said like *bed*, not *bead*—
For goodness' sake, don't call it *deed*! (T.S.W., 1970, p. 57)

One difficulty is that in English each letter does not stand for a single sound. There are, for example, 13 spellings for the sound *sh*, namely, *shoe*, *sugar, issue, mansion, mission, nation, suspicion, ocean, conscious, chaperon, schist, fuchsia*, and *pshaw*. What has happened is that the language has changed over the years but the spelling hasn't. *Knight*, used to be pronounced KUH NICKT. For Shakespeare, *meat* and *meet* were both pronounced MEYT. Changes in the English system of phonology are continuing today as people in Chicago, Buffalo, and other northern U.S. cities increasingly pronounce *can* like *Ken*, and *rat* like *Rhett*. The spellings, of course, are still not changing.

Nevertheless, sound–symbol correspondences in English are not as irregular as some people have thought. Bernard Shaw famously claimed that an alternative way to spell *fish* is *ghoti*, where *gh* has the sound in *laugh*, *o* has the sound in *women*, and *ti* has the sound in *nation*. But Shaw was wrong, as his friend Professor Henry Sweet (the real-life model for Professor Henry Higgins in *Pygmalion* and *My Fair Lady*) could have told him. *Gh* can be pronounced "f" only when it is at the end of a syllable, and *ti* can only be pronounced "sh" only when it is part of the sequence *tion*. These and other regularities of English spelling can be taught to children so that they can sound out words. For example, the letter "a" has different sounds in *cat* and *cater*. But two rules will allow the beginning reader to sort out which sound goes where. First, consider the syllable structure, which is: *cat, ca' ter*. The single syllable of *cat* is called a *closed syllable* because it ends in a consonant. Stressed vowels in closed syllables take their short sound: *e* as in *let*, *i* as in *sit*, *a* as in *cat*, et cetera. The first syllable in *cater* is called an *open syllable* because it ends in a vowel. Stressed vowels in open syllables take their long sound: *e* as in *me' ter*, *i* as in *si' lent*, and so forth. But what about *late*? Doesn't that have a long *a* sound in a closed syllable? Yes, if you just consider the pronunciation, but the spelling suggests that for reading and writing purposes there are two syllables: *la te*. The second syllable is constructed by using the famous "silent e," which is a marvelous aid to reading English, as Tom Lehrer reminded us in his nightclub act (not to be confused with his Electric Company children's version):

> Who can turn a cap into a cape?
> Who can turn a rap into a rape?
> A little glob becomes a globe instantly
> If you just add silent e!

Sometimes people aren't sure whether a syllable is open or closed, which explains why some words have two pronunciations. People who say "*eec*onomics," consider the first syllable open [e conomics], but people say who say "*ehc*onomics" consider the first syllable closed [ec onomics]. Many people use both pronunciations interchangeably. Rules like these show that English spelling is a lot more regular than Shaw gave it credit for, but there are still many exceptions. You say PA JAH MA, I say PA JAM AH.

The phonics method involves teaching children rules like those above and then giving them lots of practice reading words that follow the same rules. This restriction inevitably leads to boring exercises like the following:

cat   cater
mat   mate
latch   later

Such exercises are followed by sentences and little artificial stories written so that only a few rules are needed to decode the words, such as:

I saw an ox.
An ox in a box?
No, the ox was
Not in a box.
I saw an ox.
An ox wearing socks?
No, the ox was
Not wearing socks.

From these examples, the reader can imagine the complaints many teachers and students have about the phonics method.

Evaluation of Reading Methods

So which method is better, whole language or phonics? As in the debate over focus on form, many experts call for a balanced approach. For example, in a 390-page report, the National Research Council (1998) stresses that reading is a complex process that cannot be taught by a single approach. Nevertheless, there has been no truce in the reading wars and the latest skirmish has been a defeat for phonics. The National Assessment of Educational Progress test ("the nation's report card"), administered to 8,000 fourth graders nationwide in 2000, found that average reading scores had not changed despite the recent emphasis on phonics (Coles, 2000). What had changed was that the best readers were getting even higher scores and the worst readers were getting even lower scores. This effect is probably due to the fact that in an effort to raise scores, schools are focusing on the students most likely to succeed on the test and writing off the students most likely to fail. All of this was predicted by Ken Goodman (personal communication), who also predicted that phonics advocates would blame the lack of improvement on reading teachers and schools of education, and that, indeed, has been their response.

As in the focus-on-form argument in language teaching, it is unwise to take an extreme position on either whole language or phonics. I believe that the best reading program, like the best L2 program, should immerse students in meaningful language in a way that is enjoyable and interesting. The program should also focus on language forms when that will help children with problem words or help them express their ideas more effectively.

Teaching Mathematics

The reading wars have a counterpart in the mathematics wars, with traditionalists stressing the importance of accurate calculation and reformers stressing the importance of understanding. The back-to-basics movement has been championed by many of the same politically conservative educators who championed phonics teaching, and during the administration of Republican Governor Pete Wilson, the California School Board rejected a reform mathematics curriculum and approved a back-to-basics curriculum that mirrored the phonics curriculum.

To see the difference between the two positions, I invite the reader to try a little math problem, one which gave me a bit of trouble. Here's the problem:

$$2 \ 1/2 \div 1/4 = ?$$

After thinking for a while, I remembered that when you divide by a fraction you first change any whole number into a fraction, then invert the divisor and multiply. So, the solution is:

$$5/2 \times 4/1 = 20/2 = 10$$

But what can this possibly mean? It's not hard to understand what it means to divide by a whole number. If you divide 12 students into 4 equal groups, there will be 3 students in each group: $12 \div 4 = 3$. But dividing 12 students by $1/4$ is conceptually different. Fortunately, I could ask my daughter Marie, who is now a graduate student in physics and fully capable of giving her father a math lesson that is the equivalent of writing one-syllable words in big red letters on flash cards. Marie explained with an illustration like Figure 3.2. The problem can be made more concrete by stating it as follows: One rectangle can be divided up into four fourths $(1/1 \div 1/4 = 4)$. How many fourths can 2 1/2 rectangles be divided up into $(2 \ 1/2 \div 1/4 = ?)$? In other words, how many fourths are there in 2 1/2? Dividing 12 students by one fourth is conceptually difficult because we don't usually divide up a single student. It's easier if you use something that is often divided into parts, say a dollar. Thus, we can say $12 divided up into quarters equals 48 quarters.

If you wish I had just inverted and multiplied instead of giving an explanation with diagrams, you are a traditionalist, who mainly wants to know how to get the right answer. If you wanted an explanation, you are a reformer, who thinks that the concepts behind the calculations are important. The parallel between teaching math and teaching reading will be apparent by now. Calculation is to reform math as phonics is to whole language. The traditional approaches are centered around the teacher,

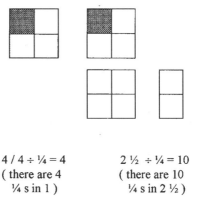

$$4 / 4 \div \tfrac{1}{4} = 4 \qquad\qquad 2\tfrac{1}{2} \div \tfrac{1}{4} = 10$$
(there are 4   (there are 10
$\tfrac{1}{4}$ s in 1) $\tfrac{1}{4}$ s in 2 $\tfrac{1}{2}$)

FIG. 3.2.   The logic of dividing by fractions.

who is the source of knowledge. Learning doesn't have to be fun or inter-esting, just effective. Basic skills like calculation and identifying words are stressed. Lessons involve memorizing and drilling. The skills are taught without meaningful context. The newer approaches are centered around the students and their interests. Conservatives characterize reform math as "fuzzy math" (a charge George W. Bush leveled against Al Gore during the presidential debates). Reformers characterize traditional math as "plug and chug."

Here is an example of the kind of problem conservatives dislike:

If Billy has twice as many apples as Bobby, and Sally has seven more apples than Chester, who has one apple in each hand plus one concealed in his knickers, then how many apples does Ned have, assuming his train leaves Chicago at noon? (Barry, 2001).

Okay, I lied. That problem is from Dave Barry. Here's the real problem, taken from a standardized test:

Estimate the answer to $12/13 + 7/8$. You will not have time to solve the prob-lem using pencil and paper. Possible answers: 1, 2, 19, 21 (O'Brien, 1999, p. 445).

The best answer is 2 because both fractions are almost equal to 1. Tradition-alists are impatient with this guesswork and want the students to calculate the exact answer. Reformers want that too, but they also want the students to understand what they are doing. Surely no student who understood fractions would answer 19 or 21. But more students gave those answers than 1 or 2, the only figures in the right ballpark. Here is the distribution of scores from the National Assessment of Educational Progress test administered during the 1980s, when no one had heard of fuzzy math and the curriculum was completely traditional (Battista, 1999):

Possible answers	Age 13	Age 17	
1	7%	8%	
2	24%	37%	
19	28%	21%	
21	14%	16%	(percentages have been rounded)

Many students must have thought that adding fractions has something to do with adding the numerators (hence the 19) or adding the denominators (hence the 21). This lack of understanding basic concepts is what worries the reformers.

Another reason conservatives don't like reform math is that the rows of calculations that older readers remember have largely been replaced by word problems. Of course, older math books had word problems too, but they dealt with politically neutral matters like laying carpet and figuring out when trains traveling at different speeds will reach Chicago. Reform math word problems tend to have a politically correct attitude.[2] Here is an example:

> In the 1960s pollution in Lake Superior became an issue of public concern. We will set up a model for how long it would take for the lake to flush itself clean, assuming no further pollutants are being dumped in the lake (Hughes-Hallet, 1994, p. 251).

---

[2]Here are more word problems that made the rounds on the mathteacher Internet bulletin board. **Teaching Math in 1960:** A logger sells a truckload of lumber for $100. His cost of production is 4/5 of the price, or $80. What is his profit? **Teaching Math in 1970:** A logger exchanges a set "L" of lumber for a set "M" of money. The cardinality of set "M" is 100. Each element is worth one dollar. Make 100 dots representing the elements of the set "M." The set "C," the cost of production contains 20 fewer points than set "M." Represent the set "C" as a subset of set "M" and answer the following question: What is the cardinality of the set "P" of profits? **Teaching Math in 1980:** A logger sells a truckload of lumber for $100. His cost of production is $80 and his profit is $20. Your assignment: Underline the number 20. **Teaching Math in 1990:** By cutting down beautiful forest trees, the logger makes $20. What do you think of this way of making a living? Topic for class participation after answering the question: How did the forest birds and squirrels feel as the logger cut down the trees? There are no wrong answers. **Teaching Math in 2000:** A logger sells a truckload of lumber for $100. His cost of production is $120. How does Arthur Andersen determine that his profit margin is $60?

I will skip over the data for this problem and get to the answer: For Lake Superior to become 99% pollution free would take over 892 years.

CONCLUSIONS

The debate that began in the early 20th century regarding instructional versus progressive teaching continues today. The instructional notion of teaching as implanting conscious knowledge in the minds of students is echoed today in the back-to-basics movement, which embraces phonics in reading instruction and calculation in mathematics instruction. The progressive notion of teaching as enculturation into a group of skilled practitioners, involving both conscious and unconscious learning, is echoed in the whole language approach to reading instruction and the reform movement in mathematics instruction. In L2 teaching, these two philosophies are evident in the debate over focus on form, or put differently, the relative importance of learning versus acquisition. Most experts recommend that specific language forms should be taught, but only within the context of meaningful language use.

SUGGESTED READING

Ravitch (2000) is a readable and opinionated history of education and educational theory in the United States. A historical overview of approaches to language teaching through the 1960s can be found in Diller (1971), and Kelly (1969) traces the roots of the discipline all the way back to the Greeks. Palermo (1978) makes the case for the behaviorist theory of language learning, and discusses how the behaviorists were challenged by the early generative grammarians. There are several excellent books on contemporary approaches to language teaching. Grabe (1998) presents an overview with attention to both theory and practice, organized according to the basic skills of speaking, listening, reading, and writing. Others include Richards and Rodgers (2001), Larsen-Freeman (2000) and Celce-Murcia (2001). The volume edited by Zamel and Spack (2002) contains important articles on approaches to language teaching covering the period from the early 1980s to the present.

The case for content-based instruction is made in Snow and Brinton (1997) and in Adamson (1993). Brinton and Master (1997) contains many practical suggestions for integrating content and language instruction. Krashen (1981) discusses the learning–acquisition distinction and argues the benefits of an acquisition approach. The case for focus on form is presented by Doughty and Williams (1998) and Hinkel and Fotos (2002).

Wildner-Bassett (1984) offers an influential treatment of interlanguage pragmatics, and Kasper and Rose (2001) provides a recent overview of the field as well as research articles.

Dispatches from the reading wars can be found in Coles (2000). The foundational document of the whole language approach to reading is Goodman (1968) and an update can be found in Smith (1994). Birch (2002) relates reading theory to ESL contexts.

Standard and Vernacular English

INTRODUCTION

The English language was in crisis and a special debate was held in the House of Lords to address the problem. The usual suspects were rounded up: Pronunciation was getting worse, slang was spreading, bureaucratic jargon was taking hold. Particular concern was expressed that the standard language was being influenced by an upstart nonstandard dialect. Lord Somers was moved to declare, "If there is a more hideous language on the face of the earth . . . , I should like to know what it is." Another peer named this dialect as the cause of increasing long-windedness and ambiguity of expression. The time was 1978 and the hideous language was American English (McCrum, Cran, & MacNeil, 1986, p. 343).

Americans have expressed similar sentiments about dialects of English that are not standard here, such as Black English. Here are some comments about this dialect that have appeared in print fairly recently:

> The Africans who were brought here didn't speak English and weren't taught it. . . . In short, they spoke [Black English] because they didn't know any better. I would like to think that we, as African Americans, know better now (Hill, 2000).

> Is there a place for Black English in the schools? Well, you certainly can't keep it out. But . . . surrendering to substandard English . . . is the wrong way to overcome it ("English Standards," 1997).

100

The occasion for these comments was the Oakland, California School Board's resolution directing the Superintendent to devise a program for incorporating Black English in the Oakland schools. When this announcement was made in December 1996, it was as though someone had declared that American English would henceforth be used in the House of Lords. Everyone had an opinion: editorial writers, columnists, teenagers, politicians, and talk show hosts. The Reverend Jesse Jackson said, "In Oakland some madness has erupted over making slang talk a second language. . . . You don't have to go to school to learn to talk garbage" (Fillmore, 1997). Later, Jackson reversed his position and supported the Board. Linguists, too, had opinions about the resolution, but it wasn't easy to get them across. The problem was that the question of what a nonstandard dialect is and what place, if any, it should have in the schools is complex. To sort out the issues requires a lot of explanation and a lot of background information on the part of the audience, and the time and attention spans required were not available on *Geraldo*.

In this chapter I am going to take the time. The chapter is mainly about Black English and its use in schools, but that discussion will come last. First, I will take the opportunity to travel unhurriedly through some linguistic territory that must be explored in order to understand the Black English controversy. This territory includes areas of language scholarship that are fascinating in their own right: language variation, Alabama English, grammar gurus, and the history of English.

LANGUAGE VARIATION

When Jimmy Carter was elected President, I was living in Virginia, and a joke that made the rounds among my neighbors was that he was the first President people could remember who didn't have an accent. Actually, everybody has an accent, or to be more precise, everybody speaks a variety of some language, including Katie Couric, Jim Lehrer, and Jane Pauley. Varieties, or dialects, of a language differ from each other in pronunciation (I say PATEYTOH, you say PATAHTOH), in vocabulary (I say *see-saw*, you may say *teeter-totter*), and syntax (I say, "I guess you don't want a sandwich"; my wife says, "I don't guess you want a sandwich"). Everyone knows that features like these make up what we think of as southern speech or Brooklynese, but it is often not realized that similar features of pronunciation, vocabulary, and syntax characterize the speech of educated Midwesterners, who are perceived as speaking Standard English. In other words, Standard English is a language variety like any other, just a more prestigious one.

When people say that they speak a dialect, they often mean that they speak incorrectly. But grammatical correctness is relative to a particular group of people at a particular time and place, and it can change. An example is the "r-less" pronunciation used by Britons who speak the prestigious dialect called *received pronunciation* (meaning the pronunciation that is received by the Queen). These speakers do not pronounce r's that occur after vowels, so that "parked car" is pronounced PAHKT KAH. R-less varieties are also found in some areas of the United States, including New York City, where in the early part of the 20th century, this pronunciation was favored by upper-class speakers. However, after midcentury, the midwestern r-full pronunciation became favored, perhaps due to the democratizing effect of World War II. Today, all speakers of New York City English "drop their r's" some of the time, but upper-class speakers do it less often than middle-class speakers, who do it less often than working-class speakers. This correlation of social class and r-full speech also occurs in some areas of Britain, but in reverse, so that working-class speakers are the most likely to retain the r.

Another example of regional variation is from my own dialect of Utah English. Most dialects of American English have 14 vowels. But in some areas of the country, including my vocalically challenged region, only 13 vowels are distinguished. The missing vowel, called "open o," is the one in *caught* (which I say just like *cot*) and *taught* (which I say just like *tot*). I remember my surprise when I was trying to learn the phonetic alphabet in my first linguistics class and was told that these words were supposed to sound different. It was a big shock to discover that I didn't speak Standard English: I was missing a whole vowel (and Western readers of this book may have just experienced a similar shock)!

Like New Yorkers, I speak a variety of English that differs from the most prestigious variety. However, 13-vowel English is more prestigious than New York City English because everyone knows that you shouldn't drop your r's, and New Yorkers try not to do it in formal speaking situations. But Westerners need not worry about not pronouncing open o because that feature is not stigmatized and is not even noticed by most listeners. Thus, some differences in how we talk make a difference in how our speech is evaluated by others and (luckily for me) some differences don't.

As all of this suggests, English (like all languages) is not a homogeneous system, but rather has many features that can vary according to the speaker's geographical region, social class, sex, race, and age. To be sure, most rules of English are used by all speakers. For example, the articles *the* and *a* must come before the noun they modify. No variety of English allows sentences like:

*Mr. Wolfe spotted red-crowned sapsucker a.

or

*Don't give up ship the!

However, there are two kinds of rules that vary among speakers, and these can be used to distinguish between dialects. The first kind of variable rule describes a syntactic or phonological alternation in which both forms are considered correct, such as:

> They are not/aren't headed for trouble.
>
> I don't like either (EETHER/EYETHER) one of the vases (VEYSES/VAHZES).

The second kind of variable rule describes an alternation in which one form of an alternating pair is not considered correct:

> John doesn't/*don't live here anymore/*no more.

Speakers of nonstandard dialects always adhere to the invariant language patterns. However, they sometimes or always use the stigmatized form of patterns that can vary. Notice that Standard English also allows plenty of variation, as in the first two examples just given. No one thinks that Standard English is unsystematic or that its speakers are lazy because they aren't consistent. But nonstandard dialects allow variation between a standard form and a nonstandard form, and this inconsistency is often attributed to a lack of systematicity in the dialect or laziness in the speaker. In fact, every variety of every language is fully systematic (but recall the discussion of pidgin languages in chap. 2), and fully capable of expressing the complete range of human ideas. The best way to make this important point, I have found, is not to preach about it, but to examine in detail a speech community that uses a dialect other than Standard English. In this way, the nature of language variation and the relationship between standard and nonstandard forms can be understood. We will examine, then, the English spoken in the fascinating community of Anniston Alabama.

Anniston English

A superb guide to the speech of Anniston is the book *Variation and Change in Alabama English: A Sociolinguistic Study of the White Community*, written by Anniston native Crawford Feagin (1979), and my discussion closely follows hers. For convenience, I will refer to the speech of Anniston as *Anniston English*, although it is not distinct from the gulf southern dialect that is spoken throughout most of Alabama, Mississippi, and Louisiana, and is very similar to other southern dialects, including midsouthern, spoken in northern Alabama and Tennessee. I have a personal interest in southern speech as my wife Alice is from Tennessee, and I have already used her speech in an example. Here are two more examples of southern speech that have caused confusion around our house. In southern English, the difference between the vowels short e (as in *pet*) and short i (as in *pit*) disappears before a nasal sound. Thus, *cinder* and *sender*, and *hymn* and *hem* are homonyms (all of these words are pronounced with the short i). To this day when Alice asks for a *pin*, I am likely to say, "You mean a straight pin?" "No," she'll reply, "a writing pen." Recently, Alice asked me, "Where's the broom?" "It's on the porch," I said. So, she went to a screened-in room that Tucsonans call an *Arizona room*, but Tennesseans call a *porch*. But the broom wasn't there; it was outside the front door on the raised, covered area that I call a *porch* but Alice calls a *stoop*.

Anniston is located in the foothills of the Blue Ridge Range, equidistant from Atlanta to the east, Huntsville to the north, and Montgomery to the south. In 1812, Andrew Jackson defeated the Creek Indians in the Battle of Horseshoe Bend, near Montgomery, and opened up the Alabama Piedmont to settlement by Whites and their Black slaves. The majority of the settlers came from Georgia and the coastal areas of the Carolinas and Virginia. Northern Alabama and Tennessee, on the other hand, were settled by immigrants from the Piedmont areas of the Carolinas and Virginia and from Pennsylvania. This settlement pattern accounts for the fact that the speech of the two areas differs slightly.

Anniston has a population of 59,000.[1] One third of its residents are African Americans. Most of the people are Baptists, with Methodists in second place. The area's largest employer is the Army Depot, located in Fort McClellan, west of the city. Other large employers are the metal industry, textile mills, and clothing factories. There are also assorted dairies, lumber mills, and two bottling companies.

Feagin's (1979) study of Anniston English focused on syntactic features in the speech of three social classes: urban upper class, urban working class, and rural working class. All of her primary informants were White, although she gives some attention to African American speech. To collect data, Feagin used standard sociolinguistic field methods. The basic technique is to locate an appropriate informant and get him or her to talk into a tape recorder at great length in as natural a way as possible. This isn't easy because when people talk to a linguist, especially one with a tape recorder, they tend to speak in formal, correct style, and it is difficult to capture the nonstandard forms that they use in everyday conversation with friends. Formal speech also tends to be used when topics like education and language are discussed. To control for topic and level of formality, sociolinguists have developed a technique known as the *sociolinguistic interview*, in which the interviewer memorizes a series of questions about set topics. The interviewer

---

[1]For convenience, I will describe the Anniston of Feagin's monograph, published in 1979, using the present tense. No doubt present-day Anniston has changed a great deal.

then tries to weave these questions into a natural conversation. A famous question, which was used by Feagin and many other sociolinguists, is the "danger of death" question: "Were you ever in a situation when you thought, 'I'm going to die. This is it?' Tell me about it." Actually, many people have been in danger of death (often in situations involving water), and as they launch into their story, natural, less formal speech emerges.

Because a major goal of sociolinguistic research is to relate speech patterns to a speaker's sex, age, race, social class, and other demographic characteristics, the researcher needs to find informants who more or less equally represent all of the demographic categories relevant to the study. The most difficult demographic to assess is the speaker's social class. For this, Feagin used Weaver's Index, which assigns a number from 1 to 100 to each informant, 100 being the highest social class. The index number is calculated using a weighted average of four characteristics: occupation, source of income, house type, and neighborhood. Feagin's 61 informants scored from 12 to 84 on this scale. Typical occupations of the upper-class informants included medicine, law, and wholesale and retail businesses. Urban working-class informants were employed mostly in manufacturing and construction, and rural working-class informants worked in farming and manufacturing.

Anniston English contains many nonstandard syntactic features. I will discuss in detail one of the most interesting: double modals ("Mrs. Kershaw *might could* tell you 'bout that"), and then briefly mention three other nonstandard features.

Double modal verbs. The modal verbs include *will, would, can, could, shall, should, may,* and *might.* They are a species of what your high school English teacher called *helping verbs* and what, in chapter 2, we called *auxiliary verbs* because they cannot stand alone but must be accompanied by a main verb (e.g., you can't say, "Marsha can Amharic," but you can say, "Marsha can speak Amharic"). Another characteristic of modal verbs is that, unlike regular verbs, they are not conjugated to agree with a third person singular subject. That is, if the subject is *Marsha*, a regular verb ends in -*s* (Marsha speaks Amharic), but *can* does not end in -*s*, as the previous example shows. Modals can combine with main verbs and with other auxiliary verbs, like *have* and *be*, in many ways including the following:

Bob *could have eaten* your lunch.

Lucy *may be eating* your lunch.

Anniston English, like many southern dialects, allows a string of two modal verbs:

Bob *might could* have eaten your lunch.

Some other examples from Feagin's corpus include the following (all speakers from Feagin's corpus are identified by pseudonym and age):

You *might could* hang a dog house [dormer window] there (Jack B., 26).
I *may can* do a lotta things later on today. (Virginia L., 61).
The kids *might would* enjoy it if you gon throw it away (Myrtice J., 62).

However, auxiliary verbs, including double modals, cannot be strung together just any way. In both Anniston English and Standard English, a modal must be the first verb in the verb string. The first modal in a double modal string is *might* or *may*. Figure 4.1 shows some of the combinations of modals Feagin observed in Anniston, and how the meaning of these combinations contrasts with the meaning of single modals in Standard English.

As Figure 4.1 shows, double modals serve to indicate shades of possibility, and their use allows for distinguishing finer shades than can be done with the modal system of Standard English. The possibilities of double modal usage shown in Figure 4.1 are not shared by all Anniston English speakers, just as the possibilities for auxiliary verb usage are not shared by all Standard English speakers. This last fact can be illustrated by the sentence:

The house *may have been being* watched by the FBI.

(For grammar fans, this tense could be called the past modal perfect progressive, passive voice.) Some speakers of Standard English find the sentence acceptable and some find it unacceptable. Similarly, some Anniston speakers use all of the double modal constructions in Figure 4.1 and others do not. The extent to which Anniston speakers use double modals can be correlated with their social class and sex. For example, for speakers over the age of 60, 28% of working-class speakers used double modals, but no upper-class speakers used them. Within the working class, 28% of women used double modals, but only 10% of men used them.

```
CERTAIN   POSSIBLE   UNCERTAIN   UNLIKELY   IMPOSSIBLE

can
          may
          may can
               might can
                    might could
                         might not could
                              might not can
                                   couldn't
                                        can't
```

FIG. 4.1.   Double modals combining may/might/can/could showing their contrast with single modals.

A-verb-ing. This form is a holdover from earlier varieties of English, but it is familiar to modern readers from nursery rhymes and folk songs, both old and modern.

A-hunting we will go,
A-hunting we will go,
Heigh ho the derry-o
A-hunting we will go (nursery rhyme).

Mister Frog went a-courting and he did ride uh-huh,
Mister Frog went a-courting and he did ride uh-huh,
Mister Frog went a-courting and he did ride,
With a sword and a pistol by his side,
Uh-huh, uh-huh, uh-huh (16th-century Scottish ballad).

I'm a-thinkin' and a-wonderin' all the way down that road,
I once loved a woman, a child untold;
I gave her my heart, but she wanted my soul;
But that's all right, don't think twice (Bob Dylan, 1963).

The underlined words are an old-fashioned form of the present participle, consisting of the base form of the verb, the suffix *ing*, and the prefix *a*. Modern present participles (which were mentioned in chap. 2) have only the first two of these elements. Wolfram and Fasold (1974), who studied the use of a-verb-ing in Appalachian English in West Virginia, say that the prefixed *a* emphasizes the duration of an action. "She's working" means that she's engaged in a relatively short-term task. "She's a-working" means that the task is of longer duration. "She's a-jumping over the fence this very minute" would not occur. Feagin (1979) did not find this temporal distinction in present participle use in Anniston. Rather, a-verb-ing was used to intensify the action or to create dramatic vividness. She found that a-verb-ing forms were common in stories about ghosts, accidents, murders, tornadoes and other dramatic topics.

To see how a good storyteller uses a-verb-ing, here is part of a "danger of death" story told by Flora P., 74:

An' another time, honey, I 'uz in a—I 'uz in a—I 'uz in a shore nuff cyclone. I lived out here at the Alston place out here at Weaver. And uh my sister and my mother 'n 'em were down in the field hoein' cotton for Mr. Herbert Sims. An' uh lemme see . . . I don't know—can't remember what year it was.

But anyhow, they'd been over there in Herbert Sims' cotton patch. I'ad seen my mother and them comin' in, an'—I kept a-watchin' it come from this direction. An', honey, when it. . . was about as far as from here to that there house down yonder from our house, and I 'uz settin' there on the back porch a-churnin'. An' I kept a-settin' there, and I said, 'well, Lord, if it hits me and kills me, I'll jus'—You intend for it to. So I kept a-settin'. I just' kep' a-churnin', watchin' it, you know, an' it was jes' like a ice cream cone, an' honey, it was *black*! I'm tellin' you, that was the blackest thing I ever seen! An' it hit that Herbert Sims' cotton patch, an' his cotton fell down for over thirty minutes! An' the cotton was that high! An' it hit a little knoll and went over cross that knoll, and it swept trees down that big around! Des went over the little knoll there an' went over into the camps [Fort McClellan]. An' them little dog tents fell, as they called 'em dog tents back then, fell in our yard there, and it blowed two big trees down right in our yard there (Feagin, 1979, p. 114).

Like all good stories, Flora's narrative begins with a background, where she sets the scene, and moves on to a foreground, where she describes the action. The foreground begins with the sentence, "An' it hit that Herbert Sims' cotton patch an' his cotton fell down for over thirty minutes!" Flora emphasizes the force of the tornado by repeating the verb *hit* once and the verb *fell down* twice. In the background, which begins with the first sentence, Flora does two things: She describes the general scene before the tornado strikes, and she describes what she herself was doing. This latter description is the main point of the story. Flora says that although others took shelter, she did not leave her porch, trusting her fate to God. She heightens the precariousness of her position by using a-verb-ing forms: *a-settin'* and *a-churnin'*. In describing her actions before the tornado struck, Flora uses seven present participles, five of them in the *a*-prefix form. By contrast, in describing the actions of others, Flora uses present participles twice, both times in the modern form. The *a*-prefix form, then, serves as a bridge between background and foreground, heightening the tension leading up to the moment the tornado hit. Storytellers who use Standard English lack this nice dramatic device.

Done.

(1) You buy a little milk and bread and you've done spent your five dollars! (Myrtice J., 62).

(2) A lot of em [towels] have done give out (Julia K., 89).

(3) I don't know if he done done it (Barbara K., 16)

In these expressions, *done* is the equivalent of the Standard English adverb *already*, and is translated by Anniston natives as such.

I done seen em;
(louder) I done seen em!
(yet louder) I already seen em (Myrtice, J., 61).

However, *done* patterns more like an auxiliary verb than an adverb as it cannot occur at the end of a sentence; it is therefore called a *quasi-auxiliary*.

Like *have, done* occurs before a main verb in the past participle form, and it can occur with other auxiliary verbs, as in (1) and (2), where it follows the auxiliary verb *have.* The longest attested string of auxiliary verbs with *done* in Feagin's (1979) data is, "should have done been give."

Like *already, done* marks perfective aspect, that is, it signals that an action is complete. To describe a tire completely worn through, Sam H., 40, says, "It's done wore out. . . . This one's done gone, y'see." Also, like *already, done* is usually used with a perfect tense. Because this tense by itself marks completion, *done* is redundant in this context, but the redundancy emphasizes the completed nature of the event, as when Myrtice J., not wishing to get out of bed to watch a TV show, said, "I've done gone to bed!" Like *a-verb-ing, done* is a holdover from earlier forms of English.

Negative agreement.   In Anniston English, several negative words can occur within the same clause.

TWO   I would*na* had a railroad man under *no* circumstances (Milly B., 77).

THREE   That's 'cause yu do*n't never* say *nothing* (Joanie W., 15).

FOUR   You did*n* have *no* money to pay *nobody* to do *nothin'* for ya (Carrie R., 72).

Multiple negation is actually an agreement phenomenon, as when the verb *be* changes form to agree with its subject: I am, you are, she is, et cetera. In many varieties of vernacular English, and in many foreign languages, pronouns and adverbs that have negative forms take those forms to agree with a negated verb. Thus, in Spanish you can say, *No tenemos ningunos problemas* (literally, "We don't have no problems"). In Anniston English, negative agreement can vary within a clause:

There wad*n no* schools then to amount to *any*thing (Lamar N., 86).

In Feagin's (1979) data, negative agreement is correlated with social class. Working class speakers used negative agreement 74.9% of the time, but the rate for upper-class speakers was only 1.1%. Feagin's negative agreement data also illustrate an unusual pattern in Anniston speech regarding differences between men and women. Sociolinguistic studies of large urban centers in the United States, including New York City, Philadelphia, and Detroit, have found that men's speech is less standard than women's speech. Linguists do not agree on why this is so, but one theory is that women are less secure socially and try to speak like members of a higher social class. However, Feagin found little evidence of such sex stratification among older speakers in the working classes. In fact, older urban working-class women used negative agreement more often than men—84% compared to 69%. Feagin emphasizes that more research is needed before concluding that older southern women are an exception to the general pattern of men's using nonstandard forms more than women, but she suggests a fascinating comparison. In developing countries including India and Iran, older women are sometimes the most conservative speakers. It is believed that this is because they have less contact with society outside the home and practically no voice in influencing it.

Anniston as a Speech Community

Feagin found that the use of nonstandard features in and around Anniston varies according to the speaker's social class, sex, and age. The largest difference is between the social classes, with the upper-class speakers using the nonstandard features far less than the working-class speakers. This large discrepancy raises the question of whether Anniston contains two speech communities or one. It is accurate to characterize the speech of the upper class as "standard southern," similar to the variety spoken by Jimmy Carter, and to characterize the speech of the working class as "vernacular southern." Feagin concludes, however, that there is no sharp boundary between the two varieties, and that Anniston constitutes a single speech community. For one thing, members of all the groups showed the ability to *style-shift*, that is, to adapt their speech to the formality of the situation. Thus, all the speakers could, to some extent, use both standard and nonstandard forms as the situation required. Also, the distinction between classes in Feagin's study is magnified by the fact that she did not include middle-class speakers among her informants. If these speakers had been included, a smooth continuum of nonstandard to standard usage would likely have emerged.

Among working-class speakers, Anniston English shows a familiar pattern of sex stratification, with men using nonstandard features more than women overall, although we have noted an exception among older women. Among the upper-class speakers, however, no patterning by sex could be detected. One possible reason was that the data were collected by an upper-class woman—Feagin herself. She speculates that when speaking to her, men of her social class may have been reluctant to shift toward the vernacular style, as they would do with other men, and that they avoided topics appropriate to the vernacular: tall tales, off-color jokes, fish stories, and adventures involving alcohol. Indeed, many studies have found that vernacular language has "covert prestige" among men, who use it to establish and maintain male solidarity. In fact, I bet that if I could get my brother-in-law from Huntsville down to Anniston with a couple of six-packs, he'd have those old boys shifting so far down the style continuum they'd make Billy Carter sound like Churchill.

In regard to differences between generations, Anniston English also shows a familiar pattern. Two archaic features are dying out, occurring less among teenagers than among older speakers. These features are *a-verb-ing* and the verbal suffix *-s* used with plural nouns, as in:

My two great grandchildren that live*s* at Oxford love*s* games bettern anything (Laura McH., 70).

Well, I cain't do much myself, but I can get anything done that I think people need*s*. I feel like sick people need*s* it worse than I do (Milly B., 77).

Other features that show signs of weakening are negative agreement and nonstandard past tense forms:

My daddy, I never *knowed* or *seen* of him doin'it, naw sir! (Myrtice J., 61).

In sum, the Anniston speech community presents a microcosm of language variation that reflects language change in progress. This variation and change can be charted on a continuum. Generally, the most conservative speakers, that is, those who favor regional forms, are older, rural, working-class men, and the most innovative speakers are teenage urban girls. This pattern is similar to that of other speech communities that have been studied, such as New York City, Philadelphia, and Martha's Vineyard, and is further evidence that Anniston is a single speech community, at least in regard to its European-American residents. All ages and social classes and both sexes have some competence in both the standard and nonstandard patterns that characterize Anniston English.

To conclude this discussion, we may ask why variation exists in speech communities. Wouldn't it be easier if everyone just spoke the same way? The answer is that social groups adopt emblems of identity to distinguish themselves from other social groups and to create solidarity among themselves. Dress is such an emblem. In the 1920s, when Ataturk wished Turkey to become a modern European state, he not only adopted the Latin alphabet for the Turkish language, but also outlawed wearing the fez. Any American high school student can identify various social groups by the way they dress: jocks, nerds, goths, ravers (don't ask), and so on. Eckert (2000) found that members of high school social groups can also be identified by how they pronounce their vowels. For better or for worse, the way we talk signals who we are, and other members of our overlapping speech communities know and share these identity markers. Some fine examples of how speech signals social distinction can be found in the writing of novelist and Anniston native Elise Sanguinetti, and this section ends with a passage from her novel *McBee's Station* (1971).

'I'm Mrs. McBee, from across the way,' said Mrs. McBee in hushed tones. 'Is there anything I can do to help here?'

'Sister's told me a heap about you.'

'You're Mrs. Flemming's sister then?'

'Yes'm.' She looked around the kitchen. 'Just trying to see what all needs to be done.'

'I presume the rest of the family has been called, relatives.'

'Yes'm. Lojean done that this morning.'

'Lojean. I haven't seen her anywhere.'

'No'm. She and buster, Junior, done took the kid and went to the funeral home to make arrange-mints.'

Mrs. McBee patted her arm. 'I know Mrs. Flemming is relieved to have *you* here.'

The woman instantly looked away. 'I thank I'm just in a spell, ain't able to take none of it in yetta while. I'm not well neither. Just got outta the hospital two weeks ago from a goiter operation.'

'Oh dear,' sympathized Mrs. McBee, 'Well, I think we're all just dazed' (p. 225).

THE GRAMMAR GURUS

Having looked in some detail at a little known variety of American English, we now examine a variety that is much discussed and often misunderstood—Standard English. We begin with a group of writers who have appointed themselves the guardians of Standard English. They have been called prescriptive grammarians, language mavens, and shamans, among other things, but I prefer the term *grammar gurus* because their pronouncements, like those of mystics like Kahlil Gibran, often sound reasonable at first hearing, but on closer examination disappear in a pretty burst of sound. The writers I have in mind include William Safire, John Simon, and Edwin Newman. Grammar gurus love to deplore nonstandard usage and language change (or, in the case of archaic forms like *a-verb-ing*, failure to change). Academic linguists, in turn, love to deplore errors of fact and logic in the pronouncements of the gurus, and I will indulge myself here.

In his article, "Why Good English is Good For You," John Simon (1983) wrote:

> If we lose the accusative case *whom*, . . . our language will be the poorer for it. Obviously, "The man, whom I had never known, was a thief" means something different than "The man who I had never known was a thief" (p. 83).

Wait a minute, John. Shouldn't that be "different *from?*" Well, let it pass. Yes, the two examples mean different things, but not because one contains *whom* and the other *who*. The difference in meaning would be preserved even if *who* were used in the first example, as it probably would be in speech. What's going on is that the relative pronoun *who(m)* has a different function in the two examples. In the first example, *whom* is the direct object of the verb *know*, and so can optionally take the objective form with *m*. But even if the less formal *who* is used, it is still the direct object of *know*. In the second example, *who* is the subject of the verb *was* and so cannot take the objective form. It is the difference in these functions of the two relative pronouns that accounts for the difference in the meaning, not the difference in the forms of the relative pronouns.[2] Our language may well be poorer if we lose the accusative *whom*, but not because it would cause the kind of confusion Simon fears.

Grammar gurus like to claim that nonstandard dialects are not logical, and refuting this claim is a regular feature of introductory linguistics books. Typical examples include:

Claim: Multiple negatives are not logical. When Anniston resident Melvin H. said, "None of them didn't hit the house," logically he has stated that the house *was* hit because the second negative cancels the first, producing a positive statement. He should have said, "None of them hit the house."

Reality: As mentioned in the discussion of Anniston English, many languages have rules of negative agreement so that in a negated sentence all adverbs and pronouns must take their negative forms.

Claim: You should say, "It is I" not "It is me" because (as we saw in the discussion of *who, whom*) the accusative form is used when a pronoun is the object of a verb. However, *is* is a copula verb (a form of the verb *to be*), which does not take an object but rather links a sentence subject and a predicate noun phrase. So the pronoun should be in the subjective case: *I*.

Reality: Many languages treat noun phrases following a copula verb as direct objects, so pronouns in that position take the accusative case. No one accused Louis XIV of bad grammar when he said, "L'état, c'est moi."

Claim: It is illogical to leave the verb *be* out of a sentence, as in Black English, "My father, he a doctor." Without *be*, the example is not a complete sentence and does not express a complete thought.

Reality: It is common for languages to allow parts of sentences to be deleted when the necessary information can be recovered in other ways.

---

[2] It is true that always using *whom* for objects and *who* for subjects would help the reader comprehend relative clauses more easily; and, in fact, reading Simon's second example the reader might momentarily be confused, thinking that *who* is the object of *known* and *the man* is the subject of *was*, as in the first example. But Simon has stacked the deck by providing an example that is only a sentence fragment. Expanding the fragment to a complete sentence produces, "The man who I had never known was a thief stole my lunch," where it is clear that *who* must be the subject of *was* because *the man* is the subject of *stole*.

For example, English commands usually don't have a subject. In "Leave me alone!" we all know that the unexpressed subject is "you"; in fact, that invisible pronoun is echoed in a polite version of the command: "Leave me alone, won't you!"

THE RISE OF STANDARD ENGLISH

How did Standard English get to be standard, and why isn't Anniston or Cockney English the standard? The traditional short answer is this: A standard language is a language with an Army. To understand the full story, we must look at the history of British English and American English.

Definitions of Standard English differ. The British sociolinguist Peter Trudgill (1984) says that Standard English is "typically used in speech and writing by highly educated... native speakers" (p. 32). Glyn Williams (1992), another Brit, insists that social class must figure in the definition, with the upper class (Williams uses the term "ruling class") choosing its own variety as the standard. Geographical region usually plays a role as well. We have seen that midwestern *r*-full speech has replaced East Coast *r*-less speech as the most prestigious pronunciation in the United States. It is widely recognized that Standard English is the variety written in books and newspapers, taught in grammar texts, and spoken on national news broadcasts (except for weather reporters like Willard Scott, who is free to use *y'all* and *might could* to his heart's content).

Standard English in England

In England, the elevation of a particular dialect to Standard English status, like so many developments in European history, is related to the rise of the middle class. In 1066, William the Conqueror installed himself, his French knights, and the French language in the English Court, and for the next 150 years, French was used for matters of state, and English for matters of everyday communication. This situation is called *diglossia*, and it is fairly common around the world. When I lived in Tigre Province, Ethiopia, for example, Amharic, the national language, was used in government offices and in the schools, but everywhere else people spoke Tigrinya. Diglossia also existed in Russia during the 19th century, where among the nobility, French was the "high" language and Russian was the "low" language. England remained diglossic until 1204 when King John lost his claim to Normandy, and France and England became enemies. The result of diminished French influence in London was to increase upward mobility for Englishmen, and people from all over the country migrated to London, bringing with them their regional dialects of Middle English. This babel of tongues in the capital city caused concern for some writers, whose worries foreshadowed those of modern-day gurus. John of Trevisa, writing in 1385, observed that a Standard English needed to be established so that everyone could understand each other. He suggested that his own southern dialect, the dominant dialect of London, would be an excellent choice because it was aesthetically more pleasing and less corrupted by foreign influence. In his own words:

> Al the longage of the Northumbres. . . ys so scharp, slyttyng and frotying, and unschapte, that we Southeron men may that longage unneth [hardly] undurstonde (quoted in Shaklee, 1980, p. 39).

John also hinted at an economic motivation for preferring southern speech:

> more in the south contray than in the north may be betre cornlond, more people, more noble cytes, and more profytable havenes (harbors; quoted in Shaklee, 1980, p. 39).

It is remarkable that John of Trevisa's modest proposal was not adopted. As it turned out, the midland dialect, spoken to the north of London, became the prestige variety partly as a result of the Black Plague, which in the 14th century killed 30% to 40% of the population of England, with much higher percentages in the cities. This devastation resulted in a shortage of laborers and craftsmen and opened the doors to immigrants from the surrounding provinces. Those who moved to London to fill critical jobs found themselves with considerable economic power and were able to rise in the social hierarchy. The result was "language change from below," where forms used by lower-class speakers become more acceptable, enter the vocabulary of upper-class speakers, and are finally accepted as correct. A more recent example of change from below is the acceptance of split infinitives, so that all but diehard prescriptivists accept "to boldly go where no man has gone before."

Change from below resulted in many midland dialect forms used by working-class speakers replacing the southern forms used by John of Trevisa; in fact, some of the features of Standard English most treasured by present-day traditionalists rose to prestige status at this time. One example is adding *-s* to present tense verbs to agree with third person singular subjects: *he speaks* not *he speak*, which was used by John of Trevisa although he usually wrote *he speketh*. A second example is the modern conjugation of the verb *be*. John sometimes used the modern *He is*, but preferred that scourge of modern gurus, *He be*.

A major force in the rise of a standard variety of English was the printing press, first brought to England by William Caxton in the late 15th century.

Caxton printed practically everything he could get his hands on, including John of Trevisa's writings, and he edited what he printed to conform to a uniform style and spelling. Caxton adopted the written style of the court clerks, called *Chancery standard*. Because many of these clerks were midlanders, many midland dialect features, such as third person *-s* and *is*, found their way into print.

The industrial revolution and the rise of the merchant class at the turn of the 18th century increased the prestige of the speech of the East Midland area—roughly a triangle that included Oxford to the north, Cambridge to the east, and London to the south—so that this variety became associated not just with a geographical area but with the influential commercial class. Williams (1961) observes:

> The class structure of England was now decisively changing, at the beginning of a period which can be summed up as the effort of the rising middle class to establish its own common speech (p. 220; quoted in Holborow, 1999, p. 159).

In her Marxist critique of the history of English, Holborow (1999) approves of this way of establishing a standard speech, namely change from below. However, she disapproves of another possible way of establishing a standard, change from above, and that is what happened in the latter half of the 18th century.

At that time, those who wished to rise in the social hierarchy paid attention to grammarians, who increasingly characterized alternate forms not as "regional" but as "incorrect." Dr. Johnson wrote books and articles about proper English, as well as his famous *Dictionary*, published in 1755. He defined a Standard English based on literary usage and the speech of the educated London middle class, of which he was a member. He wrote:

> I have labored to refine our language to grammatical purity and to clear it from colloquial barbarisms, licentious idioms and irregular combinations (quoted in Holborow, 1999, p. 162).

Standard English in the United States

In contrast to British prescriptivism, American attitudes toward language variation were liberal. Before 1850, many Americans regarded regional dialects as evidence of a healthy democracy. In the words of one observer:

> [I]n all states, there is but one language; yet come to vernacular dialects and hardly any rights will be more jealously guarded by a Virginian, a Pennsylvanian, or a Bostonian. In the polished inhabitant of New York and of South Carolina, we perceive a pride so admirably united with complacency that they

reciprocally forbear to infringe the idiomatical peculiarities of each other (Wilson, 1814, quoted in Heath, 1980, p. 13).

There were also, of course, those who argued for a national standard, among them Noah Webster, who urged that his dictionary and grammar books be adopted by all schools in order to promote a "federal English." He endorsed his own New England dialect as a good candidate for the standard, a recommendation that would mean pronouncing *deaf* as DEEF and *beard* as BIRD. Nevertheless, many Americans (Robert E. Lee is a good example) regarded themselves primarily as citizens of their states, and to them the prospect of a federal standard was abhorrent. Many grammarians, as well, were not convinced that much would be gained by standardization, and they feared that much could be lost. One of them wrote:

> There was a time, before grammars were invented to clip the wings of fancy, and shackle the feet of genius, when it was considered more important to express a thought clearly and forcibly than, as now, prettily and grammatically; when genius would as soon have stooped to accommodate itself to a rule of syntax as the eagle would to take lessons from the domestic goose; when grammarians were accustomed to *note* the movements of genious, not prescribe rules for them (Fowle, 1829, quoted in Heath, 1980, p. 21).

In the second half of the 19th century, several trends converged to change this liberal philosophy to one of strict prescriptivism. One trend was an increase in immigration, which usually raises fears of political and cultural disunity, as seen today in the movement to declare English the official language of the United States. Fowler (1887) expressed these fears as follows:

> As our countrymen . . . are brought into contact with other races, and adopt new modes of thought, there is some danger that, in the use of their liberty, they may break loose from the laws of the English language, and become marked not only by one, but by a thousand Shibboleths. Now, in order to keep the language of a nation one, the leading men in the greater of smaller communities, the editors of periodicals, and authors generally, should exercise the same guardian care over it which they do over the opinions which it is used to express (quoted in Heath 1980, pp. 28–29).

Furthermore, during a time of nationalism and expansion, uniformity of speech and writing became associated with patriotism. One grammarian wrote:

> The existence of local dialects [presents] very serious obstacles to national progress, to the growth of a comprehensive and enlightened patriotism, . . . and to the diffusion of general culture (quoted in Heath 1980, pp. 23–24).

Foreshadowing the moralistic tone of present-day gurus, 19th-century grammarians offered lists of rules for preserving the purity and logic of the standard language, including the following:

-Do not use. . . . *this here* for *this.*
-*Into* should be used after verbs denoting entrance.
-Do not use *like* . . . for *as* (an injunction repeated as late as the 1960s in reaction to the advertising slogan, "Winston tastes good, like a cigarette should"; from Harvey, 1878, quoted in Heath, 1980, p. 25).

To sum up the discussion so far, Standard American English, like other standards, is a variety that has been influenced by social and political forces, as well as by the preferences and prejudices of academics and grammar gurus. In fairness to the gurus, however, it should be said that Messieurs Newman, Safire, Simon, et al. do not merely rail against trivial matters like dropping the *m* from *whom.* They often fight the good fight against pomposity, faulty logic, deception, and euphemism. Dwight Bolinger (1980), who coined the term *language shaman,* puts it this way:

In the end, shamans and linguists share a desire: that people learn to be more interested in, and to care more about, their language (p. 180).

BLACK ENGLISH

We turn now to the variety of English that has been more in the public eye than any other. It has been referred to by many names over the years, including nonstandard Negro English, vernacular Black English, Black English, African American Vernacular English (or AAVE, the current favorite among linguists), and Ebonics. I will use the term *Black English,* although it is not the most politically correct nor the most accurate. It is inaccurate because it implies that all African Americans speak this dialect. But, as in Anniston, there exists a continuum of varieties within the Black community, with speakers like Colin Powell speaking Standard English. Nevertheless, *Black English* is the least awkward and the most widely used term; the reader should keep in mind that I use it to refer to a vernacular variety.

Description

It is remarkable how similar the vernacular speech of African Americans is in widespread American cities, from New York to Los Angeles. This similarity may be partly due to the relatively recent migration of African Americans from the south to these cities, and it is undoubtedly due to social segregation.

Black English shares many features with southern vernacular English; in fact, a description of Black English looks very much like a description of the English of working-class speakers in Anniston. Black English has all of the syntactic features of Anniston English mentioned earlier in this chapter except *a-verb-ing* although there are some differences in how the features are used, which I will mention briefly. Black English *done* very rarely occurs with the auxiliary verb *have* ("I done gone to bed" instead of "I've done gone to bed"). However, the meaning of *done* appears to be the same in White and Black varieties in Anniston, as shown by this statement from Feagin's (1979) African American informant Mattie Lou McC., 45:

We done turned it [the mattress]. (Louder) We already done turned it.

The rule of negative agreement is applied somewhat differently in the two varieties, as well. In Anniston English, negative agreement need not apply to all negatable forms within a clause:

But it didn't tear up no barns or anything (Billy H., 17).

In Black English, negative agreement is more consistently applied. In Feagin's data, as well as data collected by William Labov in Harlem, the application of the rule within a clause is near 100%. Also, in Black English, negative agreement can apply across clause boundaries, as in: We ain't never had no trouble that I can't remember (meaning in Standard English: that I *can* remember). Some scholars have claimed that negative agreement across clauses distinguishes Black English from southern vernaculars. However, Feagin found some examples of this structure in Anniston English:

No, I'm *not gon* stay home when I *ain't married* (meaning when I *am* married); me and . . . my husband can go on campin' trips (Dioane B., 15).

Feagin points to this as an example of how vernacular southern and Black English are more similar than some scholars have thought.

The degree of difference between Black English and southern vernacular English has been a continuing controversy. The two varieties are, in fact, not too different (Labov, 1972a). Many of the differences do not involve different forms, but differences in the frequency or contexts in which identical forms are used. For example, all dialects of English can delete a final consonant from a consonant cluster, so that *next* is pronounced "neks," and *called* is pronounced "call' ". However, the rate of this deletion is higher in Black English than in southern vernacular varieties (Wolfram & Fasold,

1974, p. 134). In addition, only Black English can delete a final consonant that is not in a cluster, so that *played* is pronounced "play' " and *ride* is pronounced "ri' ".

Of course, Black English also has some unique features. For example, Black English uses the term *mother wit* for Standard English *commonsense*. Several years ago, a scandal occurred at the University of Arizona when it was discovered that an African American administrator in the Office of Minority Affairs had used public funds to sponsor what was described in announcements aimed at the Black community as a "family reunion." More than a few indignant letters were printed in the campus newspaper before it was made clear that in Black English, a "family reunion" does not mean a gathering of one's own family but a public gathering to which all families are invited.

The best known syntactic feature unique to Black English is invariant *be*, so called because it is usually not conjugated (although occasionally forms like "It bees that way" are heard). For example, a Detroit teenager said,

My father, he work at Ford. He be tired. So he can't never help us with our homework.

He be tired means that the father is usually tired. If the speaker had wished to say that her father was tired now, she could have said, "He is tired," "He's tired," or "He tired." Invariant *be* can also be used with a present participle to indicate habitual action.

BLACK ENGLISH: They be playing basketball everyday.
STANDARD ENGLISH: They play basketball everyday.

The invariant *be* plus present participle form contrasts with:

BLACK ENGLISH: They playing basketball right now.
STANDARD ENGLISH: They're playing basketball right now.

In questions, invariant *be* can be combined with the auxiliary verb *do*:

BLACK ENGLISH: Do they be playing everyday?
STANDARD ENGLISH: Do they play everyday?

Lacking invariant *be*, Standard English uses the simple present tense to express both habitual and present action or state of affairs. Thus, Black English makes a distinction that Standard English cannot make by verb tense alone.

A final feature of Black English is the absence of *is*, as in these examples:

She fast in everything she do.

That a bear book.

He coming over to my home.

White southerners very rarely omit *is*. The Anniston rural working-class informants omitted it only 6.8% of the time compared to Labov's Harlem teenagers, who omitted it 42% of the time. Both White and Black dialects omit *are* much more often. The Anniston rural working-class speakers omitted *are* 56% of the time, and higher percentages are found among Black English speakers. In sum, there are only minor differences between Black English and the speech of working-class Whites in Anniston. Black English and Anniston English are also similar in a more important respect. Although speakers of both varieties comprise a coherent speech community, there is considerable variation within the community. Moreover, like Anniston English speakers, Black English speakers can, at least to some extent, style shift, using more standard or more vernacular forms as appropriate. We now consider the question of what place Black English and other nonstandard varieties should have in the schools. As usual, the presence of a racial element makes the question highly controversial.

Ebonics in the Schools

The controversy about Ebonics in the schools has two aspects. The first is the public policy aspect, which includes judicial decisions and school board resolutions along with reactions of the public. The second is the classroom aspect, which includes choosing textbooks, writing curricula and lesson plans, and researching the effectiveness of teaching methods that use vernacular language.

As mentioned at the beginning of the chapter, Black English made headlines in 1996 when the Oakland School Board issued a proclamation stating, among other things, that Ebonics (I will use the Board's term) was not a dialect of English but a separate language and that it should be used in the schools. Old linguistics hands could only sigh at the subsequent furor because we had seen it all before. So, before examining the 1990s Ebonics controversy, let us review the 1970s version, which started in Michigan.

In 1979, the parents of 11 African-American school children sued the Ann Arbor Board of Education claiming malpractice on the part of their children's school, Martin Luther King Jr. Elementary. The malpractice claim was based on the 1964 Civil Rights Act, which says:

> No state shall deny equal educational opportunity to an individual on account of his race, color, sex, or national origin by . . . failure . . . to take appropriate action to overcome language barriers that impede equal participation

by its students in its instructional programs (Public Law 88-352, Section 601, July 2, 1964).

The case centered around the fact that the children had been diagnosed by a speech therapist as "linguistically handicapped" and placed in special education classes on the basis of a test of Standard English. Judge Joiner ruled in favor of the plaintiffs. He noted, first, that the special education classes had delayed the students' academic development and, second, that the diagnostic test was inappropriate for these students, who were unfairly asked to perform using Standard English when the dialect they spoke was Black English.

The judge directed the Ann Arbor School District to take the language spoken by students into account in its academic program, in regard to both testing and teacher training. Specifically, the district had to develop tests that would identify students who truly had developmental problems and needed special education classes, and it had to provide training for teachers of Black English speakers to make them aware of the differences between Black English and Standard English. The judge did not mandate that teachers use Black English in the classroom or that it be taught to students, as was reported in the press.

The Oakland School Board Resolution

The Black English battle of the 1990s was fought with a lot more rancor and misinformation. The misinformation began with the Oakland School Board's resolution. In it, the Board proclaimed that Ebonics was not a dialect of English but a separate language, that it was the first language of the Black children in the district, and that the Oakland schools would immediately begin an academic program featuring Ebonics. The resolution was, in linguist Robin Lakoff's words, "a blooming, buzzing confusion." She noted that in much of it, "practically every word . . . is misleading or incorrect" (Lakoff, 2000, p. 230). Here is an excerpt from the resolution:

> WHEREAS, numerous validated scholarly studies demonstrate that African American students as part of their culture and history as African people possess and utilize a language described in various scholarly approaches as "Ebonics" (literally "Black sounds") or "Pan-African Communication Behavior" or "African Language Systems"; and
>
> WHEREAS, these studies have also demonstrated that African Language Systems are genetically based and not a dialect of English; and
>
> WHEREAS, these studies demonstrate that such West and Niger-Congo African languages have been officially recognized and addressed in the mainstream community as worth [sic] of study, understanding or application of its principles, laws, and structures for the benefit of African American students both in terms of positive appreciation of the language and these students' acquisition and mastery of English language skills; . . .

NOW THEREFORE, BE IT RESOLVED that the Board of Education officially recognizes the existence, and the cultural and historical bases of West and Niger-Congo African Language Systems, and each language as the predominant primary language of African American students; . . .

BE IT FURTHER RESOLVED that the Superintendent in conjunction with her staff shall immediately devise and implement the best possible academic program for imparting instruction to African American students in their primary language for the combined purposes of maintaining the legitimacy and richness of such language whether it is known as "Ebonics," "African Language Systems," "Pan-African Communication Behaviors," or other description, and to facilitate their acquisition and mastery of English language skills (Oakland School Board, 1996).

All of the misstatements here are too numerous to mention, but perhaps the two worst errors are these:

Statement: Ebonics is not a dialect of English.

Reality: We have discussed the relationship between Black English, Standard English, and southern vernacular varieties. Labov sums up his own opinion, and that of most linguists, as follows: "[W]e are plainly dealing with a dialect of English which is not . . . very different from other developments within the language" (Labov, 1978, p. 42).

Statement: Studies have demonstrated that Ebonics is genetically based.

Reality: This statement aroused more furor than any other because it appears to endorse a popular misconception, routinely refuted in introductory linguistics textbooks, that the ability to speak a particular language is genetically transmitted. Some people think that Swedes, for example, pass on a Swedish language gene to their children the way they might pass on a blond hair gene. This is wrong. A child born to Swedish parents but brought up in Hungary will learn Hungarian in exactly the same way as a child of Hungarian parents. As we saw in chapter 2, genetic information is critically involved in language acquisition in the form of universal grammar, but this information facilitates the learning of any language. Black English scholar John Baugh (1999) has noted that a related error in the Oakland School Board's resolution was the claim that all African-American students speak Black English. We have seen that not all African Americans use all the features of Black English all of the time. Furthermore, many Whites and Hispanics who have grown up in African-American neighborhoods use many Black English features. In the King School Children case, the judge ruled that the language variety spoken by individual Black students had to be identified using an appropriate linguistic test. The fact that the Oakland School Board equated skin color with language variety reinforces the impression that it believed that Black English is genetically programmed.

After the furor following the release of its resolution, the Board, with the help of a public relations firm, issued a revised version of the resolution and a number of clarifications. One clarification was that the phrase, "genetically based" did not mean based on genes, but rather was "used according to the standard dictionary definition of 'has origins in' " (Quan, 1996). In other words, Ebonics has its origins in Africa. It is quite true that some features of Black English originated there, as the discussion of creole languages in chapter 2 showed. But the linguist Charles Fillmore points out that "there is no easy way to substitute either 'genesis' of 'has its origins in' into the phrasing of the resolution and come up with something coherent . . ." (Fillmore, 1997).

Robin Lakoff (2000), who watched the controversy from the nearby University of California at Berkeley, critiqued the resolution in precisely the right terms:

> When you make a statement that you suspect may have controversial aspects; when you make this statement publicly; . . . when you represent education—it is incumbent on you to be clear and precise. You cannot claim to be "misunderstood" (as the Board was quick to do) when your explicit written statement is laden with obfuscations, baroque pomposities, and idiosyncratic usages (p. 232).

It happened that the Ebonics controversy reached its height while the Linguistics Society of America (LSA) was holding its annual convention across San Francisco Bay at Stanford University. It seemed appropriate for the LSA to issue a statement on the matter as it fell directly within the area of its professional expertise. However, the members of the LSA faced a dilemma. Professional ethics required them to bring their expertise to bear on the matter and correct the many errors in the Oakland School Board's resolution. However, if they wrote a statement along the lines of Lakoff's critique, it would appear to undercut a beleaguered school district and support the district's right-wing critics. Torn between professional responsibility and political correctness, the LSA came down four-square on the side of political correctness. The Society's statement reads as follows:

> Whereas there has been a great deal of discussion in the media and among the American public about the 18 December 1996 decision of the Oakland School Board to recognize the language variety spoken by many African American students and to take it into account in teaching Standard English, the Linguistics Society of America, as a society of scholars engaged in the scientific study of language, hereby resolves to make it known that:
>   a. The variety knows as "Ebonics," "African American Vernacular English" (AAVE), and "Vernacular Black English" and by other names is systematic and rule-governed like all natural speech varieties. In fact, all human linguistic systems—spoken, signed, and written—are fundamentally regular.

b. The distinction between "languages" and "dialects" is usually made more on social and political grounds than on purely linguistic ones. For example, different varieties of Chinese are popularly regarded as "dialects," though their speakers cannot understand each other. But speakers of Swedish and Norwegian, which are regarded as separate "languages," generally understand each other. What is important from a linguistic and educational point of view is not whether AAVE is called a "language" or a "dialect" but rather that its systematicity be recognized.

c. As affirmed in the LSA Statement of Language Rights (June 1996), there are individual and group benefits to maintaining vernacular speech varieties and there are scientific and human advantages to linguistic diversity. For those living in the United States there are also benefits in acquiring Standard English and resources should be made available to all who aspire to mastery of Standard English. The Oakland School Board's commitment to helping students master Standard English is commendable.

d. There is evidence from Sweden, the United States, and other countries that speakers of other varieties can be aided in their learning of the standard variety by pedagogical approaches which recognize the legitimacy of the other varieties of a language. From this perspective, the Oakland School Board's decision to recognize the vernacular of African American students in teaching them Standard English is linguistically and pedagogically sound (Linguistics Society of America, 1997).

Points a, c, and d are well-taken, and help to clarify some of the misunderstanding that arose on all sides during the controversy. Point b, however, seems designed to justify the Board's erroneous claim that Ebonics is not a dialect of English. It is true that the distinction between language and dialect is often made on political grounds, as with the Chinese government's claim that many mutually unintelligible languages in China are dialects of Chinese. But it is precisely the linguist's duty to point out that this claim is political and not scientific. It is also true that there is no clear-cut scientific way to distinguish between a language and a dialect; there is a fuzzy boundary between the two concepts. But we deal with fuzzy concepts all the time. For example, readers may have noticed that sport utility vehicles (SUVs) seem to be morphing into trucks, and vice versa. When does an SUV become a truck? When you replace the back seat with a truck bed? When you take away 4-wheel drive? We can't turn to the Department of Transportation for technical advice because they classify even minivans as trucks so that the manufacturers can escape tough emissions standards. But the fact that it can sometimes be hard to classify a particular vehicle doesn't mean that people go around mistaking Explorers for pickups. They are clear examples of their respective categories, and Black English is a clear example of a dialect. Thus, in regard to the question of the difference between a language and a dialect, the LSA resolution muddies the waters.

The main problem with the resolution, however, is its silence on the many errors and confusions in the Oakland School Board's statement. For this, the LSA deserves to be reprimanded, and I wish that Lakoff had done that because she does it so well. Instead, let me offer my own critique of the LSA's statement along the lines of Lakoff's comments on the Oakland School Board's resolution.

When you make a statement in regard to a controversial question; when you make this statement publicly, and when you are a professional academic society, then it is incumbent on you to be scientifically accurate and to address all important questions and misunderstandings relevant to the controversy without regard to the political positions of the parties involved.

We now move on to consider some of the important work that has been done on how best to teach reading to speakers of Black English.

Classroom Aspects of the Ebonics Controversy

In the 1960s, educators noted that a disproportionate number of Black children were not reading at grade level. Teachers and researchers realized that many factors contributed to this problem, but some wondered whether one factor was the difference between the children's language and the language of the reading textbooks. An obvious problem was in the teaching of phonics. As discussed in chapter 3, many phonics lessons teach children the various vowel sounds by drilling the difference in *word families*, groups of words that differ by a single sound. Thus, the difference between the vowels in *bet* and *bit* might be taught by having the child read the following groups of words:

pet   pit
letter   litter
set   sit
tent   tint
pen   pin

In this lesson, confusion could arise because Black English, like southern dialects, does not distinguish these vowels when they occur before nasal sounds, as in the last two examples. Thus, *tent* and *tint*, *pen* and *pin* are homonyms in these dialects. The same problem would occur in teaching the vowels in *caught* and *cot* to many westerners. There are a number of other phonetic differences between Black English and Standard English, as well, which would interfere with teaching phonics from a Standard English textbook.

There might also be problems related to syntax and morphology, involving Standard English forms that the child may not have mastered, such as *any*, third person -*s*, irregular past tense, and past participles. Furthermore, many Black English patterns do not appear in the Standard English textbooks, such as completive *done*, invariant *be*, and multiple negation. On the basis of these considerations, a number of linguists in the 1960s and 1970s proposed that reading materials written in Black English should be used in the schools.

Several dialect readers were written, the most ambitious of which was the *Bridge* reading program, published in 1977 (Rickford & Rickford, 1995). These materials included passages in three forms: nonstandard, standard, and an intermediate variety, with standard spelling used throughout. Teachers were encouraged to let students pronounce the Standard English passages in their own way, without correcting nonstandard pronunciation (similarly, Miss Dolan, my fourth-grade teacher in Cambridge, Massachusetts, did not require her students to quit saying "Cuber" for Cuba or "Africar" for Africa and neither, obviously, did Senator Kennedy's teacher). The *Bridge* materials also included exercises and an audiotape featuring spoken Black English. Here is an excerpt from a vernacular passage.

DREAMY MAE

This here little Sister name Mae was most definitely untogether. I mean, like she didn't act together. She didn't look together. She was just an untogether Sister. Her teacher was always sounding on her 'bout day dreaming in class. I mean, like, just 'bout every day the teacher would be getting on her case. But it didn't seem to bother her none. She just kept on keeping on. Like, I guess daydreaming was her groove. And you know what they say: "don't knock your Sister's groove." But a whole lotta people did knock it. But like I say, she just kept on keeping on (Rickford & Rickford, 1995, p. 127).

The *Bridge* program was field tested with 417 seventh- and twelfth-grade students in several cities. These students showed significantly larger gains on the Iowa Test of Reading Comprehension than 123 control group students, who were taught with "regularly scheduled remedial reading instructional activities." Despite evidence of their effectiveness, the Black English readers met with resistance from many parents and teachers. Comments like those of Jesse Jackson quoted at the beginning of this chapter were typical. As a result, the dialect readers were quietly dropped.

Opinions about the value and appropriate place of Black English in the schools have recently changed within the Black community, as the Oakland School Board resolution illustrates, and dialect readers, including the *Bridge* series, have come back—this time to a more positive, though still mixed, reception.

The Stanford linguists John and Angela Rickford (1995) have conducted research on the use of the *Bridge* readers in East Palo Alto, California. One goal of their small-scale study was to gauge the attitudes of students and teachers, White and Black, toward dialect readers versus Standard English readers. The attitudes were mixed. Teachers of both races rated the Standard English readers as better written and more helpful to students. One Black teacher remarked:

> Every Black kid knows that there is language for the playground, and then there is language for the classroom, and if you want anyone to take you seriously, you'd better not mix the two. . . . I just don't think it's the right approach for teaching Black kids English (Rickford & Rickford, 1995, p. 118).

The students, on the other hand, preferred the vernacular materials and there was a sharp distinction between boys and girls, with boys much preferring the Black English materials.

In one of the studies, the African-American students were asked (1) whether they preferred the vernacular or Standard English version of a story, and (2) which version was most like the way they talked. To both questions all of the boys answered "vernacular" and all of the girls answered "standard." This split reflects the sex stratification that was mentioned in the discussion of Anniston English. In general, women and girls seem to be more sensitive to the social significance of linguistic forms than men and boys, and are better able to shift toward the more prestigious forms (Labov, 1972c). As a result, males, particularly teenage males, often speak the purest form of the vernacular.

A number of studies besides the Rickfords' have been made to assess the effectiveness of using dialect readers and other vernacular language materials in the classroom, and their results have been mixed. Leaverton (1973) found that students' reading performance rose when they used both Standard English and Black English texts. Simpkin and Simpkin (1991) found that students learned to read faster when taught with dialect readers. Tayler (1989) found that college students in Chicago improved their skills in writing Standard English when they were taught to translate Black English into Standard English. However, other studies have found that using dialect materials makes no difference. In a second small study made by Rickford and Rickford (1995), the students performed better using Standard English materials (thus, the Rickfords' research as a whole does not support either position). Nolan (1972) found that there was no difference in Standard English test scores between a group of children taught using dialect readers and a group using Standard English readers. In our discussion of bilingual education research in chapter 7, we will also encounter contradictory research findings, and conclude that educators cannot expect to find a single model of instruction that is best in all circumstances. Rather, they need to look at studies that have been done in schools with students and resources similar to their own in order to get ideas about what is likely to work best in their situation.

In the discussion of reading in chapter 3, we noted that traditional primers, such as the McGuffy Readers, included material of genuine literary merit, and currently there is pressure from both conservative educators and parents to include quality literature in a reading instruction program both for its aesthetic and didactic value. The *Bridge* series appears to be a good way to teach basic literacy, but its specially written passages are not, of course, real literature. A program that includes literature, and that could be used along side introductory materials like the *Bridge* program, was also tried out in East Palo Alto by Angela Rickford (1999).

Rickford was educated in the Caribbean, where she read local authors such as V. S. Naipaul. Remembering the excitement and sense of participation she felt reading about her own culture, she decided to create a reading program that would feature traditional Black folk tales, such as the Brer Rabbit stories, and contemporary African-American short stories. The language used in these stories varied from formal, Standard English to Black English. Rickford (1999) notes, "The vernacular is maintained as an important cultural marker, but idiosyncratic [forms] are avoided" (p. 241). Julius Lester, who wrote the version of the Brer Rabbit story that Rickford used, described the language as a modified contemporary southern Black English, a combination of Standard English and Black English, as in this example.

> Yes, Brer Rabbit had fallen in love, and it was with one of Miz Meadows' girls. Don't nobody know why, 'cause he'd been knowing the girl longer than us folks have known hard times, but that's the way love is. One day you fine and the next day you in love (Rickford, 1999, p. 242).

Perhaps the use of such dialect literature would satisfy both the Oakland School Board, who wish to acknowledge Black students' language and culture, and traditionalists, who wish, like Rickford, to expose students to the beauty and excitement of good literature.

CONCLUSIONS

Discussing the proper place of nonstandard dialects in the classroom is probably the most cautious and uncertain conversation that takes place in a linguistics course for teachers. Most teachers and linguistics professors are ecumenical in regard to language. Like the 18th-century American grammarians, they value diversity of expression, as well as the diversity of their students' linguistic and cultural backgrounds.

The problem with using vernacular language in the public arena is not a problem with the language; it is a problem with the public. But teachers cannot (quickly at least) change social prejudice, whereas they can change their students' chances for public success by teaching them to read and write Standard English. Usually the most popular position among a group of teachers is that students should be bidialectal. In regard to reading, both standard and vernacular materials should be used, as in the *Bridge* program. Students should be allowed to pronounce the standard materials according to their own phonological systems. In regard to writing, students should be encouraged to use the vernacular in appropriate contexts, such as writing a personal journal, a letter to a friend, or dialogue for a short story. Of course, there should be assignments that elicit Standard English, as well. An especially useful exercise is asking the students to recast a piece of writing for a different audience, requiring that Standard English be rewritten in vernacular, and vice versa.

If bidialectal competence is the goal, the Oakland School Board's resolution makes perfect sense (if, like the LSA, we ignore the errors and focus on what the Board really meant). The resolution stated, first, that all Ebonics speakers should be taught Standard English, and that Ebonics should be used as a resource to this end, much as a student's first language should be used as a resource in teaching a second language. The resolution also stated that Ebonics should be included for the purpose of "maintaining [its] legitimacy and richness. . . ." I strongly endorse this notion. Black English, and all vernacular varieties, should be studied and cultivated in the schools where they are spoken. In the section on Anniston English, we saw some fine examples of vernacular language, both in the novel *McBee's Station* and in Flora's tornado story. This literature, written and oral, is an important part of the culture and history of Alabama and the south, and it should have a valued place in the school curricula in those places. Exactly the same is true for literature in Black English, as Angela Rickford's (1999) reading program demonstrates. But traditional literature is only one resource available to teachers. African-American communities have a rich store of oral literature in the form of tales, sayings, proverbs, jokes, and toasts. African-American students should be encouraged to record, write down, discuss, and disseminate this folk literature. In doing so, they would not only be creating their own dialect readers, but making available to the larger American speech community a rich literary resource that is accessible to us all.

SUGGESTED READING

Good introductions to sociolinguistics and language variation include Romaine (1994) and Wardhaugh (1992). Williams (1992) provides a Marxist perspective. Two books by Labov defined the field of the quantitative study of language: *Sociolinguistic Patterns* (1972c) covers New York City English, among other topics, and *Language in the Inner City* (1972b) focuses on Black English. Feagin's (1979) book on Anniston English is *Variation and Change in Alabama English: A Sociolinguistic Description of the White Community*.

The definitive book on grammar gurus is Bolinger (1980). Lakoff's *The Language War* (2000) discusses this topic as well as her take on the Oakland School Board's proclamation and the LSA's statement on the resolution. Discussions of the history of English and the rise of Standard English include the very readable McCrum et al. (1986) and Trudgill (1984). Holborow (1999) provides a Marxist interpretation. A more technical discussion can be found in Labov (1994). My discussion of the rise of prescriptivism in the United States closely follows that in Heath (1980).

A good article-length introduction to Black English is Smitherman (1985). Black English and other nonstandard dialects are discussed in Wolfram and Fasold (1974). Baugh (1999) discusses the structure, politics, and legal entanglements of Black English. The 1960s controversy over Black English readers is discussed in Baratz and Shuy (1969) and Laffey and Shuy (1973) and is updated in Rickford and Rickford (1995). Rickford's use of dialect literature is discussed in her book *I Can Fly* (1999). McWhorter (1998) provides an authoritative overview of the entire field and is also fun to read. He is one of the few linguists to disapprove of the use of Black English in the schools, presenting a position similar to that of Richard Rodriguez in regard to bilingual education, which we will review in chapter 7.

5

Learning in a Second Language

INTRODUCTION

In chapter 1, I described my experience tutoring George, a student from Colombia who was attending high school in a Washington, D.C. suburb, which I call Fairview County. Fairview is one of the richest counties in the country, and its citizens, who include a lot of government workers, are very civic minded. They insist on (are willing to pay for) excellent schools, parks, and libraries, and they get them. My children started school there, and my only complaint was that they had to study too hard. Fairview attracts a large number of immigrants. The largest groups are Koreans, Vietnamese, and Hispanics, but the public schools enroll children from over 100 countries. When I lived in Fairview, the main way of integrating immigrant children into the schools was through English as a second language (ESL). Children who spoke little or no English were placed in ESL classes for 3 hours a day and nonlanguage intensive classes, such as music and physical education, for the rest of the day. When they were ready, the students took 2 hours of ESL and one or more mainstream classes, such as math or science, and later one ESL class with more mainstream classes. For advanced-level students, there were some sheltered classes (see chap. 3) in literature, history, and science (George was taking all mainstream classes except for one ESL class and the sheltered literature class in which I helped him).

While I was tutoring George, my colleagues Virginia Collier and Wayne Thomas were carrying on some of the most important research in the

132

field of second language (L2) education (Collier, 1989; Collier & Thomas, 1989). Fairview administered the California Achievement Test in Grades 4, 8, and 11, and Collier and Thomas looked at how students learning English did on these tests compared to native English-speaking students. They found that the native speakers did very well. The average score for both 8th and 11th graders on the reading section of the test was 68 (the national average is 50). It is expected that the scores will not change much between the 8th and 11th grades because if the students are 18 points above the national average in Grade 8, they should maintain that advantage throughout high school. The 8th-grade English language learner (ELL) students also did well on the reading section of the test, with an average score of 45—well below their native speaker classmates, but pretty darn good for students who had been in the United States for an average of less than 2 years. But on the 11th-grade test, something unexpected happened. The ELL students did not close the gap with the native speakers, but fell further behind. Their average score on the reading section was 35. In fact, the 11th-grade ELL students' scores were lower than the 8th-grade ELL students' scores on all sections of the test except mathematics.

Collier and Thomas believed that one problem was that the 8th-grade test and the 11th-grade test were different kinds of tests. The 8th-grade test was more of a competency test than an achievement test; that is, the test did not assume a lot of background knowledge on the part of the students. On the social studies section, for example, the answers to the questions could be found in the reading passages of the test itself. However, on the 11th-grade test, students needed a lot of background knowledge about social studies to answer the questions correctly. An even bigger problem for the ELLs was that although they had learned a great deal in 3 years, the native speakers had learned even more. The troubling fact is that in the upper grades, English language learners often fall further and further behind mainstream students. For this reason, it is important to understand how both groups learn academic material, and in this chapter we will review some research relevant to this question.

MODELS OF LEARNING

We saw in chapter 2 that theories of language learning can be divided into cognitive and social/cultural varieties, and the same is true of theories of academic learning. Before examining studies of learning from these two perspectives, we will take a look at the philosophical underpinnings of learning theories.

Philosophical Background

Two of the oldest questions in philosophy are the ontological question and the epistemological question. The ontological question asks, "What is the nature of reality?" and the epistemological question asks, "How do we know what we know?" Modern philosophy has two different answers to these questions, and they provide the underpinnings for two different views of how best to learn academic subjects. The two rival theories of knowledge are *objectivism* (or *positivism*) and *social constructionism.* Objectivism is the philosophy endorsed by many scientists, and it is compatible with the grammar–translation method, phonics, and traditional mathematics teaching. Social constructionism is endorsed by many humanists and, as you might guess, is compatible with communicative language teaching, the whole language approach, and reform mathematics.

Objectivism has been the dominant philosophy in the West since Aristotle. One reason for its popularity is that objectivism provides a common-sense answer to the ontological question and the epistemological question. The objectivist's answer to the ontological question is that the natural world consists of objects, which have certain properties, such as weight and density, and which exist in certain relationships to each other; for example, *the rock is in the river,* or *the bird is flying over the tree.* The objectivist's answer to the epistemological question is that the mind constructs an accurate model of reality, which reflects the objects, properties, and relationships that exist independently in the world. However, according to objectivism, it is important not to confuse external reality with mental models of reality. Therefore, objectivism endorses the *independence assumption* (Lakoff, 1987, p. 164), which says that no true fact can depend on people's believing it, on their conceptualization of it, or on any other aspect of human cognition. Thus, objectivism posits a "God's Eye" view of the universe, independent of human perception, in which all objects, properties, and relationships are correctly characterized. If you ask an objectivist, "If a tree falls in the forest and no one hears it, does it make a sound?" the answer will be "yes."[1]

Objectivists claim that there are two kinds of facts. *Brute facts* involve the external world and form the grounding of scientific theories, which therefore can be objectively evaluated. Theories that correspond to and predict the actual brute facts of nature are true; other theories are false. *Institu-*

---

[1]Social constructionists might reply with this limerick:

There once was a man who said, "God
Must find it exceedingly odd,
When he sees that this tree
Simply ceases to be,
When there's no one about in the quad."

tional facts, on the other hand, depend on human understanding. They include laws, customs and agreed on states of affairs like the fact that Phoenix is the capital of Arizona and that George W. Bush was elected President of the United States (or was he? You can begin to see that there may be a problem here).

Objectivist epistemology is compatible with *schema theory* in psychology (Osherson & Smith, 1982; Smith & Medin, 1981), which claims that the mind constructs internal models of brute and institutional facts called *schemas*. A schema is an abstraction that leaves out the details of a particular instance. For example, the schema for *bird* contains the information that birds lay eggs and have feathers, but it does not specify details like the color of the feathers. The central assumption of objectivist psychology is that schemas accurately represent the brute facts in the world—that the mind is a mirror of nature.

Social constructionists (Geertz, 1983; Kuhn, 1973, 1977; Rorty, 1979, 1989) have several objections to the objectivist story. One concerns the absolute dichotomy between brute facts and institutional facts, which social constructionists claim are not that different. Obviously, institutional facts depend entirely on human understanding and do not correspond to any physical objects. Social constructionists emphasize that the sum total of a society's institutional facts makes up a social reality that can differ drastically from one culture to another. Furthermore, this reality is in constant flux as participants in social events act and interact, thereby "constructing" a new reality. For example, in Eastern Europe, institutional facts involving national boundaries and political alliances have recently changed.

Social constructionists emphasize that different institutional facts in different societies are equally valid. It doesn't make sense to argue about whether a custom like that of the dowry is "true." Different customs are appropriate in different societies. In regard to brute facts, social constructionists and objectivists agree that knowledge of these facts consists of mental schemas constructed from perceptions of the world. However, social constructionists say that these schemas do not mirror external reality. They point out that schemas for *bird, chair,* and so on do not exist in isolation, but are part of a complete model of the world, which is largely represented in language. Our knowledge of what a chair is depends in part on our knowledge of what it is not: how it contrasts with a couch, stool, pouf, et cetera. Social constructionists claim that the dividing lines between individual schemas, such as those for pieces of furniture, do not coincide with naturally occurring joints in nature. Rather, these dividing lines are supplied by the lexicon of a language, and different languages supply different dividing lines. For example, languages divide the color spectrum into as few as 2 and as many as 11 basic colors. Because our knowledge of brute facts depends to some extent on language and other social institutions, the independence principle cannot stand. No form of knowledge is grounded solely in reality. There is no "God's Eye" view of nature. Language and mind do not reflect, but rather create, human reality. Social constructionism proposes a relativistic theory of knowledge, including scientific knowledge, in which truth can only be judged in relation to a particular culture at a particular time.

Actually, not all social constructionists hold this strong relativistic position. For example, philosopher of science Thomas Kuhn places a high value on universal sensory experience in evaluating scientific theories. Kuhn asks "[Is] sensory experience fixed and neutral? The [objectivist] viewpoint . . . dictates an immediate and unequivocal Yes! In the absence of a developed alternative, I find it impossible to relinquish entirely that viewpoint" (1973, p. 126).

Teaching implications. The objectivist and the social constructionist views of knowledge suggest two very different ways of thinking about teaching. The objectivist believes that knowledge about brute facts, and by extension "proven" scientific theories, is authoritative: Certain claims are true and others are false. The ultimate authority is nature, but next in authority is the researcher who understands nature; thus, there is no point in discussing or debating scientific facts. The classroom analog of this view is instructional teaching, where an authoritative teacher stands at the front of the room and supplies facts to the students.

The social constructionist, on the other hand, believes that all knowledge, including scientific knowledge, is collaboratively constructed. Authority resides in a society of experts who agree that certain assumptions and explanations are fruitful. Members of this society interact in conversations, by writing books and articles, and by sending letters and e-mail messages. The process of expounding, criticizing, and revising ideas within a scholarly community is called the *hermeneutic circle*. In science, the hermeneutic circle includes reports of experiments, but experimental results are suggestive rather than conclusive. As Kuhn (1973) points out, no scientific theory is without exceptions and problems, and scholars must interpret experimental data and assess how new data affect a dominant theory. Sometimes when experimental results call a theory into question, scholars consider the results to be a special case or a convenient fiction that does not change the basic theory. For example, for at least 50 years after Copernicus proposed the heliocentric universe, astronomers accepted the utility of his model for calculating the location of the planets, but they did not believe that the model was literally true. Furthermore, sometimes experiments cannot decide between competing theories, and the scientist must hold several theories in mind, using whichever theory seems most helpful for dealing with a particular phenomenon. As Richard Feynman (1998) observed,

> Every theoretical physicist who is any good knows six or seven different theoretical representations for exactly the same physics. He knows that . . . nobody is ever going to be able to decide which one is right at that level, but he keeps them in his head, hoping that they will give him different ideas for guessing (p. 168).

The classroom analog of the social constructionists' model of knowledge is a circle of scholars constructing the network of schemas for a particular area of knowledge. Such construction can be observed at professional conferences, where someone will read a paper presenting new data, and members of the audience will ask questions or make comments that assess how the new data fit with previously known data, and whether the new data support the dominant theory. The job of the teacher, according to English professor Kenneth Bruffee (1984, 1986), is to engage students in the ongoing conversation of an academic discipline, that is, to introduce them into the hermeneutic circle. He states:

> Our task must involve engaging students in conversation among themselves at as many points in both the writing and reading process as possible, and that we should continue to ensure that students' conversations about what they read and write are similar in as many ways as possible to the way we would like them eventually to read and write (1984, p. 642).

The similarity of Bruffee's ideas to those of Dewey discussed in chapter 3 is obvious.

When I introduce students to social constructionism and the relativity of knowledge, they often don't like it, especially students in the sciences. If all knowledge is relative and there is no such thing as truth, they ask, how have we learned to make airplanes fly, and why aren't doctors still using leeches? I reply that social constructionism doesn't deny that some knowledge systems are better than others, just that none of them can ever be true in an absolute sense. Scientific theories and models are just more or less useful ways of thinking about the world. But my students make an excellent point when they observe that social constructionism has no explanation for why some knowledge systems are better than others for dealing with nature. There is no explanation of our sense that science is progressing, and surely an explanation for this progress should be of considerable interest to philosophy. One school of philosophy that has addressed this question (and that just happens to be closely associated with language study) is *experiential realism.*

Experiential realism. Experiential realism endorses the social constructionist claim that mental models of institutional facts are entirely socially constructed, but it rejects the claim of some social constructionists that mental models of physical reality can differ radically in different societies. Rather, it holds that such models are constructed and constrained by an interaction between the human perceptual and cognitive apparatus and the physical world. Experiential realists say that human beings have a concept-making capacity (analogous in some ways to Slobin's Language Making Capacity, discussed in chap. 2) that allows us to learn about reality directly (in social constructionists' terms to "construct" reality directly) as well as by means of language. Because this cognitive apparatus is universal in the species and because basic experience with physical objects is similar in all societies, "directly known" knowledge is similar as well. Such knowledge provides a grounding for schemas of brute facts, which explains why, in all societies, people do not try to walk through walls or expect water to run uphill. Thus, experiential realists claim that schemas of brute facts are grounded not in reality but in the human concept-making capacity, and thus are universal. Schemas for institutional facts, of course, are relative to the societies and languages that have produced them.

A Cognitive Study of Learning

Cognitive psychologists are on the objectivist side of the objectivist–social constructionist continuum because they emphasize the cognitive, rather than the social, aspects of learning. An example is a study by Perfetti, Britt, and Georgi (1995), who looked at text-based learning of American history by six college students. Though none of these students were ELLs, there were considerable differences in their background knowledge and academic skills (though not their intelligence), differences that often distinguish ELL students from mainstream students. The subject matter of the study was the history of the building of the Panama Canal from the California Gold Rush in 1846 until the signing of the Treaty that awarded the Canal Zone to the United States in 1903. The students read four texts about the Canal, one each week. Each text covered basically the same material, but each subsequent text added more information or told the Canal story from a different point of view. Each week after the students had read a text at home, the researchers asked them questions about the material. The students also wrote summaries of the texts. By examining the students' oral answers and summaries, the researchers were able to measure what they had learned and how their understanding of the historical episode increased.

Perfetti et al. (1995) assumed that to understand the Canal story, students needed to construct a mental schema that represented the main facts of the story and their relationships to each other. To measure how the students learned these facts and relationships, the researchers constructed a *causal model*, similar to the one shown in Figure 5.1. The causal model represents not only events and states relevant to the Canal Story, numbered

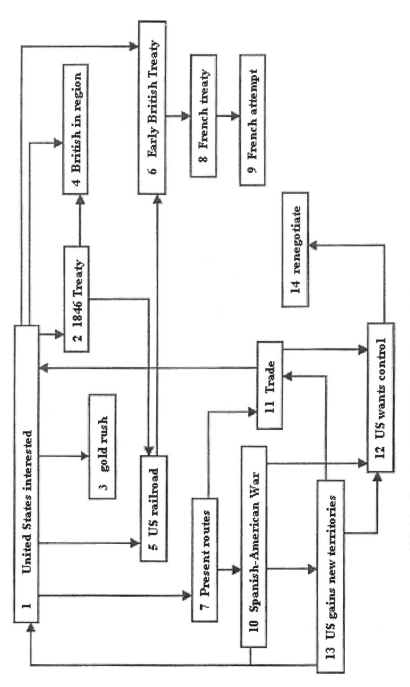

FIG. 5.1. Causal model of the history of the acquisition of a U.S. canal in Panama.

chronologically, but also the causal connections between them, which are represented by arrows. Thus, event 10 (The Spanish American War) caused event 13 (United States gains new territories), which, in turn, caused an increase in state of affairs 11 (Trade [between the United States and the new Pacific territories]), which caused an increase in state of affairs 1 (United States interested [in building a canal]). Causal models like Figure 5.1 are also used to model human knowledge in a computer, which suggests a basic assumption of the cognitive approach to learning: Human beings and computers store and process information in similar ways (Kintsch, 1988).

The least successful learner among Perfetti et al.'s subjects was the freshman Robbie, who had the least amount of initial knowledge about the Canal and about world events in general. (He was the only one of the six students who had not heard about the revolt in Tiananmen Square.) Perfetti et al. (1995) characterize Robbie's learning as "gradual and difficult" (p. 100). He failed to master all the events of the story, learned new facts slowly, and was confused about key relations in the story and about the vocabulary of historical research in general. For example, Robbie understood "revolution" to mean "war," and this misconception interfered with his ability to understand that Panama fought Colombia in order to gain its independence. Although Robbie had high reasoning ability, his reasoning about the Canal Treaty was hampered by his lack of background knowledge, and, unlike the other students, he did not change his opinions regarding the motivations for and fairness of the treaty as the course progressed. In chapter 6, we will see how lack of background knowledge is similarly vital to ELL students' learning and critical thinking.

Perfetti et al.'s (1995) research is compatible with objectivist philosophy because it assumes that the facts represented in Figure 5.1 (though social facts) are indisputable and are to be internalized, not "constructed," by students. It also assumes that neither the circumstances of learning nor individual or cultural differences in the learners are important. Thus, it does not seem to matter whether Perfetti et al.'s students gained the information through readings, discussions, or lectures. Nor does it matter what academic and cultural backgrounds the students came from. The cognitive perspective assumes that human minds, like human spleens, work in the same way, so learning need not be affected by the social situation in which it takes place.

A Social/Cultural Study of Learning

Studies of classroom learning conducted within the social constructionist framework have a very different flavor. Like Heath's (1983) research reviewed in chapter 2, they often focus on the learning of discourse conventions within different social groups and how these conventions affect learning in an academic setting. For example, Gee (1996) studied how a story was understood by African-American and European-American high school students. Here is the story:

The Alligator River Story

Once upon a time there was a woman named Abigail who loved a man named Gregory. Gregory lived on the shore of a river teeming with man-eating alligators, and Abigail lived on the opposite shore. Abigail wanted to cross the river to be with Gregory. Unfortunately, the bridge had been washed out. So she asked Sinbad, a river boat captain, to take her across. He said he would be glad to if she would consent to go to bed with him preceding the voyage. . . . Abigail felt her only alternative was to accept Sinbad's offer. Sinbad fulfilled his promise and delivered Abigail into the arms of Gregory.

When [Abigail] told Gregory about her escapade, Gregory cast her aside with destain. Heartsick, Abigail turned to Slug with her tale of woe. Slug, feeling compassion for Abigail, sought out Gregory and beat him brutally. Abigail was overjoyed at the sight of Gregory getting his due (pp. 168–169).

After the students had read and discussed the story, Gee asked them to rank the characters from "most offensive" to "least objectionable." Then each group appointed a representative, who summarized the discussion. Let's look at the two summaries.

The African-American student's summary

All right. As a group we decided Sinbad was the worst because he should have never in the first place asked her to go to bed with him just to get her across the water to see her loved one. Then we had Gregory because when she arrived over there he just totally disowned her you know like I don't want you after what you did which is wrong. We got Slug for third. True, Abigail told him to beat him up, but he didn't have to. He could have said no and he just, you know, brutally beat him up. Abigail is . . . fourth because she never should have told Slug to beat him up and then laughed, you know. . . (p. 169).

The European-American's response

OK, our findings were that um the most offensive spot was Sinbad mainly because for no other reason he just wanted to sleep with Abby—you know—for his own benefit—you know—kind of cheap. OK. Coming in second was Gregory mainly because he didn't really listen to a reason from her and he kinda. . . kinda. . . tossed her aside, you know, without thinking—you know— he might have done the same if he was put in the same position—you know— for love was why he did it. Then we put Abigail in the third spot only because we took a vote (laughter). No, because we figured she didn't really do anything. She didn't—I mean—she didn't tell Slug to beat up Sinbad. She didn't tell Slug to beat up Gregory, so she really didn't have any bearing. She was just dejected, so now Slug we figured was the fourth because his only reason for beating up Gregory was through compassion, so he wasn't really that offensive. . . . And that's our ranking (pp. 170–171).

Gee makes several observations about the differences in the two reports. The first has to do with style (note that Perfetti et al., 1995, never mention the style of their subjects' reports; they are interested only in the facts). In the second sentence, the African-American student uses the pronoun *her* for Abigail without explicitly introducing this character. This is logical as there is only one woman in the story, and the audience knows who she is. In fact, this student uses pronouns without a previous referent in the text a total of four times. The European-American student, on the other hand, never uses a pronoun unless its referent is explicitly mentioned earlier in the text. Logically, this is unnecessary, but it represents a formal, explicit style that is more appropriate for school discourse.

Another difference in the two students' summaries is the interpretation of Abigail's role in Gregory's beating. The African-American student says that Abigail "told [Slug] to beat [Gregory] up." The European-American student says that Abigail "didn't tell Slug to beat up Gregory." Here, the African-American student is willing to make an inference that goes beyond the written text. The European-American student treats the text as autonomous, and is unwilling to speculate beyond what it says. This scholarly caution is also more appropriate for a school context.

A final observation is that the African-American student uses terminology that we associate with morality, such as *right, wrong, should*, and *have to*. The European-American student does not use traditional moral terminology, but the more neutral language of explaining. Sinbad is offensive because he didn't have a good enough reason for what he did. Slug wasn't that offensive because he had a reason (compassion) for what he did.

In sum, the African-American student is more personally involved with the text. His use of pronouns assumes a familiarity with the characters; he is willing to make inferences that are not explicitly stated, and he makes judgments about the characters using the vocabulary of personal morality. The European-American student, on the other hand, creates a distance between himself and the text by explicit pronominal reference, by refusing to draw inferences that go beyond the given information, and by adopting a less moralizing stance toward the characters. In short, the students employ different discourse styles: one more appropriate for an informal conversation, the other more appropriate for an academic discussion.

Discussion

Perfetti et al. would probably call their approach to the study of learning objective and fact based. Gee would probably call it positivistic and naive. He would say that there is no simple universal perspective, like the one in the causal model, from which to discuss the Canal Story. Rather, there are many Canal Stories, some of which may be mutually contradictory. For example, according to the Causal Model, the United States wanted to build a canal to get to California faster in order to extract gold and to exclude the British from the region. Both of these reasons are utilitarian, and do not involve moral questions. But Gee does not hesitate to bring up questions of morality. He might say, for example, that an underlying motivation for building the canal was the American notion of Manifest Destiny, that is, the belief that the United States had a God-given right to expand westward to the Pacific Ocean. He would certainly say that the Colombians would tell a very different story of the Canal, one that involved moral questions of imperialism and intervention in the internal affairs of another country. He might also point out that including questions of morality in the study of history appears to be more compatible with the discourse style of at least one minority ethnic group.

The cognitive school of psychology has become dominant during the last 40 years, but there are problems with its basic assumptions that are similar to the problems with objectivist philosophy. Cognitive psychology adopts the computer metaphor of the mind; this metaphor, however, will take us only so far in understanding how the mind works. The greatest difficulty in getting computers to perform like human beings is called the "frame problem," that is, knowing which elements of a context are relevant for human purposes. For example, a citizen of the future might ask the household computer whether there is any water in the refrigerator. After checking the refrigerator's contents (broken down by chemical composition) the computer might reply, "Yes, there is water in the refrigerator—in the cells of the eggplant." The computer has incorrectly framed the water question in terms of chemistry rather than in terms of human needs. Similarly, Perfetti et al. (1995) framed their learning study in terms of expository academic teaching without regard to whether this style of discourse is familiar to their subjects (they just assume that it is). Gee's (1996) study shows that students who are less familiar with academic discourse conventions may frame a task differently than students who are familiar with these conventions, and, therefore, the two groups may come to a different understanding of a text.

In regard to language learning, some theories lend themselves to a cognitive account. For example, in universal grammar (UG) theory, all that the child requires from the environment is exposure to the triggers contained in the language input. The mind does the rest of the work, building a grammar the way cells in the jaw build teeth. However, the learning of discourse conventions requires a theory that acknowledges different social circumstances and conventions, as can be seen by comparing 3-year-old Mark's conversation with his mother to 3-year-old Lem's reply to Lillie Mae, described in chapter 2. So far, UG scholars and discourse scholars have not found much common ground, but we will now consider a school of psychology that is interested not only in the workings of the mind, but also in the culture and society that surrounds it, and, in fact, claims that internal and external factors in learning cannot be studied separately. Its founder was the Russian psychologist Lev Vygotsky.

Vygotsky

Vygotsky did his most important work from the mid-1920s until 1934, when he died of tuberculosis at the age of 37. Although he was a dedicated Marxist, Vygotsky disagreed with the Russian behaviorist Pavlov, whose work won official favor, and, consequently, Vygotsky's writing was suppressed. However, his ideas were preserved and extended by his students and colleagues, Luria and Leontiev, and eventually his work became known in the West during the 1960s, where it has become especially influential among educational researchers. Discussions of Vygotsky (Frawley, 1997; Lantolf & Appel, 1994; Moll, 1990; Newman & Holzman, 1993; Wertsch, 1985) usually include the ideas of Luria and Leontiev, and I shall follow that tradition here.

Luria (1976) tells the story of a literate Russian peasant to whom he put a counterfactual problem.

> Experimenter: It is twenty versts from here to Uch-Kurgan, while Shakhimardan is four times closer. [Actually, the reverse is true.] How many versts is it to Shakhimardan?
>
> Peasant: What! Shakhimardan four times closer?! But it's farther away.
>
> Experimenter: Yes, we know. But I gave out this problem as an exercise.
>
> Peasant: I've never studied, so I can't solve a problem like that! I don't understand it! Divide by four? No . . . I can't . . .
>
> [The experimenter repeats the problem.]
>
> Peasant: If you divide by four, it'll be . . . five versts . . . if you divide twenty by four, you have five! (quoted in Frawley, 1997, p. 13).

In this dialogue, the peasant is grappling with the frame problem. The first framework he tries is that of everyday discourse and commonsense reasoning, but it does not prove helpful: "What! Shakhimardan four times closer?! But it's farther away." At the experimenter's suggestion, the peasant then frames the problem within school discourse, which allows for counterfactual reasoning, and he is able to solve the problem. This shift of frameworks illustrates that problem solving is not simply a matter of internal information processing, as cognitive psychology assumes, but rather that problem solving is *mediated* (assisted) by cultural conventions, the most powerful of which is language. Vygotsky (1986) provides a clear example of how mediation works. A patient with nerve damage is having difficulty learning to walk again, so his doctor draws footprints on the floor indicating where the patient should place his feet. The footprints mediate the process of learning to walk. Similarly, in Luria's story, as the peasant struggles with the distance problem, we can almost see him following in the pedagogical footprints laid down by his mathematics teacher.

Gee (1996) observes that everyone is born into a discourse community, and so learns one type of discourse "free," but other kinds of discourse can be learned (in Vygotsky's term, "appropriated"). When the peasant adopts school discourse in order to solve the distance problem, he employs a cultural tool from another discourse community. Vygotsky called such appropriated discourse "inner speech." He observed that when people are grappling with a problem in the company of others, they often employ oral reasoning, like the peasant. Privately, people sometimes talk aloud to themselves, but more often they engage in a dialogic thinking process that is the internal equivalent of the peasant's external speech.

Activity theory. What is a "bachelor?" It seems simple enough: A bachelor is an unmarried man. But it is odd to say that the Pope is a bachelor although the Pope fits that definition. Apparently, a bachelor should be not only unmarried but eligible for marriage. In fact, bachelors apparently have to live in a society that includes eligible women as it also sounds odd to say that Tarzan was a bachelor. Lakoff (1987) suggests that many concepts, like BACHELOR, are understood in terms of an *Idealized Cognitive Model.* Our Idealized Cognitive Model of BACHELOR is something like "a single man who dates several women but who chooses not to marry for the time being." When a real-world situation does not fit this idealized model, we usually modify the word *bachelor* in some way. Thus, it seems better to say, "Technically, the Pope is a bachelor." Similarly, the concept MOTHER is understood in terms of an Idealized Cognitive Model of a woman who conceives, bears, and nurtures a child. If a real-world case does not fit this prototype, we speak of a stepmother, adoptive mother, genetic mother, or surrogate mother.

Activity theory, developed by Leontiev, is similar to the theory of Idealized Cognitive Models because it situates how we conceive of what we do within a cultural model. The effect that cultural context has on an activity is illustrated by an experiment performed by Wertsch, Minick, and Arns

(1984) in rural Brazil. The researchers recruited teams consisting of a mother and a child or a teacher and child and asked them to solve a problem that involved making a model of a farmyard. They found that the mother–child teams finished the task more quickly because the mothers did most of the work, assigning only easy tasks to the children. The teachers, on the other hand, let the children do tasks that they did not completely understand, allowing them to make mistakes and learn from them.

Both ways of approaching this activity made sense given the different cultural frameworks that the adults adopted. The mothers interpreted the activity as labor, which should be accomplished as efficiently as possible. The teachers interpreted the activity as a lesson to benefit the children, in which making mistakes is allowed as it is an integral part of learning. This experiment, like Gee's (1996) Alligator River study, suggests that human activity is performed within cultural frameworks that influence how the activity is conceived and carried out. Next, we will see how cultural frameworks influence ELL students' academic work.

The Zone of Proximal Development.   Wertsch et al.'s (1984) experiment also illustrates another important Vygotskian concept: the Zone of Proximal Development (ZPD), defined as "the distance between the actual development level as determined by independent problem solving and the level of potential development as determined through problem solving under adult guidance or in collaboration with more capable peers" (Vygotsky, 1978, p. 86). The children could solve the farmyard puzzle (or at least parts of it) with the help of an adult; thus, they were working within their ZPDs. Scholars agree that the ZPD is Vygotsky's most useful contribution to education, but opinions differ as to exactly what it is. The ZPD involves three concepts, which different scholars understand somewhat differently. The first concept is *learning*, which can be understood in Perfetti et al.'s (1995) cognitive terms as adding pieces of information and the logical connections between them to a mental schema.

The second and most problematic concept is *development*. Development is similar to maturation, and perhaps the most well-known theory of development in both Vygotsky's time and our own is that of the Swiss psychologist Jean Piaget. Piaget (1972) claimed that as children mature, they go through four cognitive stages. In the sensori-motor stage, from about birth to age 2, children learn to coordinate their physical actions. In the preoperational stage, from about age 2 to age 7, they learn to represent actions in thought and language. In the concrete operational stage, from about age 7 to age 11, they learn to think logically about physical reality, and in the formal operational stage, about age 11 and older, they learn to think abstractly. Piaget believed that learning builds on these developmental stages. Thus, his theory predicts that it would be a mistake to try and teach the laws of flotation to 5-year-olds because they have not yet reached the concrete operational stage, a level of development that is necessary for understanding the physical relationships these laws embody.

Piaget also believed that although development cannot occur without adequate stimulation from the surrounding language and culture, it unfolds according to built-in biological principles. An analogous case in language acquisition theory is the UG account of article learning. A child learning English articles must first set the head direction parameter for head initial, thus specifying that articles will precede nouns (as specifiers precede their heads). This is a developmental stage involving UG and requiring minimal exposure to input. Only after reaching this stage can the child proceed to learn the semantic restrictions regarding when to use *a* and *the* (as described in chap. 2).

Piaget believed that learning and development are separate processes, and that the course of development is not affected by learning. Vygotsky disagreed, claiming that learning contributes to development: "Instruction is useful when it moves ahead of development [where] it impels or awakens a whole series of functions that are in a stage of maturation lying in the zone of proximal development" (1987, p. 212). As to what, exactly, development is, Vygotskian scholars are usually not as specific as Piaget (or Chomsky), but they understand it to involve increasing powers of memory, reasoning, concentration, and other mental faculties.

The third concept involved in the ZPD is *social.* As we have seen, Perfetti et al. (1995), like other cognitive psychologists, study learning within the minds of individuals and assume that social circumstances are largely irrelevant. However, Vygotsky believed that learning cannot be studied without attention to the social environment in which it takes place. An example of such a study is Wertsch et al.'s (1984) puzzle-solving experiment, in which learning is embedded within an activity that is socially constructed (like the concept BACHELOR), and which may be understood somewhat differently by different social groups, such as mothers and teachers. Similarly, the two social groups studied by Gee (1996) understood their task in culturally influenced ways.

Notice, however, that Wertsch's notion of the ZPD is not that different from the cognitive science notion of learning. Cognitive science does not address the question of development. Wertsch, as a Vygotskian, believes that learning leads development, but does not really address the question of what development is: the focus is on teaching and learning. This focus is shared by other Vygotskian educational researchers, such as Tharp and Gallimore (1988, 1990), who state that teaching consists of "assisting performance through the ZPD. Teaching can be said to occur when assistance is offered at points in the ZPD at which performance requires assistance" (1990, p. 31). This sounds very similar to the notion of *scaffolding*, which was developed by the cognitive psychologists Wood, Bruner, and Ross (1976), who did not mention Vygotsky. Scaffolding is the process by which a teacher helps a student understand new concepts by filling in necessary background information. Newman and Holzman (1993) argue that the close relationship between cognitive psychology and Vygotskian psychology is a bit too cozy, and label Wertsch and Tharp and Gallimore "neo-Vygotskians." Newman and Holzman believe that the ZPD is located more in a group than in an individual, and that it should be studied as part of a culture, rather than a context or "activity setting" that can be as small as a mother and child or teacher and student.

I will adopt the neo-Vygotskian position here. I have found the notions of scaffolding and the ZPD to be very useful in understanding how ELL students learn academic material when tutored by an adult. Of course the ZPD includes more than scaffolding; it assumes that scaffolding occurs within particular educational and cultural contexts and that these contexts cannot be ignored. In chapter 6, we will see some examples of learning by ELL students within the broader context of their overall school and home situations. However, Newman and Holzman have in mind an even broader interpretation of the social dimension of the ZPD, which will be illustrated in the next section.

Another important Vygotskian notion, related to the ZPD, is the difference between spontaneous concepts and scientific concepts. Spontaneous (or everyday) concepts like BOAT, BROTHER, and PAST TIME are acquired naturally in the course of living, perhaps in the same way the child acquires the non-UG aspects of the native language. They do not necessarily have logical relationships with other concepts and cannot be voluntarily controlled. Scientific concepts like MAMMAL, ARCHIMEDES LAW, AND ATOMIC NUMBER, on the other hand, are logically structured, can be consciously manipulated, and must be consciously learned, usually at school. A spontaneous concept can become part of a system of scientific concepts through instruction. Thus, a child may spontaneously learn what a whale is, but the concept changes radically when the child learns that a whale is a mammal. Vygotsky (1987) observes:

> Both types of concept are located in one and the same child and at more or less the same level of development. In the thinking of the child, one cannot separate the concepts that he acquires in school from those he acquires at home. Nonetheless, these concepts have entirely different histories. [The scientific] concept reaches the level it has attained while having undergone a certain portion of its development from above. The [spontaneous concept] reaches this level having completed the lower portion of its development path (p. 219).

Readers may have noticed that Vygotsky's notion that concepts can develop "from above" and "from below" is similar to Labov's (1994) notion of linguistic change, discussed in chapter 4. "Change from below" is unconscious and usually unnoticed; it is not under the control of the speaker. "Change from above" is conscious and often inspired by grammar lessons at school. The two kinds of change occur in the cognitive system of the same individual. In change from above, conscious knowledge leads to change in unconscious knowledge and thus to change in an individual's linguistic system. Similarly, Vygotskian theory claims that scientific concepts build on an already existing system of everyday concepts. Panofsky, John-Steiner, and Blackwell (1990) put it this way:

> It is through the use of everyday concepts that children make sense of the definitions and explanations of scientific concepts; everyday concepts provide the "living knowledge" for the development of scientific concepts (p. 10).

Professor Luis Moll has employed these and other Vygotskian insights in an exciting research program involving the instruction of Hispanic students in Tucson schools, which we now consider.

Teaching within a Vygotskian framework.   Moll (1990) and his colleagues and students at the University of Arizona (many of them in-service teachers) have used ethnographic methods similar to those of Heath (1983; discussed in chaps. 1 and 2) to study learning by Hispanic children in Tucson. They visit students' homes and interview their parents, siblings, friends, and neighbors, usually in Spanish, in order to document areas of expertise that are available in the community. Most of this expertise consists of everyday concepts, which the researchers call "funds of knowledge." Their goal is to exploit this knowledge as a bridge to learning scientific concepts in school. Moll and Greenberg (1990) found that their informants know a lot about a wide variety of subjects, many of which are related to their rural farming backgrounds, including plant cultivation, animal husbandry, veterinary medicine, carpentry, masonry, automobile repair, folk remedies, and herbal cures. They also found that friends and neighbors are accustomed to sharing this knowledge with each other, a practice they call *confianza* (mutual trust).

Let me relate a personal experience that illustrates both *confianza* and the broad-based practical knowledge that working-class border people possess. One weekend, my family and I drove to Puerto Peñasco, a beach town on the Gulf of California that is a favorite vacation spot for Tucsonans. In the middle of town, my car stopped and wouldn't start—dead battery. Just about every car driving down the street was from Arizona, so I stuck out my hand, a driver stopped, and he gave us a jump start that enabled us to get back to the hotel. But, we would have to buy a new battery for the drive home, and it was Saturday night, and the stores wouldn't open until Monday. The hotel janitor, Señor Ruiz, offered to help. He said he knew the owner of the car parts store and was sure he would sell me a battery on Sunday.

The next day Señor Ruiz's friend opened his store and sold us a battery, but it didn't fit my car. Mexican batteries are taller than American batteries, and the positive cable wouldn't reach all the way to the terminal. I despaired, but Señor Ruiz got out his tools and some wire and spliced an extension onto the cable. He refused to accept any money for his work, but I finally forced some on him. The battery worked fine and lasted longer than most batteries I have purchased in the States, thanks to Señor Ruiz's practical knowledge of electrical repair and the tradition of *confianza*.

Through his ethnographic studies, Moll has found that expertise in construction is one of the funds of knowledge often found in working-class Hispanic homes in Tucson, and he has developed teaching modules around this subject. For example, in one bilingual sixth-grade class, students visited the library to find information on the different professions involved in construction, such as carpentry and plumbing. Then they built miniature model homes and wrote essays about construction and how it related to their models. One student compared a home to the human body:

> El esqueleto de una casa no está construido por huesos como los nuestros, sino que hormigón armado. *The skeleton of a house is not constructed of bones, like ours, but of reinforced concrete* (Moll & Greenberg, 1990, p. 338).

Extending the module, the teacher invited parents and relatives who worked in construction to visit the class, thus accessing the funds of knowledge in the community. One visitor, a student who was studying drafting, presented his drawings to the class and explained how he had developed them. The children discussed and wrote about all of these activities in Spanish and English. Finally, the teacher was able to connect the construction module to the mainstream curriculum in several ways. For example, the curriculum required the students to write biographies, and some of the students were able to interview their classroom visitors to find out the details of their lives other than those connected to their profession.

Moll's funds of knowledge project attempts to relate schooling to students' daily lives both cognitively and culturally. For this reason, Newman and Holzman (1993) regard it as more "Vygotskian" than the one-on-one tutoring studies of the neo-Vygotskians. According to Newman and Holzman, the ZPD in Moll's research does not reside in the minds of individual students, but rather in the immigrant Hispanic community as a whole. It is in this larger social context that everyday concepts and scientific concepts interact, and in which the learning and development of individual students must be studied.

ACADEMIC DISCOURSE

As we saw in chapter 2, learning a language involves learning both linguistic forms and how to use them appropriately within some kind of discourse. Similarly, learning an academic subject involves learning facts and skills and how to employ them within the discourse appropriate to that subject. In this section, we will discuss how different discourses require different ways of using language, and how learning American academic discourse conventions is a major challenge for many English language learners.

Register Variation

A useful concept for analyzing variation in written and spoken language is the notion of *register*. Register, as I use the term here, refers to the linguistic (but not the rhetorical) features of a discourse. For example, a study of the registers that Gee's (1996) subjects used in discussing the "Alligator River Story" would focus on the speakers' use of pronouns and antecedents, but not on whether they were willing to draw conclusions from partial evidence. Examples of written registers include instruction manuals, letters to friends, and academic articles. Examples of spoken registers include academic lectures, conversations, and stories. Like social dialects, registers do not usually differ because they contain unique linguistic forms (e.g., Black English *be*) but because they use the same forms at different frequencies. An example is how relative clauses are used in spoken versus written registers. Before looking at some relevant studies, we need to review some facts about relative clauses.

Recall from chapter 3 that relative clauses can be classified according to *focus*; that is, according to whether the relative pronoun functions as the subject, direct object, or prepositional object of the clause. The examples given in chapter 3 are repeated here:

Subject focus: The forest [*which* burned down] was in Arizona.

Direct Object focus: The balloon [*which* I lost] was found.

Object of preposition focus: The people [with *whom* you talked] were very nice.

A fact not mentioned in chapter 3 is that in object focus clauses, the relative pronoun can be deleted. Thus, an alternative form of the direct object focus clause above is:

The balloon [I lost] was found.

An alternative form of the object of preposition focus clause is:

The people [you talked with] were very nice.

There are speakers who sometimes delete relative pronouns from subject focus clauses as well, and some of my favorites are the tough characters in Ed McBain's detective novels. Here are three examples from *Candyland* (co-authored by Evan Hunter and Ed McBain, who are the same person):

Bartender: [t]here was a guy [who] came in around seven-thirty last night
             [who] might be him.
Detective: There's this guy [who]'s a bartender in an after hours joint on
             Second Avenue . . . (Hunter & McBain, 2001, p. 168).

However, sentences like these are very rare, even in working-class speech.

Relative pronoun deletion from object focus clauses is found in all spoken varieties of English but is more frequent among working-class speakers, as I found in a study of the speech of Philadelphia residents (Adamson, 1992). My data included 300 hours of recorded speech, which contained 2,240 relative clauses. I found that the working-class speakers deleted object focus relative pronouns about 68% of the time whereas the upper-class speakers deleted them only about 40% of the time. At least one best-selling author represents this style stratification in fictional dialogue fairly accurately. Prideaux and Baker (1986) analyzed the speech of two characters, an Army sergeant and a Supreme Court Justice, in the novel *The Vicar of Christ* by M. F. Murphy. The Sergeant deleted 75% of object focus pronouns while the Justice deleted only 25%.

Biensenback-Lucus (1989) found that different sections of the *Washington Post* contained different registers, and that these registers were distinguished by their rates of relative pronoun deletion. There was no deletion at all in the World News section. The percentage of deletion in the other sections of the *Post* was as follows: Front Page 3%, Business 6%, Letters to the Editor 11%, and Sports 25%, an order that reflects the formality of the writing.

Douglas Biber (1988, 1995; Biber, Conrad, & Reppen, 1998) has done extensive studies of variation in written registers, looking at how the frequency of key features distinguishes them. He found that academic texts in different fields, such as biology and history, constitute different registers, a fact that has important implications for preparing ELL students to succeed in biology and history courses. In order to distinguish different registers, Biber looked for linguistic features that tended to co-occur in similar kinds of texts. He found, for example, that across all registers, writing contains high frequencies of passive sentences, conjunctions, and subordinate constructions, whereas speaking contains low frequencies of these features, and he suggests that this difference contributes to the less personal tone of written texts. Having determined the frequencies at which particular features are used in very formal and very informal texts, Biber was then able to place any individual text, spoken or written, on a continuum ranging from "highly impersonal" to "highly non-impersonal," according to the percentage of relevant features that the text contained. Going one step further, Biber combined a number of texts representing a particular register (say research articles about history) and calculated where that register as a whole fit on the impersonal–nonimpersonal continuum.

Figure 5.2 (Biber et al., 1998, p. 164) shows how four registers—ecology research articles, history research articles, general fiction, and face-to-face conversation—fit on the impersonal–nonimpersonal continuum. Ecology research articles are highly impersonal in style, containing many passive and subordinate constructions. Passives are to be expected in scientific articles because human agents are usually not important to the natural phenomenon being discussed, as in this sentence from an article on biology: "Seeds *were taken* from canopies of hosts not normally *used* and *transferred* into canopies of normal hosts . . ." (Biber et al., 1998, p. 166). Here the author used the passive voice because it doesn't really matter who does the taking and transferring of the seeds. In history articles, on the other hand, it usually does matter which human or political agents perform which actions, as in this sentence from Perfetti et al.'s (1995) study: "Panama *fought* Colombia in order to gain independence" (p. 34).

Research on register variation suggests that ELL students must acquire more than general proficiency in English. If they are to write like physicists, ecologists, or historians at the college level, they need to acquire the subtle features that mark the appropriate registers for those fields. The foundation for this competence must be laid at the pre-college level, where ELL students must learn the different conventions for writing lab reports, book reviews, journals, and other kinds of academic discourse. For this, they will need considerable exposure to a variety of academic registers.

Douglas and Selinker's Study

The fact that different linguistic forms and varieties are appropriate in different contexts is usually well known to language learners, who find that their competence varies with the situation they are in. One can be fluent when making small talk but completely tongue-tied when the conversation turns to politics. I personally have planned entire evenings around avoiding the Spanish subjunctive. In fact, according to Selinker and Douglas (1989), learners may employ different interlanguage systems depending on the register they wish to use. These researchers report the case of a Korean graduate student working as a teaching assistant (TA) in the chemistry department of an American university, who apparently used modal verbs, such as

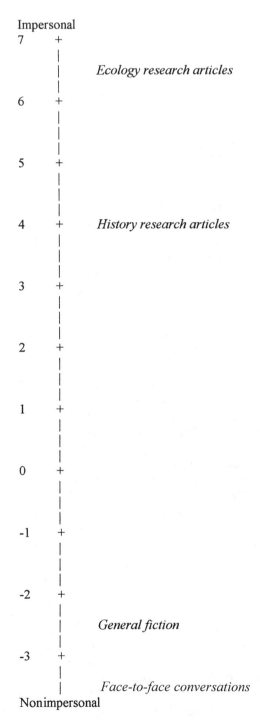

FIG. 5.2.   Impersonal versus nonimpersonal style.

should, can, supposed to, and *have to,* differently when discussing chemistry than when discussing his private life. Here is an example of his English when discussing chemistry with an American student.

> Q: You're working on a research project now, right . . . , what's that about?
>
> TA: Solid state chemistry, it's hard to explain.
>
> Q: uh-huh yeah—try.
>
> TA: OK [laugh] then—first of all when I—whenever I talk to somebody about solid state chemistry I should talk about the difference from the solid state chemistry . . . and traditional chemistry . . . in traditional chemistry for example take a cup of water and all the water molecules in the—in the cup behave (then) differently—individually (I mean) so we can create such a system as a—accumulation of such a small molecules . . . but in solid state chemistry—all the molecules or sup- any units which are supposed to be -uh—supposed be acting as molecule—atom—in such a system are linked or bonded to each other—so we have to treat them as a -just a—a starting unit—no—not accumulation of many such a molecules or atom—you just treat them as a unit depending on their size.
>
> Q: Mm-hmmm mm-hmmm (Selinker & Douglas, 1989, p. 117).

This explanation is fairly coherent, and the use of the modal verbs is appropriate. But when the TA talks about his personal life, he is less coherent and his use of modals resembles that of a less advanced English learner:

> Q: Why were [your students in Korean] learning mathematics?
>
> TA: Um—first of all they couldn't have opportunity to advance for higher school and almost all of them are working—were working in the factory and (skill) they couldn't have a way for their desire for advanced study—and whenever they are qualified in an exam which is . . . umm . . . which is given by the government they could advance of higher school—so sometimes they can skip certain level of school and so they can advance from the elementary school to the university or higher school directly (Selinker & Douglas, 1989, p. 120).

Here the TA uses *couldn't* in a distinctly non-native way, and he abruptly changes from past tense *could* to present tense *can.* Selinker and Douglas conclude that the TA is accessing two different internal grammars for modal verbs in the two domains of talk.

Biber's and Douglas and Selinker's research supports a point that Cummins (1980, 1989; Cummins & Swain, 1983) has been making for a long time: Academic discourse and everyday discourse are different, and students are often proficient in one discourse but not the other. Highly educated ELL students who have learned English abroad, like the Korean TA, are usually more proficient in academic discourse, whereas students in

American schools (like George, described in chap. 1) are usually more proficient in everyday discourse. Cummins' theory, which distinguishes between Basic Interpersonal Communication Skills (BICS) and Cognitive Academic Language Proficiency (CALP) is often cited as a theoretical rationale for bilingual education; we will examine this more fully in chapter 7, which is devoted to that subject.

Rhetorical Discourse Conventions

Becoming proficient in academic discourse involves much more than learning the vocabulary and linguistic structures associated with academic registers. As we saw in the "Alligator River Story," competence in academic discourse also involves knowing how to interpret a text, present an argument, cite evidence, and draw conclusions. We examine these rhetorical aspects of academic discourse in this section.

Several years ago, I taught an introductory linguistics course to 25 freshmen and sophomore students. For three weeks during the semester we were joined by 15 ELL students, who were enrolled in the university's intensive English program. During these weeks, the ELL students did all the work of the course: They took notes on lectures, participated in class discussions, completed a small research project, and took a short quiz. In comparing the work of the ELLs and mainstream students, I discovered was that the ELL students had not yet mastered all the rhetorical conventions of American academic discourse (Adamson, 1993).

One example occurred on the quiz, where the students were asked, "What is the critical period hypothesis for language acquisition? Discuss the evidence on which the hypothesis is based." In grading the answers to this question, I looked for a number of points: The student should state the hypothesis, mention some of the evidence for and against it, and briefly evaluate the evidence. My schema for a good answer looked like this:

CRITICAL PERIOD HYPOTHESIS:

Complete language acquisition occurs only between the ages of birth and the onset of puberty.

Direct evidence (anecdotal)

1. Genie, a girl who was raised in an attic without exposure to English until after the onset of puberty, did not learn native-like English.
2. Another child (Mason's, 1942 unnamed subject), who was first exposed to English at age 6½, did learn native-like English.

Indirect evidence

1. Brain lateralization is complete at the onset of puberty (this implies that brain function changes at that time).
2. Few adults learn a second language with native-like competence.

First, consider the essay written by Turi, one of the mainstream students. Turi received most of her education in Iran, but had graduated from a U.S. high school. She wrote:

> The critical period for language acquisition occurs between the ages of 2-3, until 14. Lenneburg says that after this age, which is the beginning of puberty, children's ability to learn language slows down, the individual becomes less sensitive to stimuli. the basics of a language are not taught during the "critical period," therefore it is to late.
>
> Taking the example of Genie, her case is the evidence proving that language acquisition occurs within the critical period. Genie has lived in isolation during the critical period, therefore the development of language in her case has bee limited, although she acquired stages of language beyond the "critical period."
>
> Genie hasn't been exposed to any language learning during the "critical period." She started learning English at the time of a second-language acquisition, which is out of the critical period. Normally, the process of lateralization occurs after the critical period (and the language acquisition), but Genie's case proves that lateralization can precede language acquisition.
>
> Genie's case shows that at some degree, language acquisition seems to be possible beyond the critical age.

Now let us look at the essay written by Mouna, an ELL student from Iran who had recently arrived in the United States.

> The critical period for language acquisition is when one reaches puberty and has not learned a language then in Lennenburg theory it is stated that he never will. I don't believe in Lenneburgs theory because even if one never learned a language their brain does not ceaze to function. If a person had been in a wheel chair and can now walk with the help of artificial legs he not learn all over again I believe the same in terms of langage. Genie who was isolated virtually after birth learned to speak of course not to the same extent as a natural child but this is because of psychological effect.
>
> ii) A child must learn to imitate if he is to learn Genie did not see anybody but her mother for a couple of minutes. Genie also could not talk because she could not breath large quantities of air in and out in order to speak. this brought her a lot of physical pain. . . .

There is not a lot of difference in the quality of the two essays (Turi's received a C– and Mouna's received a D+), but some of the differences shed light on how the students are acquiring academic discourse. First of all,

Turi's essay is fairly well organized. The first paragraph defines the critical period; the second paragraph cites the case of Genie. The first part of the third paragraph continues the discussion of Genie and the second part of that paragraph mentions the brain lateralization argument. It would make more sense to include the discussion of Genie in paragraph two, but that would leave the third paragraph with only one sentence, which Turi has probably learned doesn't look good. The fourth paragraph summarizes Turi's thesis and contains a nice example of scholarly caution with the word *seems*. It is true that Turi seems to contradict herself when she says, "Genie's case proves that lateralization can precede language acquisition." But in the next sentence, she says that this is possible only "at [to] some degree," which is consistent with her endorsing Lenneberg's theory. In short, Turi has learned to write a barely acceptable short theme that conforms to many of the rhetorical conventions taught in American high school English classes.

Mouna's essay violates many of these conventions. One problem is that the second paragraph inexplicably begins with the number *ii*. A more serious problem is that Mouna mentions the fact that breathing was painful for Genie (in a sentence that was copied almost directly from the book) without relating this fact to her argument. The most serious problem in Mouna's essay is the evidence she cites against the critical period hypothesis. Whereas Turi sticks to reviewing the evidence for the critical period hypothesis that was presented in class, Mouna brings in her own ideas about language acquisition. One of them is, "A child must learn to imitate if he is to learn." Unfortunately, this commonsense idea is false in regard to language acquisition. Here Mouna has violated an academic convention similar to one violated by the African-American student who analyzed the "Alligator River Story." She has gone beyond the text (not just the textbook but our whole unit on language acquisition) and supplied her own interpretation. Furthermore, Mouna challenges Lenneberg's claim that normal language acquisition cannot occur after the critical period. To justify her opinion, she uses the analogy of a crippled person who learns to walk using artificial legs. But the two cases are not comparable because language acquisition is a cognitive ability and walking is a physical ability. Turi just presents Lenneberg's views and cites the case of Genie as evidence. This is a less ambitious but safer strategy.

In sum, Turi did not write a very good answer because parts of it are confused and because it lacks critical analysis. It is a safe answer. Mouna, on the other hand, has attempted to be analytical and independent, but she has not pulled it off. She shows more involvement and curiosity in the issue of a critical period and therefore is possibly a more promising scholar than Turi, but she has not yet learned how to make a convincing academic argument.

Access to Academic Discourse

Studies of classroom discourse like those just discussed have shown that the linguistic and rhetorical conventions of textbooks, lectures, and classrooms are different from those of everyday conversation. However, measurements of students' English proficiency often ignore the distinction between the two varieties. For example, a national survey conducted by the U.S. Census Bureau ("Study Finds," 2001) reported that 18% of school age children in the United States speak a language other than English at home (up from 14% in 1990). The survey also found that two thirds of these children (mainly the younger ones) rated themselves as speaking English "very well." Proponents of English-only education have cited findings like these to claim that bilingual and extended ESL programs are not necessary: Most ELL students speak English well, so just put them in with the native speakers. But discourse studies show that general English proficiency is not enough. ELL students need to learn the language of academic discourse.

What kinds of ESL programs are best for achieving this goal? A traditional answer has been sheltered and adjunct courses, and these can be effective provided the material is at an appropriate level for the students. Unfortunately, this is often not the case, as we saw in chapter 1, where George was struggling in his sheltered literature course because the material was too difficult. Fairview County was not the only place where ELL students did not have access to academic discourse because they were assigned to inappropriate courses. In a recent book, *Learning and Not Learning English: Latino Students in American Schools*, Guadalupe Valdés (2001) describes a three-year study of four ELL students as they moved from ESL to mainstream courses in middle school. She found that the quality of their ESL courses differed greatly. It is instructive to compare two of Valdés' subjects: Lilian, who eventually dropped out of school and got a job in a fast food restaurant, and Manolo, who went on to graduate from high school and got a job as a technician in an electronics firm.

Both Lilian and Manolo were the children of immigrants from Mexico; both of their fathers came to the United States in search of a better life, found employment, and after a number of years sent for their families. The two families, however, were from different social classes. Lilian's father had little education and worked for a gardening service; Manolo's father had been a police officer in Mexico City and was able to find better paying jobs (which he usually worked at two or three at a time). As a result, Manolo's family lived in a better neighborhood, and there was less pressure on Manolo to go to work at an early age.

Lilian and Manolo were 12 years old when they came to the United States, and they both enrolled in Garden Way Middle School, where the ESL program could be described as the program from hell. Both students were stuck for two years in the same basic-level ESL class. During the second year at Garden Way, their English abilities were much better, but because of school policy, they were kept in a class with raw beginners. The teacher of the basic ESL class, Mrs. Gordon, had taught language arts to native speakers in elementary school and her lessons used materials appropriate for these students but not for ELL students. Most of Mrs. Gordon's lessons emphasized linguistic form and betrayed a fear of letting students make mistakes. Her class was instructional and teacher centered; the activities were largely mechanical; and the content had no relation to the academic material that the students eventually needed to know. In fairness, it should also be said that Mrs. Gordon maintained discipline in her classes and that her students liked her and her way of teaching.

During the first year, when Lilian and Manolo took Mrs. Gordon's ESL class for 3 hours a day, they were also enrolled in sheltered courses in science, math, and home arts taught by teachers without ESL training. These teachers worked hard to modify their lessons so that ELL students could understand them, but they could not do this successfully because the students lacked the necessary vocabulary, background knowledge, and academic skills; they needed backup support in these areas from the ESL faculty, as provided in an adjunct course. The curriculum at Garden Way stated that students should be at an appropriate level of English proficiency before they enrolled in sheltered classes, but this requirement was ignored, and the hapless science and math teachers were given an impossible task.

Valdés also notes that the academic situation was not the only problem with the sheltered classes. The behavior of some of the students was a problem as well. Describing the science class, Valdés (2001) writes,

> When the teacher attempted to explain a concept using overheads and pictures, and as she asked for student feedback, an especially unruly group of youngsters made comments aloud in Spanish. These remarks were intended to be funny, and, in general, they had the desired effect. Students would break into laughter and would respond, returning insults and humorous remarks. Mrs. Morton tried her best to maintain order by varying class activities, by providing stimulating opportunities for hands-on science, and the like, but during most of the year, the unruly students created disruptions almost daily. Manolo angrily stared down at his desk when explanations were interrupted. . . . He really wanted to know the results of the experiment that the teacher had begun (pp. 113–114).

In chapter 6, we will see further examples of how difficult it is to provide content instruction at an appropriate level for ESL students and how the need to maintain classroom order limits the possibilities of doing so.

During their second year, Lilian and Manolo enrolled in some mainstream classes with native English speakers, where they encountered problems similar to those in the sheltered courses because they were not prepared to handle the material, and no backup support was provided. Manolo had taken a sheltered social studies course during his first year, but it did not teach him the background knowledge expected in the mainstream social studies course. For example, he had never heard of the Boston Tea Party, did not recognize the names of the founding fathers, and was unfamiliar with the structure of American government. Furthermore, it was difficult for Manolo to fill in this information on his own because his ESL class focused on reading at the sentence and paragraph levels, not on the extensive reading that is necessary to gain background knowledge.

During his third year in the United States, Manolo's family moved, and Manolo enrolled in the J.F.K. Middle School, which had a much better ESL program than the one at Garden Way. The teachers at J.F.K., like the teachers of the middle-class Cuban immigrants at Coral Way Elementary School discussed in chapter 1, believed that bilingualism was an asset, and also that their students were fully capable of doing rigorous academic work if given proper support. That support was provided by integrating ESL instruction into the overall academic program. For example, the beginning ESL teacher did not focus only on language forms, but included lessons on American history. She emphasized understanding and communication rather than mechanical accuracy. She also taught academic skills, like notetaking, and gave assignments that required her students to interview their mainstream peers in order to encourage peer contacts beyond the ELL community. Most important, the teacher showed students that they could deal effectively with difficult academic material even though they did not understand every word, a topic we will return to later.

There were no sheltered classes at J.F.K.—students moved immediately from ESL into the mainstream—but the school was fortunate enough to be able to provide a good way of supporting ELL students in mainstream classes: They were assigned tutors who spoke their native language, which is an alternative form of adjunct teaching. Valdés does not explain who these tutors were or how they were paid, but it is safe to assume that not many schools could afford this system. However, the regular adjunct course as described in chapter 3 also provides a way of helping ELLs develop the background knowledge, discourse competence, and academic skills required in mainstream coursework, as long as the material is appropriate to their level, or, in (neo-)Vygotskian terms, within their ZPDs. In chapter 6, we will see more examples of ELL students struggling to learn academic material both within and beyond their ZPDs.

Academic Strategies

In this final section on academic discourse, I will suggest ways in which ELL students can be taught to deal with difficult academic material, preferably in a sheltered or adjunct course. My suggestions are based mostly on research (Adamson, 1993) that I conducted in Fairview County, where my graduate students and I tutored 34 ELL students at the middle school, high school, and college levels in mainstream and sheltered courses. We observed the students in their classes and helped them with their homework, tape-recording the tutoring sessions and taking field notes. The result of this effort was 34 case studies that described how the students read textbooks, studied for tests, asked questions, took notes, and in other ways handled their academic assignments.

We found that the students varied greatly in their use of learning strategies: Some used much more effective strategies than others. A common example of an ineffective strategy was overuse of the dictionary, which resulted from an inability to tolerate less than a full understanding of a text. For example, Ahmed, a college student from Tunisia, looked up practically every word of his engineering text in an Arabic–English dictionary (even words he knew, like *toy*) and wrote the Arabic translations in the book. He also filled three notebooks with English words and their translations, which he memorized. This strategy was not optimal because he could not finish his reading assignments on time. On the other hand, Duc, a Vietnamese college student, was able to vary his reading strategies to match the difficulty of the material. He read easy material much as a native speaker would, underlining important points and making notes in the margin. He read more difficult material three times, first to get a general idea of the meaning, then using a dictionary, and finally underlining and making notes.

The ability to vary strategy use to match the difficulty of the material was a characteristic of the more successful students. Elizabeth, a college student from Korea, was (like many of the students) frustrated because she could not understand everything her geography professor said in lectures. She remarked, "I usually didn't miss the main parts. . . . Some details I miss. I'm curious about the details. I want to understand her lectures perfectly." But Elizabeth had developed effective strategies for taking notes. She took notes in English, but when she encountered a word she didn't understand, she wrote it phonetically using the Korean syllabary, and afterward asked a friend what the word meant. She also kept a tape recorder handy and recorded parts of the lecture that she did not understand and later transcribed the tape. She did not record everything because transcribing is a very time-consuming task.

A number of students reported another way of varying their notetaking with the difficulty of the material. They found that for easy material they could both understand the lecture and take notes in English. However, for more difficult material, they could follow what was being said only if they took notes in their native language. With very difficult material, the students could not both follow the meaning and take notes. Some preferred just to listen and try to borrow notes from friends. Others wrote down as much as they could in English without understanding what they were writing and tried to make sense of it later. This strategy was used in classes where the lectures contained information that was sure to appear on a test, in which case it was important to write down dates and formulas even if they were not understood during the lecture. We also found that some students never took notes except for copying what was written on the board. These students were very print oriented, and relied exclusively on their textbooks. They had not learned how to deal with difficult spoken English.

We found, like Valdés, that many of the ELL students were in over their heads, submerged in mainstream classes where they could not keep up, and we found that they had developed strategies for completing their assignments without understanding them, which we called *coping strategies*. The two main coping strategies were copying and memorization. One copying strategy was to look for a keyword in a question, then skim the reading passage for a sentence in which the word appeared and copy that sentence as the answer. For example, Manny, a high school student from Cambodia, answered a question about tectonic plates as follows:

Q: What did people notice about the shape of continents?
A: Notice how the continents seem like pieces of a jigsaw puzzle that might just fit together.

This answer is copied almost word for word from the book. Although Manny did not know what a jigsaw puzzle was, he was able to locate the appropriate sentence from the text because of the keywords *notice* and *continents*. Of course, the keyword strategy sometimes produced nonsense. Manh, a high school student from Vietnam, answered a question from his world history text like this:

Q: Why did Ulysses decide to put his ships in harbor?
A: Ulysses wished to put as much open water as possible between him and the Island of Winds, but after six days he realized he would have to put his ship into harbor.

Here Manh had found a sentence with word *harbor*, but it was not relevant to the question. It is interesting to compare Manh's copied answers to his meaningful answers. For example, after much help and encouragement from his tutor, Manh wrote the following definitions:

looting	The thief taken something.
skillful	It skillful to do something well.
archer	it helps people to make animal die by bow and arrow.
overboard	something drop in the water from the ship.

Manh's tutor remarked, "Most teachers would look at the above definitions and just cringe, [but for me] they were meaningful, and that is what counted."

Memorization is a favorite learning strategy in many countries. One reason the audio-lingual method was popular in Ethiopia is because some of the students had memorized entire books of the Bible in Ge'ez, the ancient liturgical language of Ethiopia, not understanding a word of what they were saying. Similarly, one of the tutors in the Fairview County study who was from Palestine reported, "We used to memorize the whole lesson word by word. . . . I still suffer from this memorization strategy that our schools emphasize." Mark, a middle school student from Japan, was a champion memorizer. Sometimes this strategy served him well. He successfully learned 15 or 20 new vocabulary words every week by writing them many times. But sometimes he used memorization to compensate for a lack of understanding. For example, Mark miscopied the definition of *prey* as, "an organism that is lucnted [should be *hunted*] by another organism." He memorized this definition and supplied it on the test.

The studies just reviewed suggest that a crucial factor in ELL students' success is how well the ESL and mainstream programs are integrated. ELL students need special help to learn the background knowledge assumed in the mainstream curriculum, become familiar with the conventions of academic discourse, and develop effective strategies for dealing with difficult material. Unfortunately, as Valdés found, some ESL programs concentrate only on teaching language, with no attention to these other essential areas. In fact, both Valdés and I independently came to very similar conclusions about how best to prepare ELL students for mainstream classes, even though we studied different populations at opposite ends of the country, and this chapter concludes with the comparison of these recommendations in Table 5.1. In chapter 6, we will take a closer and more personal look at three English language learners struggling and sometimes succeeding in a Tucson middle school.

SUGGESTED READING

For academic discussions of objectivism and experiential realism, see Lakoff (1987) and Johnson (1987). An extension of Lakoff and Johnson's ideas to the field of literary criticism can be found in Turner (1991). Good discussions of the social constructionist view are provided in two articles by Bruffee (1984, 1986). The classic thesis of how scientists construct knowledge is Kuhn (1973). A book-length treatment of how discourses differ in interpretive communities can be found in Gee (1996). Perfetti et al. (1995) is a readable discussion of learning from the perspective of cognitive psy-

TABLE 5.1
Recommendations for Effective Schooling of ELL Students

Valdés (2001)	Adamson (1993)
Schooling must build on the existing strengths of immigrant students, including language-learning and metacognitive strategies.	Academic strategies should be explicitly taught on an individualized basis.
Students must be offered ESL courses that are designed to develop the English-language skills needed for unrestricted access to challenging academic subjects.	Students can best learn strategies in a content-based course that uses authentic text that is studied in depth.
Schools must find a way to end the isolation of immigrant students.	The course should provide contact with native English speakers.
Students must be given access to the mainstream curriculum while they are learning English.	The content subject should be one that the students will need to know when they are mainstreamed.

chology. The definitive volume relating Vygotskian theory to education is the collection of articles in Moll (1990); the chapter by Moll and Greenberg describes the funds of knowledge project, and the chapter by Goodman and Goodman points out the similarities between Vygotsky's theory and the whole language approach to reading. The articles in Wertsch, Rio, and Alvarez (1995) discuss Vygotskian theory in relation to psychology, sociology, and anthropology. Lantolf and Appel (1994) provides a Vygotskian perspective on second language acquisition, and Frawley (1997) discusses the relationship of Vygotsky to cognitive science. Valdés (2001) tells the stories of six Hispanic students struggling in Bay Area schools. An article length discussion of Chinese American students living on the other side of the Bay can be found in Harklau (1994). This article is reprinted in Zamel and Spack (2002), a book that contains other interesting ethnographic studies of ELL students.

School and Family

H. D. Adamson
Ellen Courtney

INTRODUCTION

The research reported here was carried on over the course of a year by Doug Adamson and Ellen Courtney. Doug began the project during a spring semester and Ellen continued it in the fall. During that time, we visited classes at the middle school we call "Cholla" (pronounced CHOYA), interviewed teachers, and tutored the three Cortez children who are the focus of our study. Ellen's contributions and insights to the project were particularly important because she and her family lived in Latin America for many years and are bilingual and bicultural. Since our year at Cholla, much has changed because of the passage of Arizona's Proposition 301 (discussed in chap. 7), which severely limits a school's options for offering both English as a second language (ESL) and bilingual classes. Nevertheless, the program for English language learner (ELL) students that we observed at Cholla is still common in many districts throughout the country.

This chapter is offered as a case study that illustrates the opportunities and challenges that face schools enrolling substantial numbers of ELL students. Most of the students at Cholla were "at risk," and for them to learn and achieve in the unfamiliar academic environment that the school represented was no easy matter. Nor was it easy for the teachers to create an environment in which these students could succeed.

SCHOOL

Cholla Middle School, comprising Grades 6 through 8, is located in a Hispanic neighborhood in the south of Tucson that was once one of the nicer neighborhoods in the city. Favored with wide streets, old-fashioned street lamps, and southwestern Victorian style homes, it has a character that is so lacking in the stucco and tile housing units that have been thrown up since people started moving to the "sunbelt." There are some signs of urban decay in the neighborhood, with a few abandoned houses and trash-strewn lots, and at night cars cruise the streets thumping out rap music. Drugs and gang activity are problems, and homeless men camp out in the public park next to the school. But overall this barrio is spacious and clean—an open time capsule of the Old Pueblo.

Cholla is one of the oldest schools in the district, occupying an attractive campus with a historic, territorial-style building, which houses the main office, Principal's office, and classrooms, and a newer building containing classrooms and laboratories that are fitted with computers and other high-tech equipment. In Arizona, as in many states, schools are funded by property taxes from each school district, so schools located in richer districts have many amenities, whereas schools located in poorer districts (and especially on reservations) often lack basic necessities. (The Legislature recently changed this method of funding after the Arizona Supreme Court threatened to shut down all public schools, and the state must now pay to improve the physical facilities in all districts.) Cholla is not in a rich district, but it has adequate facilities, in part because the District chose Cholla to specialize in science teaching and has supplied it with computer laboratories, science equipment, and a staff that includes some first-rate science teachers.

Cholla draws from six elementary schools, each of which has a different ESL and/or bilingual program. It also accepts students who have just arrived from Mexico. As a result, entering students have differing levels of proficiency in Spanish and English. Students whose records indicate that they may have limited English proficiency are given a standardized test of written and spoken English. Students who are classified as English language learners (about 20% of entering students) are assigned to a mix of ESL, bilingual, and mainstream classes. Monolingual Spanish-speaking students take ESL for 3 hours a day along with a mix of bilingual classes, Spanish for native speakers, and mainstream classes, as their schedules allow. After each semester the ESL teachers, in consultation with content area teachers, decide whether a student should take fewer ESL courses and more mainstream courses. Cholla offers a traditional ESL program, such as the one in Fairview County described in chapter 5. There is no first language support for speakers of languages other than Spanish, but during the period of this study there were no such students attending Cholla. As we will see, Cholla boasts some teachers of formidable talent and impressive educational credentials (and, as in every school, some who are less qualified), as well as some excellent physical facilities. But the school faces major challenges. One goal of this chapter is to try to assess how well Cholla is meeting them.

A notable feature at Cholla is the triad system, in which the students in Grades 7 and 8 have the same teachers for science, English, and social studies. These teachers coordinate their syllabi so that the subject matter taught in one course is reinforced in another. For example, students doing a science fair project involving satellite mapping of Arizona might write biographies of rocket scientists in their English class and give a report on the settlement of different parts of Arizona in their social studies class. The system appears to work well and is popular with the teachers who participate in it. Unfortunately, many ELL students are pulled out of one or two of the triad classes in order to attend ESL classes, and thus are not fully a part of their peer group. This arrangement, however, is better than enrolling the students in all three of the content classes as they often struggle to keep up in just one. The ideal arrangement would be for the ESL class to coordinate with the content classes, but this is impossible because students from both grades may be in the same ESL class. Nevertheless, there is considerable communication between the ESL teachers and content teachers about the progress and problems of individual students.

A number of the teachers at Cholla informally classify the students as monolingual Spanish, bilingual, and monolingual English. The nature of the monolingual Spanish group has been changing in recent years, and this has been a cause for concern. These students are almost all new arrivals from Mexico. In past years, Mexican immigrants came mainly from urban areas with good schools, and thus were literate and numerant in Spanish. But recent arrivals have come from rural areas and do not have a strong educational background. Dr. Linda Clark, the Principal of Cholla, believes that this change in the composition of the student body is responsible for a recent drop in the scores on one of the standardized tests the district administers. This test contains both English and Spanish sections (the latter is administered only to students who have some knowledge of Spanish), and the scores on both sections have been falling, an outcome that has consequences for school funding. One language arts teacher, who normally offers individualized writing instruction organized around her students' interests, has been spending more time preparing her students for the grammar and punctuation questions on the test, and even the Spanish for native speakers teacher has been devoting class time to helping her students with basic English and preparing them psychologically for their inevitable poor performance.

Another problem involving the new arrivals is that many of their parents do not speak English, which makes communication difficult with the teachers who do not speak Spanish. In addition, students sometimes "disappear" for 2 or 3 months to visit family in Mexico. Although they may attend school there, they do not complete a full year in either system.

FAMILY

The Cortez family, with whom we worked, is a good example of a bicultural family that has ties in both the United States and Mexico. The family includes Mr. Cortez, Señora Beatriz (this is how we addressed them), and three children, Juan, age 14, Eva, age 12, and Joel, age 11. Mr. Cortez was born in El Paso, Texas, about 40 years ago and grew up in El Paso and Juarez, Mexico, just across the border. He attended both Mexican and American schools, including El Paso Community College. Spanish is his native language, and he speaks good English. Over the years, he has worked mainly as a cook, and several times tried to make a go of running his own Mexican restaurant, but these ventures have not worked out. At present he works in the landscaping business, holding down two jobs.

Señora Beatriz is from Chihuahua, Mexico, one of nine children. Most of her siblings live in Juarez, and the families visit each other frequently. Señora Beatriz was born on a ranch, but then moved to Juarez, where the schools were better. She left school after the sixth grade although some members of her family went on to higher education, and one of her brothers is a doctor. Señora Beatriz makes crafts at home, which she sells on weekends at the swap meet, usually accompanied by one or more of her children, who act as translators because Señora Beatriz speaks little English, although she understands a great deal.

The family is very religious, and their social activities center around their evangelical church, where services are conducted in Spanish. Spanish is spoken almost exclusively at home. The only use of English is among the children when they are reporting conversations in English or joking around. There are no newspapers or magazines in either language in the home although there is electronic entertainment. The radio is usually tuned to the Spanish evangelical station, and the family enjoys watching their newly acquired television, almost always tuned to one of the Spanish stations. Señora Beatriz shops at supermarkets and pharmacies where English is spoken. She can handle routine transactions in English but takes one of her children along if something must be discussed. Neither parent is able to help the children much with their homework: Mr. Cortez is seldom at home because he works so many hours, and Señora Beatriz has had too little schooling. However, she does monitor her children's activities and whereabouts. She might be characterized as a typical "mama latina"—caring and a bit controlling.

Juan was born in Albuquerque but lived in Juarez between the ages of 2 and 4. He has been schooled entirely in the United States and intends to stay in this country. Juan speaks excellent Spanish and good English. When he meets other American children, he begins a conversation in

English, but if they speak Spanish, he continues in that language because he feels more comfortable. Juan's interests include playing the guitar and sports. When playing basketball and soccer, Juan uses English. He doesn't have any Anglo friends and speaks Spanish just about everywhere except at school, where he usually converses with classmates in English, speaking Spanish only if he needs to. Juan is in the eighth grade and is taking all mainstream classes except for one period of ESL and Spanish for native speakers.

Eva is in the seventh grade and is taking all mainstream classes. Born in El Paso, she lived in Mexico between the ages of 1 and 3, but has attended only U.S. schools. She says that she started learning English at age 4 from a caretaker. Eva plans to return to Mexico to live because most of her extended family lives there. She has many bilingual friends and often code-switches, but if one member of the group speaks only one language, the conversation is limited to that language. Eva's interests include basketball (her favorite), soccer, bike-riding, skating, and playing the saxophone. The Christian Spanish station is also her favorite. At Fry's, the grocery store where her mother shops, Eva sometimes helps out monolingual Spanish speakers who need to ask a question in English. At school Eva uses both languages with her friends ("half and half"). With her teachers, she sometimes speaks Spanish in one-on-one situations because they want to practice their Spanish.

Joel is in the sixth grade. Born in El Paso, he lived the first two years of his life in Mexico. He started kindergarten in Tucson, and used only Spanish in school until the second grade, when English was introduced. Joel says he wants to live in El Paso. He usually speaks Spanish with his friends unless they speak only English. His activities include going to the park, attending church, and going to the swap meet. He loves to play the drums, and is about to start piano lessons with a Spanish-speaking teacher. At school Joel speaks Spanish with friends who speak that language and English with those who don't. Joel's English is the weakest of the three siblings, a fact that his mother attributes to his having lived in Mexico for the first two years of his life.

LANGUAGE CLASSES AND MAINSTREAM CLASSES

Juan is taking two language classes: Spanish for native speakers (usually called "Native Spanish") and Advanced ESL. A description of the two classes conveys some of the flavor of Juan's daily routine at Cholla and illustrates some of the points about language teaching that were discussed in chapter 3.

Spanish for Native Speakers

The Native Spanish course is taught by Ana Palacios, an intense woman in her 30s with an air of no-nonsense competence. A native of Mexico who speaks excellent English, Ms. Palacios also teaches bilingual social studies. The primary goal of the Native Spanish class is to teach literacy skills to students who speak at least some Spanish; these are usually students like Juan, who were educated in the United States. Another goal is to show students the difference between the Tucson variety of Spanish, which is heavily influenced by English, and the Spanish of educated Mexicans. Ms. Palacios must also pay some attention to basic structures and vocabulary because some of the students in the class are not proficient in Spanish.

The Native Spanish class described here was conducted entirely in Spanish. [The researchers' impressions and comments are enclosed in brackets.] Juan and the other students enter the classroom and take their seats at one of seven tables. There are approximately 30 students in the class. Ms. Palacios tells the students that they will have a few minutes to study their notes before taking a quiz. Juan sits at a table near the back of the classroom. His friend Miguel, whom we have also observed and tutored, is sitting at the table behind him.

Teacher: ¡Atención! (Everyone quiets down, but not completely.) La palabra 'atención', ¿Qué quiere decir? Hay que mirar a la maestra. *Attention! The word "attention," what does it mean? You have to look at the teacher.* (There is complete silence.)

Ms. Palacios begins the lesson with some mime and clowning. She holds up wrinkled pieces of paper and drops them on the floor.

T: Aquí abajo hay papeles. Por favor, la tarea. Aquí tiene, Señora. *Here on the floor there are some papers. (In a stage "teacher voice") Your homework, please. (Playing the role of a student) Here it is, Ma'am.*

Ms. Palacios picks the papers up off the floor; the students laugh. She sticks papers up her sleeves, in her shoes, in her pant legs.

T: La tarea, por favor. Por aquí está, Señorita.
Momentito, Momentito, sí la hice . . . yo me acuerdo que la hice. ¿Dónde la dejé? Si me acuerdo. Aquí está, Señora. *Your homework, please. (In her student's voice) It's right here, Miss. (She pulls papers from her sleeve) Just a minute, just a minute, I did it . . . I remember that I did it. Where did I put it? I remember. Here it is, Ma'am (she pulls paper from her pants).*

Ms. Palacios moves to the front of the class and mimes ironing the homework papers, while whistling. All the students are focused on the teacher.

T: Para poder calificarla, así. Así quiero la tarea. *To make it clear, this
            . . . (holds up a clean sheet of paper) this is how I want your homework.*
Student: ¿En blanco? *A blank paper?*
T: ¡No! Escrito con la lección. Papel planchado y almidonado. Con
            nombre y fecha. Van a entrar Uds. al salón y van a aprender como
            hacer las cosas muy bien hechas. *No! Written with the lesson. Paper
            ironed and starched. With name and date. You all are going to enter the
            classroom, and you're going to learn how to do things correctly.*

[This sketch was very effective. The students were attentive and, judging
from their laughter, thoroughly enjoyed the teacher's antics. The point was
very clear even to those who may not have understood all of the Spanish
words.]

Ms. Palacios then reminds the students of their general responsibilities
in her class: Don't chew gum, study, clean up your mess before you leave
the class.

T: Tienen diez minutos para estudiar y luego el examen. *You have ten
            minutes to study, and then we'll have the exam.*

Most students are studying their notes and a few are talking. The three boys
at Miguel's table are just fooling around. Ms. Palacios begins a quick review
by asking questions about the rules for dividing words into syllables. She
also reviews key definitions—dipthongos, vocales abiertas, vocales cerradas
dipthongs, open vowels, closed vowels. The students answer by reciting memorized rules in chorus. The teacher moves around the room to answer individual students' questions, occasionally including the whole class in an answer.

T: (To the whole class) ¿Cuándo no es un diptongo un diptongo?
            When is a dipthong not a dipthong?

Without raising his hand, Miguel calls out the rule [This is a breech of pro-
tocol because Miguel has not been called on]. Ms. Palacios scurries up to
him and shakes both his hands.

T: Chócala y chócala. *Put 'er there, and there.* [Miguel smiles, happy to
            receive positive attention.]
T: ¿Cuál es la regla para sílabas? *What is the rule for syllables?*
Students: (In chorus) Una palabra tiene tantas sílabas como tiene vocales y
           diptongos. *A word has as many syllables as it has vowels and dipthongs.*

T: ¿Cuáles son las vocales abiertas? *What are the open vowels?*
            The class recites them in chorus.

T: ¿Y las cerradas? *And the closed ones?*
            The class recites them.
            ¿Qué es un diptongo? *What is a dipthong?*
            There is a choral response.

Ms. Palacios does a quick review of how vowels are combined. She moves around to individual students who have questions. Some of the students are reciting the rules to one another; others, like Miguel, are fooling around. After several minutes, the class settles down and all the students are reviewing their notes or reciting aloud.

Ms. Palacios announces that the quiz is about to begin and the students should get ready.

T: Papel, lápiz, nombre, fecha. Tienen que estar listos para comenzar
            a 70 millas por hora porque va a tocar la campana. Tres preguntas.
            Paper, pencil, name, date. You have to be ready to start at 70 miles per hour
            because the bell is about to ring. (You should each answer) three questions.

Ms. Palacios then assigns each student a number from 1 to 4 and tells them to answer only the questions with that number. The purpose is to prevent cheating. As the quiz unfolds, however, it is clear that the students at each table could easily help one another. The teacher's aide then turns out the lights and projects the quiz on the board. There is silence.
Here is the exam.

EXAMENCITO

1. ¿Qué es un diptongo? *What is a dipthong?*
2. ¿Cuáles son las vocales abiertas? *What are the open vowels?*
3. ¿Cuáles son las vocales cerradas? *What are the closed vowels?*
4. ¿Cuándo no es un diptongo un diptongo? *When is a dipthong not a dipthong?*
(four more definition questions follow)
Dividan la palabra en sílabas: *Divide the word into syllables*
1. ESPIRITUALES
2. SIMPLEMENTE
3. CONSTANTINOPOLIZADOR
4. RECUERDE

The quiz ends after exactly 10 minutes, with some time left before the bell, which Ms. Palacios fills up telling stories, mostly about student behavior. She compares turning in poor homework to going to the cafeteria and being served a bad hamburger. Throughout Ms. Palacios' comments, the students listen attentively and laugh. The bell rings and before Ms. Palacios has finished talking, everyone stands up and leaves without saying goodbye.

FROM ELLEN'S FIELDNOTES:

The students clearly love this teacher, and, if they have ever studied in Latin America, where students recite memorized rules in chorus, her teaching style will be familiar. I am sure Ms. Palacios reminds her students of their teachers there, with her emphasis on learning rules by rote and on specific formal aspects of turning in work. In that sense, the students are well-served by having this teacher, who, in addition, is so full of fun. However, in this lesson, at least, too much emphasis was placed on matters of form and not enough on matters of substance—rule-learning at the expense of meaningful practice. The questions on the quiz mostly elicited the memorized rules recited moments before. There is only a single application of one of the rules, and the rules are not contextualized in any way. I guess this is what you would call the opposite of the whole language approach. Also, as in other classes I have observed at Cholla, a great deal of time is wasted, especially at the end of the class!

Advanced English as a Second Language

Mr. Young's ESL class provides both similarities and contrasts to Ms. Palacios' class. Ernest Young, a man in his mid-20s, has a clean-cut appearance that gives the impression of a business-like informality. He lives in a predominantly Hispanic section of Tucson, speaks excellent Spanish, and mixes with his students and their families at church socials and norteño music concerts. Mr. Young is the senior of the two ESL teachers at Cholla, and so has considerable responsibility for designing the ESL program, testing students for English proficiency, and assigning ELL students to an appropriate mix of classes.

As the students enter his classroom, chatting in Spanish, Mr. Young is writing on the board. When the bell rings, he raises his hand for silence. In response, the students raise their hands until the class is quiet. Mr. Young reminds the class that yesterday they wrote one-paragraph themes about their families, incorporating structures that he had provided. He has written a list of these structures on the board:

Topic sentence
Adjective sentence
When sentence
Restate topic

Mr. Young has also written on the board a paragraph about his own family, and he points out how he has incorporated the structures into his paragraph.

TOPIC SENTENCE

My family is the most important thing in the world to me.

ADJECTIVE SENTENCE

My wife and two children are very *loving* people.

WHEN SENTENCE

When I play with my 3-year-old son, I forget all of my problems.

RESTATE TOPIC

When I am separated from my family, I feel that my heart is breaking.

As Mr. Young reads this last sentence, some of the students groan.

Teacher: It's important to write with your heart (more groans).

On a board at the side of the room there are some suggested topics for other one paragraph themes, all of which relate to the students' personal interests and experiences. Mr. Young asks which topic the students would like to write about in class today. The winner is "my favorite food." Mr. Young instructs the students to write a paragraph about their favorite food, again using the structures listed on the board. The students begin to write.

FROM ELLEN'S FIELDNOTES:

The 18 students are seated at individual desks arranged in six rows of four desks each. Juan sits in the second row. The six students in the two rows nearest the teacher's desk get on task immediately. They work silently writing their paragraphs, occasionally calling on the teacher for help or asking each other for help. Juan asks me how to say "quesadilla" in English. ["Grilled cheese sandwich"? No—you can't say it in English.] A boy sitting in the first row has great difficulty getting started. His paper has only a title, *My favorite food*, for about 10 minutes. The boy sitting next to him has problems with spelling. He writes a number of words phonetically, "on till" (until). He later asks me how to spell "Thanksgiving," "force me," and "hate."

After 30 minutes, Mr. Young announces that time is up.

Student: ¿Mister, lo tenemos que leer frente a la clase? *Sir, do we have to read it in front of the class?*

Teacher: (Ignoring the question [probably because it was in Spanish]) Okay, now let's try something. Put your finger on your *when* sentence. Now write it on the board.

The students take about 5 minutes to write their sentences. Juan writes, "When I eat pizza I like whit a lot of chess." The noise level increases considerably, and Mr. Young raises his hand for silence. Mr. Young reads each sentence aloud, congratulating the students on their good ideas. He then calls on the class to suggest corrections in grammar, spelling, and punctuation for each sentence. Many of the students address him in Spanish ("¿Así, Mister? ¿Está bien?" *Like this, Sir? Is this good?*), and Mr. Young sometimes ignores them and sometimes answers them. To elicit punctuation corrections, he points to charts that are displayed next to the blackboard. After the *when* sentences have been corrected, the students write their adjective sentences on the board, and Mr. Young asks for corrections. Before the class has finished this task, the bell rings and all the students stand up and start putting away their things. Mr. Young quickly dismisses the students by rows. They leave. Only one student says good-bye to the teacher.

Ms. Palacios' and Mr. Young's classes provide some interesting comparisons. Mr. Young's class is more communicatively oriented as he asks students to provide information that he himself doesn't know. Although both classes focus mainly on matters of form, Mr. Young allows his students to use the required forms (*when* sentences, adjective sentences, etc.) in their own way, whereas Ms. Palacios requires her students to memorize definitions and rules without the opportunity to use them on their own. Ms. Palacios, however, provides a lot more target language input (which is important for those students who do not speak fluent Spanish): She speaks to the class at length and uses actions to make her meaning clear. Also, her class is a lot more engaging. Mr. Young does not talk much with the class, but moves from one activity to another with a minimum of explanation and instruction. Ms. Palacios' class is noisy with the target language. Mr. Young's class is quieter, and English is spoken mainly by the teacher. The students use only Spanish with each other and usually address the teacher in Spanish. Of course, Ms. Palacios has a much easier time getting the students to use the target language because it is the most comfortable language for most of them.

There is another important comparison between the two classes that so far has been mentioned only briefly: the matter of discipline, which can be seen in how each teacher handles the same student—Miguel.

Miguel goofs off in both classes—talking to his friends and ignoring the assignments—and both teachers allow him to do this as long as he is not too disruptive. But in both classes, Miguel goes farther and challenges the teacher. The challenge to Ms. Palacios is not too serious. Miguel calls out the answer to a question without raising his hand, but he gets the answer right. Nevertheless, Ms. Palacios does not just let this pass, nor does she rebuke Miguel, but rather makes a show of congratulating him. It's a joke, but it sends the message that a shouted answer will not just be ignored. Later in the class, Miguel calls out an answer again and is treated in the same way.

Miguel behaves a lot worse in Mr. Young's class. First he talks to his neighbor, and Mr. Young moves him to the rear of the class (this isolating approach is the opposite of Ms. Palacios's approach, which is to give Miguel positive attention), but Miguel continues to cause trouble, talking to the girls in front of him, laughing out loud, and walking around the room. Finally, Mr. Young asks Miguel if he has brought some requested materials. He hasn't and says he won't. Mr. Young says that he intends to speak to Miguel's mother about this, and Miguel shouts out his phone number, in effect saying "Go ahead and call." At this point, Ellen wrote in her field-notes: "I don't understand why the teacher ignores Miguel's disruptive behavior. I wonder what he can do about it within the school norms."

As we will see in the description of other classes, discipline is a continuing problem at Cholla. Scenes like Mr. Young's class where students shout to their friends, wander around the room, and directly challenge the teacher were not uncommon in the classes we observed. Visitors to Cholla, including college students who volunteer to tutor, are often shocked at what appear to be scenes of utter chaos. In fact, even in these classes, there is usually some structure and learning does take place. For example, although Miguel and other students acted up in Mr. Young's class, many students stayed on task. The experienced observer learns to ignore the background level of disruption and see the learning that is going on. But every teacher must have strategies for controlling students or true chaos will emerge, and we believe that these strategies are an integral part of how teachers structure their classes. Or, to speak more plainly, the possibilities for communicative teaching are limited by the constant need to control the students' behavior.

Ms. Palacios' effective strategies are rooted in the traditional way she teaches. Her lessons are teacher centered: She tells stories or leads the class in group recitation. These techniques by themselves do not guarantee that the students will stay on task, but Ms. Palacios' dynamic presentation and no-nonsense demeanor captivate the students' interest and focus their attention. During the class already described, Ms. Palacios did allow the students to work in groups at their tables, an activity that can lead to chaos, but because they had a specific and well-understood assignment (i.e., memorize rules and definitions for an upcoming test), they stayed on task. Several Cholla teachers mentioned that it is easier for them to maintain discipline when lessons are highly structured, so they do not allow much student creativity. This could well have motivated Mr. Young's writing lesson, which could be characterized as "controlled composition." His assignment allowed students to communicate original ideas, but only within a very structured framework, which included limiting the topics to those provided by Mr. Young. A more communicative technique would be to let each student select an individual topic of personal interest, but that would probably not work in Mr. Young's class because it would require him to work with individual students rather than with the class as a whole, a technique that could quickly lead to chaos among the unsupervised students. The need to maintain order effectively eliminated a more individual approach to teaching writing in this particular class and has fostered an emphasis on highly structured and less interactive teaching throughout the school.

Mainstream Language Arts

Eva is enrolled only in mainstream courses, including Ms. Wirthlin's seventh-grade language arts class, a triad class team-taught with the social studies teacher and coordinated with the science teacher. Ms. Wirthlin gives the impression of a young teacher with a great deal of experience and authority. She often allows her students some freedom in deciding what they want to study. For example, the students choose their own books for book reports and some books in Spanish are allowed. Ms. Wirthlin's way of teaching shows a marked difference from the two language classes just described.

The English–social studies class is currently studying Native-American culture and the lesson for today mostly involves watching a film on that topic. The students have already seen the first part of the movie in a previous class session. From the outset of the lesson, Ms. Wirthlin makes it clear to the 25 students in the class that they are expected to watch the movie carefully and thoughtfully because they will be writing about the film in the next class.

Right at the beginning of the lesson, Ms. Wirthlin displays the day's activities and reminders on the overhead projector:

1. Movie notes out
2. Turn in behavior essay (anyone want to read theirs?)
3. Talk about test on Thursday:
You will need your notes.
Two parts—essay and facts.

The teacher briefly explains item 3, which relates to the test scheduled for the following day.

> T: I will let you use your notes. . . . The first part of the test asks for facts: who was the movie about? what year? what is the conflict? who are the major players? The second part of the test is an essay, in the format of a persua-

sive essay about something you learned from the film. You will need to use
your notes on the movie to write the persuasive essay.

S: The conflict is the problem, right?

T: Yes, the conflict is the problem.

In this way, the teacher communicates a clear focus and purpose for viewing the movie, with specific tasks to be performed later on.

While the students are watching the movie and taking notes, the teacher
shows Ellen some of the students' work, which includes retelling Native-
American myths and writing their own "myths" using given words (*sun god,
rattlesnake*). She also explains some of the contracts that every student signs
spelling out what readings the student will complete during the semester.
These documents, together with the teacher's enthusiastic explanations, reveal the great emphasis placed on reading and writing in this course and on
the actual use of language for different purposes. The students read required and optional books, and they write reports on each book using a variety of formats with different focuses and tasks. For one book report, they
might write an essay; for another, a free verse poem. Finally, instead of
learning teacher-compiled lists of spelling words, the students create their
own weekly lists, with additions made by the teacher of any words misspelled in their essays. The students give each other spelling tests from
these personal word lists.

The students in Ms. Wirthlin's class behave well and stay on task during
the lesson. At only one point during the lesson do a few students start talking. The teacher counts to three, and there is silence. Thereafter, there are
no further instances of misbehavior, even though this group of students is
capable of unruly conduct: In a previous class, they behaved badly for a substitute teacher. We will suggest how Ms. Wirthlin is able to maintain discipline in the following discussion.

The challenge to critical thinking and the relentless emphasis on reading and writing practice in this mainstream language arts class contrast
sharply with the lessons we observed in Juan's Spanish and ESL classes, in
which the students either recited rules or produced required forms. The
students in Ms. Wirthlin's class enjoyed a great deal of freedom in the selec-
tion of writing topics, books to read, and personal spelling lists. In their assignments, the format or genre of the writing task, not a list of required
forms, provided the structure.

Only a year apart in age, Eva and Juan are experiencing very different access to English and academic discourse in their language classes. Eva's reading and writing capabilities are developing through frequent, varied, and
stimulating literacy experiences. Unfortunately, Juan does little reading or
writing for his language courses, either in Spanish or in English.

BILINGUAL CLASSES

Cholla is not one of the designated bilingual schools in the district and so does not offer a full bilingual program; however, it does offer a number of classes taught bilingually. The Cholla bilingual education (BE) program was set up by a team of teachers, using guidelines provided by the District, to take advantage of the bilingual personnel at the school. The program specifies a sequence of BE classes offered at each grade level but does not address the question of what method of BE teaching will be used, so teachers are free to use the two languages in their classes as they see fit. This eclectic arrangement is probably necessary because the Spanish proficiency of the BE teachers, as well as the Spanish and English proficiency of the students in any particular class, varies greatly. Before looking at some bilingual classes, let us listen to some of the opinions the BE teachers at Cholla expressed regarding their program and BE in general.

Interviews

Mr. Lorca is Joel's sixth-grade teacher. At Cholla, sixth grade is organized along an elementary school model with students staying with one teacher throughout most of the day. Mr. Lorca teaches his students math, physical education, social studies, language arts (the four monolingual Spanish speakers in Mr. Lorca's class are pulled out of language arts for ESL instruction), and exploratory. The exploratory segment covers different subjects (currently civil rights), emphasizing the use of technology. For example, the students might prepare oral reports on videotape or produce projects for presentation on a computer, complete with graphics and animation. Mr. Lorca teaches all of these subjects bilingually to some extent, when possible using bilingual textbooks. His usual teaching method is to switch back and forth between the two languages, a method necessitated by the fact that he has four monolingual English and four monolingual Spanish speakers in his class. Mr. Lorca also individualizes the instruction when possible, giving explanations and making assignments in the language in which the student can best understand the concepts. His students are a mixed group. In addition to the monolingual students, Mr. Lorca has 12 bilingual students (he places Joel in this last group). Four of the students (including two of the monolingual Spanish speakers) are also special education students, who are joined in Mr. Lorca's classroom for part of the day by a special education teacher.

Mr. Lorca is a supporter of BE (although he criticizes Cholla's lack of a more comprehensive BE model), and he emphasizes that it is important for teachers to share some of the culture and language of their students. For this reason, he occasionally uses some Spanglish and barrio language in his classes. He believes, however, that all the students in a bilingual class should be bilingual. As we will see, the wide range of his students' language abilities, as well as the necessity to cover the mainstream curriculum, makes it very difficult to teach at a level appropriate to all the students. Mr. Lorca also emphasizes that teaching in two languages requires a lot of extra work.

Mr. Lorca observes that Joel refuses to write in English in his class. He believes that Joel could do his assignments in English, but that he is afraid to try, and Mr. Lorca does not believe in pressuring the students. Some of Mr. Lorca's comments about Joel reveal a pattern we have come to expect when we tutor an ELL student: We often get to know the student better than does the teacher (who, after all, teaches up to 150 students per week), and we disagree with the teacher's assessment of the student. Ellen agreed with Mr. Lorca that Joel was a sensitive boy and something of an outsider. However, she disagreed that his English was good enough to handle all of Mr. Lorca's writing assignments.

Mr. Kingsly, Eva's math teacher, has tried a number of ways of teaching bilingually but is not satisfied with any of them. First he tried delivering his lessons in English and then covering the same material in Spanish, but he found that it took twice as long to prepare a class, and that the class only covered half as much material as a monolingual class. Then he tried teaching entirely in Spanish, but this did not work very well because some of the students were not fully proficient in Spanish. At present, Mr. Kingsly is not teaching any bilingual classes and uses English exclusively. He does, however, offer help to the Spanish dominant students by pairing them up with students more proficient in English. Although this arrangement tends to isolate the students working in pairs from the rest of the class, he says it can work fairly well provided the students cooperate. Sometimes, however, they just fool around.

Mr. Kingsly also mentioned that he has taken workshops in sheltered instruction, but that he doesn't think he could teach that way: It would require much extra work revising materials written for native speakers and would not cover the syllabus required by the district. In the end, Mr. Kingsly has arrived at a very conservative position. He disagrees with the district's policy of providing bilingual or Spanish instruction and thinks that given Cholla's limited resources, monolingual Spanish speakers should take a year of intensive English and then be placed in mainstream classes. This is the system that is now mandated by Arizona's Proposition 203.

Mr. Franco, Juan's social studies teacher, says that he has become disillusioned with academic discussions of BE because there is a disconnect between the ideal programs discussed in teacher training courses and reality. In the ideal program, students start BE in kindergarten, learn basic academic skills in Spanish, and then move on to English. But in practice,

BE programs don't always get kids in kindergarten: Some enter Cholla at age 12 or 13 with no English and are put in bilingual classes. The experts, he says, are not looking at reality. Mr. Franco also mentions the lack of direction in how to teach bilingually, which he attributes to the fact that school administrators don't know much about BE. A recent administrator told the teachers to teach in the students' dominant language; if that language was Spanish, it would be up to the ESL program to enhance the students' English skills. Mr. Franco has taught this way ever since, and he notes that the English–Spanish mix that he uses in the classroom is determined by the language abilities of the students in a particular class. If there are no monolingual Spanish speakers, he will use about 75% English, but if there are some monolingual Spanish speakers, he will use about 85% Spanish. Mr. Franco does not agree with Mr. Kingsly's strategy of paring a monolingual Spanish student and a bilingual student because it makes the ELL students very dependent and places too much responsibility on the bilingual student.

Mr. Franco also mentions the problem of the changing nature of Cholla's student population, with the recent increase in the Mexican students who lack academic skills. He says that these students often have trouble reading Spanish as well as English, and he notes that some of them have given up trying to read either language. He adds that both monolingual Spanish and bilingual students often lack background knowledge of American history, and so he now devotes 75% of his course to that subject, which will become increasingly important as the students move on to high school.

Mr. Franco speaks briefly about some differences of opinion he has with Mr. Young regarding language teaching. He says that Mr. Young works more with vocabulary and sentence structure, whereas he recommends more "phonetic teaching," adding that if he were teaching the Native Spanish class, he would emphasize grammar and pronunciation. In fact, Mr. Franco teaches quite a bit of Spanish in his social studies class, and often stops in the middle of a lesson to write out words phonetically for the students. He mentions the importance of a structured classroom for ELL students as a means of keeping discipline.

When asked what changes he would like to see at Cholla, Mr. Franco repeats Mr. Lorca's observation that all the students in a bilingual class should be bilingual. An even better system would be the dual language approach where all the teachers are bilingual, and monolingual Spanish and monolingual English students are mixed together, so that each group can help the other learn their language. This would eliminate the present tracking system in which ESL and some bilingual classes are taken only by Spanish-speaking students, who are thus separated from the monolingual English students for part of the day. This division creates a social gap between the students.

The bilingual teachers at Cholla have a broad range of opinions about how to teach bilingually, but all of those we interviewed are to some extent dissatisfied with the BE program as it now exists. We will return to a discussion of this problem at the end of this chapter.

Observations

Bilingual social studies.   We now take a look inside Mr. Franco's bilingual social studies class, which is currently studying geography. As the students enter the class, they find atlases and worksheets laid out on the tables. Mr. Franco calls the class to order by ringing a bell on his desk.

Teacher: Ahora, su atención aquí, por favor. *Now give me your attention, please.*

Mr. Franco rings the bell again. He moves a boy in a back seat to the front. He explains that the lesson today involves geography. The class is not yet quiet.

T: ¿Quién va a continuar hablando? *Who's going to go on talking?*

Mr. Franco threatens to add names to the detention list he has started on one side of the board.

T: Ayer estuvimos haciendo un ejercicio en las hojas de trabajo. *Yesterday we were doing an exercise on our worksheets.*

Mr. Franco writes on the board: Dónde está la tabla del contenido? *Where is the table of contents?*

T: ¿Qué explica allí? Levanten la mano para responder. *What does it explain there? Raise your hand to answer.*

Several students raise their hands. The atlases are in English and Mr. Franco provides a Spanish translation of important terms in the table of contents, pointing out that most of the terms are English cognates. He writes on the board:

physical = físico

T: Los que están en la clase de inglés como segundo idioma con el Señor Young ya deben de saber todos estos términos. Es un cognado. ¿Qué es un cognado? *Those who are in the English as a second language class with Mr. Young should already know all these terms. It's a cognate. What is a cognate?*

The students protest that they have never learned what a cognate is. Mr. Franco writes on the board: ¿Cognado? Palabras que suenan igual en I o E. *Cognate? Words that sound the same in E[nglish] or [S]panish.* He asks for examples, and the students supply *Africa, America,* and *chocolate.*

T: (to the student who said "chocolate") ¿Es que ya es la hora de la merienda? *What is this? Snack time?*

Mr. Franco continues to point out cognates in the table of contents, bringing in examples from other fields as well.

T: ¿Cómo se dice 'político' en inglés? Ésta es parte de aprender el inglés o el español. *How do you say "political" in English? This is part of learning English or Spanish.*

T: En geografía es muy raro que vayan a cambiarse los nombres. *In geography it's very rare for the names to change.*

Mr. Franco writes on the board:

Russia / Rusia
continent / continente
combustibles / combustibles

He reminds the class that yesterday a student had said he didn't know what the word *continent* meant, but he should have guessed because the Spanish equivalent is very similar. Mr. Franco then shifts the focus of the lesson from geographical terms to other subjects they have been studying.

T: ¿Cómo se dice la palabra "combustibles" en inglés? *How do you say the word "combustibles" in English?*

S: Combustibles. [Everybody laughs.]

Mr. Franco now uses English for the first time in the class.

T: Combustible is anything that will make a sudden explosion.

He writes on the board:

combustible: oil > petróleo
                      petroleum
              coal > carbón

T: ¿Quién puede explicar lo que es carbón? *Who can explain what coal is?*

A student begins to explain, but is drowned out by an announcement from the loudspeaker about a magazine drive.

T: Como dijo Alberto, lo usan carbón para echar al horno del tren. ¿De qué otro combustible estaban hablando? *As Alberto was saying, coal is used to put in the fire box of a train. What other fuel were they talking about?*

S: Gas natural. *Natural gas.*

Mr. Franco adds this term to the list on the board, noting that in Spanish the adjective goes after the noun.

T: Los americanos ponen todo al revés. Nosotros lo hacemos bien, donde va. Dicen "natural gas." *The Americans get it backwards. We do it right, where it goes. They say "natural gas."*

Mr. Franco's lecture is more of a language lesson than a social studies lesson, but it should be valuable to the students, who are learning to negotiate the interface between English and Spanish in an academic context because it emphasizes that many technical words in the two languages are cognates. Like the language classes described earlier, Mr. Franco's lesson focuses on the form of academic language rather than on content, and in this respect it also resembles some of the other bilingual classes we observed. Perhaps one reason for this emphasis is the fact (mentioned by all of the bilingual teachers interviewed) that preparing a bilingual content lesson requires a great deal of extra work. It is understandable that teachers sometimes lecture more or less informally about language rather than prepare a content lesson in two languages. The next class we observe, Mr. Matthews' eighth-grade engineering class, does focus primarily on content.

Bilingual engineering. Sam Matthews is a red-haired man of about 30, who has a degree in engineering from the University of Arizona. His wife is from Mexico, and they usually spend 1 or 2 months during the summer living in Guanajuato with his mother-in-law. Mr. Matthews speaks excellent Spanish though sometimes he has to ask his Spanish-speaking students to repeat things or slow down. The engineering class is not officially a bilingual class, but some of the students are not very proficient in English, so Mr. Matthews uses a good deal of Spanish in the class.

The class is doing a unit on accessing and manipulating databases that are available on the Internet. The classroom has been set up with six computer stations, each of which consists of a table with an Apple computer connected to the Internet, four chairs, and a project sheet that tells the students what activities to do at that station. There is a different project sheet at each station so that students, working in groups, can access the appropriate database and complete the project. After the students have finished one project, they move on to another station. Everything in the databases and on the worksheets is in English, but Mr. Matthews has written Spanish translations of important terms on the board. During the class, he walks around and answers questions, which are often asked in Spanish. He usually answers in English, but if he thinks the student will understand better in Spanish, he uses that language. He sometimes asks the Spanish-dominant students or the class as a whole how to translate a phrase or technical term into Spanish (even though they often don't know), thus conveying the message that Spanish has a place in the class and that he, too, is a language learner.

As Doug enters the classroom several minutes late, the students are sitting at the tables working on their projects. Mr. Matthews is at his desk at the front of the classroom talking to two students about their project. Doug pulls up an extra chair and sits down at a table with Tracy, Mazda, Jessica, and Ana, who are working on the computer and talking excitedly. Ana is at the computer controls, and it becomes apparent that she is the computer expert in the group. She is also the student with the weakest English, so the talk is mostly in Spanish, but because the project sheet is written in English, a lot of English vocabulary gets mixed in. The project sheet requires students to find and manipulate information about hurricanes that is contained on a Web site. The first question reads:

1. Hurricane Victor
   A. In what month and year did Hurricane Victor come ashore in Mexico?
   B. In what province did it come ashore?
   C. What states in the U.S. did it affect?

The answers to these questions are not provided in regular text. Rather, the students must bring up several satellite pictures of the hurricane and trace its progress across Baja California and into California and Arizona. The answers to the questions can be found by reading the information provided with each picture.

The girls talk and argue about the answers, mixing other topics into the discussion, such as who is dating whom, how their hair looks, and what they are doing after school. Practically all of this discussion is in Spanish. Ana is usually the one who brings the conversation back to the project. After the answers are agreed on in Spanish (with English words mixed in), they must be translated and written in English on the worksheet, and this is mainly

Mazda's job. Mazda asks Doug for help, and he shows the students the trick of using the words of the question in the answer.

> B. In what province did it come ashore?
> It came ashore in the province of Baja California.

One of the questions asks whether the eye of the hurricane was larger over water or land. The instructions require the students to bring up the four available photographs on the screen and measure the eyes with a ruler. The diameter of each eye in millimeters is to be entered on the project sheet. Ana is in charge of this operation and manages to bring up the required images without much help from her friends. Doug asks her what she is doing, and she explains in Spanish. Mazda produces a ruler, makes the measurements, and writes them on the project sheet (the eye is larger over water).

Although Mr. Matthews' class was not officially a bilingual class, we believe that a lot of acquisition of both languages took place. The conditions for language acquisition described in chapter 2 were all present in the class. The students in the group Doug observed used both languages to communicate about matters that were interesting to them. The meaning of what was spoken and written was clear to everyone because the girls were engaged in a collaborative project in which they all participated. The affective factors in the group were also optimal: The girls were all friends and if one of them didn't understand something, she did not hesitate to say so.

In addition to improving their language abilities, the students in both Mr. Matthews' and Mr. Franco's classes were learning content material, but we think Mr. Matthews' class was more effective for several reasons. First, Mr. Matthews' students were learning an obviously important skill, how to use computers, and that fact gave the class a sense of seriousness and rigor. Second, the quality of the instruction was very high. Notice that Mr. Matthews did little personal teaching; rather, the quality was contained in the interesting, real-world projects he had designed. Third, Mr. Matthews' class involved hands-on learning, where the students were actively engaged with electronic tools. The value of learning by doing has been known at least since John Dewey's time. Fourth, and most important, the material was not beyond the students' abilities. In Vygotskian terms, the students were working within their Zone of Proximal Development (ZPD). In fact, the group Doug observed was a good example of Moll and Greenberg's (1990) point (discussed in chap. 5) that a ZPD can be the property of a group as a whole. Ana knew more about computers and helped her friends understand how to access the Web site, but she received help from them in the area of English. One reason that all the students could engage material within their ZPD is that the learning was collaborative. There was plenty of give and take, trial and error, argument and clarification—opportunities that do not exist in a lecture class.

What about the matter of discipline? We have claimed that the need to control behavior works against individualized instruction and motivates teachers to walk the class in lock-step through lectures and mechanical exercises. Mr. Matthews' class was far from quiet, but the commotion was mainly that of exuberance. As in Ms. Wirthlin's class, the quality of the teaching and the rigor of the subject matter focused the students' attention and captured their interest. However, things did not always go smoothly, and sometimes chaos took over. When this happened, Mr. Matthews fell back on the technique that many of his colleagues had adopted as standard: He convened the class as a whole, reviewed his rules of conduct, wrote the names of disturbers on the board for future detention, and gave a lecture followed by a quiz. But these classes were the exception. In general, the students were eager to get to work on the projects Mr. Matthews provided, and many of them stayed after school to do more science in the science club that Mr. Matthews supervised. There, as in his classroom, English and Spanish mixed usefully in pursuit of real-world goals.

LEARNING

We now consider how two of the Cortez children, Juan and Joel, handle the task of learning unfamiliar and difficult academic material in a language in which they were not completely comfortable.

Juan Studies Chemistry

Juan is taking science from Mr. Daniels and has to prepare for a test on the periodic table of the elements and atomic structure. The course is taught bilingually to some extent, but the textbook and most of the worksheets are in English. The test will be entirely in English. The format of the course is lecture/discussion, followed by worksheets. There are few demonstrations or hands-on activities, and Mr. Daniels' tests reflect this expository approach to teaching; so, to pass the test Juan needs to learn abstract concepts from his notes and from the textbook. This task is made more difficult by the fact that he is not allowed to take the textbook home, a policy that holds for most of his classes. Asked why this was so, Principal Clark explained that textbooks are very expensive, costing as much as $75. She did not have to mention that if a book is lost, it would be impossible for many parents to replace it. Another problem is that many of the boys refuse to carry books home from school even when they are available. The taunt of "school boy" from classmates or cruising cars is a strong insult. Many Cholla teachers try to provide handouts and worksheets that duplicate textbook material, but these are not available in Mr. Daniels' class, so Ellen checked some chemistry books out of the school library to use in tutoring Juan.

We will quote at length from the tutoring transcript because it illustrates how a student learns in Vygotsky's ZPD when helped by a teacher. Juan has some background in atomic structure because he studied it in his science class the previous semester when Doug tutored him, and he understands how protons, neutrons, and electrons combine to form atoms. But he has not been able to understand from Mr. Daniels' lectures how atoms and atomic particles are related to the periodic table, and this is the main task of the session described here. Our comments regarding Juan's ongoing learning are in bold type, enclosed in brackets. The session begins at 7:15 in the evening. Ellen and Juan are seated at the dining room table in Juan's home. (In order to follow the lesson, the reader may wish to refer to the Appendix of this chapter for a short refresher on how to read the periodic table.)

Ellen: Well, what do you need to know for your test? The periodic table?

Juan: The neutrons because, um, ... those protons, and . . . . . today we were talking about the protons that they's the same that the neutrons, the same like 72 protons is the same as 72 protons [**Juan means neutrons**]. And, um, the teacher told me that, um, just I look up atoms, um, and isotopes and atomic mass and numbers and periodic table. That's gonna be about the test. [**Juan understands what he needs to know for the test, and he has some understanding of a central fact: Usually the number of protons and neutrons in a nucleus is the same. However, the fact that he mistakenly calls neutrons protons shows that he does not use this vocabulary easily. Furthermore, as we will see, he is not always able to apply this general proposition to answering questions about the structure of specific atoms. Juan also knows some of the terms that will be on the test:** *isotopes, atomic mass, and atomic number,* **but his knowledge is very sketchy.**]

E: That's what the test is going to be about? Okay, fine. Did you understand what we talked about last night?

J: Uh, huh. . . .

E: Do you understand what's in this picture (pointing to a picture of a helium atom)? [**Ellen moves from the abstract concept of nucleus to the concrete picture of a helium nucleus.**] Yeah? Um . . . let me just show you a couple of pictures, all right? . . . This is a helium atom. That's one of the elements, and, if you look at it, in the nucleus, how many protons are there?

J: Two?

E: Good. And how many neutrons?

J: Two? [**So far, so good. Juan understands that the number of protons and neutrons is equal in the example they have discussed.**]

E: What kind of charge do the protons have?

J: Positive.

E: Great. And what about the neutrons?

J: Negative.

E: Neutrons? [**Juan confuses neutrons and electrons.**]

J: Oh, no charge.

E: Right. Remember, *neutro*—neutrons. [**Ellen uses Spanish to reinforce a fact that Juan keeps forgetting.**] That's why they're called neutrons. Okay, where are the electrons?

J: The electrons are around the nucleus.

E: Good. And what kind of charge do they have?

J: Negative?

E: Perfect. Okay. Here are some keywords. Do you understand what an element is?

J: Um. . . . An element is like, uh, like the electrons?

E: [**Now Ellen moves into material that Juan did not study last year.**] No. Okay, look (pointing to the periodic table). The periodic table of the elements. All of these are elements. Each one of these is a different element. They're the basic substances that the whole universe is made of. So you've got helium, carbon, sodium, magnesium, all right? And each one of these is called an element. And in Spanish they're called *elementos*, which is exactly the same.

J: Uh, huh.

E: You understand what an *atom* is, right?

J: An atom is a, um, is, um, inside of the electrons? [**Juan is not clear about a basic term that he had known before, so Ellen goes back to a familiar example.**]

E: No. What does it say here?

J: The helium atom.

E: Okay, this is a picture of a helium atom (Ellen draws a rough picture bigger than the one in the book).

J: Uh, huh.

E: This is what they think a helium atom looks like, okay? Every atom has a nucleus with some electrons going around it.

J: Uh, huh.

E: But every element has a different-looking atom, okay? The atom for each element looks different. Some have three protons, some have four protons, some have three electrons, you see?

J: Uh, huh.

E: So if it looks like this, if it has two protons, two neutrons, and two electrons, that means that's a helium atom. Let's find helium here (Ellen points to the symbol for helium on the periodic table). That means helium. That's the formula. Okay, what does that mean (points to the atomic number for helium)? It has a two here. What does that mean?

J: Two protons?

E: And what does that mean (points to the atomic mass for helium)?

J: Five neutrons? [**Juan has misread the number, which is 4.003, or perhaps he incorrectly rounded it to a higher number. The remainder of the session involves getting Juan to understand the concept of atomic mass.**]

E: Well, is that what that means?

J: The number at the bottom is not, um, exactly the same because it has, um, extra. [**That is, the atomic mass is not exactly the same as the number of the protons and neutrons. Juan may be paraphrasing something Mr. Daniels said in class.**]

E: Okay, you're very smart. Is that the atomic mass?

J: Uh, huh.

E: Why is it about four?

J: Four.

E: Why is it about four? There's a good reason for this. (No response.) This is interesting, Juan. Look (Ellen points to oxygen on the periodic table indicating that the atomic mass is approximately twice the atomic number), for oxygen you have 8 and 16; (pointing to fluorine) 9, 18. How are they alike? What do you see there?

J: Um, that the neutrons are the same as the protons? [**This doesn't answer the question, but it is a true statement. Juan may be using a coping strategy that usually gets partial credit on a quiz.**]

E: Okay. Why?

J: Ummmm. . . .

E: This is the number of protons.

J: Uh, huh.

E: This is approximately the mass, right?

J: Uh, huh.

E: Why is this [**the atomic mass**] twice this [**the atomic number**]? Why is this two times this? (No response.) He's gonna ask you this on the quiz tomorrow. (No response.) Okay, let's go back to our helium, okay? Remember, this is helium (pointing to the hand-drawn helium atom). How many protons does it have?

J: Two?

E: Okay, point to them. Where are they?

J: Here.

E: Right. Are they the black ones? Yeah, the two black ones. Okay. How many neutrons?

J: *Uno?* Neutrons? Two?

E: Good. Okay. Now, how much mass does that whole nucleus have?

J: 4.003?

E: Yeah. Why? . . . Why is this (pointing to 4.003, the atomic mass) twice this (pointing 2 to the atomic number)? *¿Por qué es el doble de esto?*

J: It's **[i.e. the atomic mass]**the mass of the . . . it's the mass of the pro-tons and neutrons? **[Juan provides an acceptable answer.]**

In the remainder of the tutoring session, Ellen asks about the relationship of atomic mass and atomic numbers for other atoms, and Juan gets them right, reading from the periodic table. As part of the lesson, she tries to re-late the abstract notion of an element to something Juan knows.

E: This symbol [pointing to Ca on the periodic table] means calcium. You know what calcium is, don't you? What kind of food can you find calcium in?

J: Um . . . In vegetables?

E: I think so. It's also in milk. That's why we always give babies lots of milk so they get nice teeth and bones. So that's what calcium is.

The tutoring session shows that Juan has the background knowledge to learn to read the periodic table, but that he does not understand the tech-nical terms and their relationships well. He is working in the ZPD. In order to teach Juan these relationships, Ellen first reviews the basic concepts of atomic structure. Then she uses the familiar example of the helium atom to show how these concepts are related to the new concepts of atomic number and atomic mass. The textbook and the teacher's lectures were enough to orient Juan to this material, but he remained confused until a tutor could probe his understanding of atomic structure and then relate it to the new concepts. In the case studies reviewed in chapter 5 (Adamson, 1993), Doug found this pattern of imperfect learning time and again when ELL students were confronted with material within their ZPDs but had no tutor or more advanced peer who could help them to understand the material.

Joel Studies History

The notion of the ZPD is important for understanding why Joel was failing Mr. Lorca's American history unit. As we have seen, Mr. Lorca teaches bilin-gually, so Joel had some first language support, but he lacked the English vocabulary and background knowledge to understand the required English texts, even with this support. First, let us take a look at a passage from Joel's textbook *Taming the West*.

Millions of Acres

Together, the two railroad companies had laid almost 1,800 miles of track. For each mile of track, the government had given the railroad companies ten square miles of land to sell. The companies advertised all over the East for settlers. They sent agents to Europe to spread news of cheap land for sale in America. Many thousands came. The rush to settle the plains had begun.

In 1862 Congress passed the Homestead Act. Under this law, any person could have 160 acres of land free if he or she built a house on the land and lived there for five years. This brought thousands of people from the East and from Europe. As these people soon found out, life on the vast and windswept plains was far from easy.

The daring men and women who settled the plains had to find new ways to

—build houses
—find water
—farm the land
—protect their crops
—plow the soil

New inventions helped the pioneers solve some of the problems. The pioneers had to find the solutions to other problems for themselves.

Now consider how Joel did on a true or false test that covered this and other material.

Practice Quiz

x   1. __F__   The first people that migrated to North America came from Europe.

     2. __T__   The frontier separated the colonies in the East from the wild, unsettled West.

     3. _____   In 1848, gold was discovered on the Great Plains.

     4. __T__   The area between the Missouri River and the Rocky Mountains was an "ocean of grass."

     5. __F__   It was easy to settle in the plains because there were a lot of trees there, and the climate was beautiful.

     6. __T__   Pioneers were brave people who crossed the frontier to settle in new territory.

x   7. __T__   A blizzard is a violent wind that picks things up.

     8. __T__   People called the plains the Great American Desert.

x   9. __T__   The earliest settled area was the Central Plains.

x 10. __T__   Europe is in North America.

Joel got only five correct answers, no better than chance. The textbook was simply too difficult for him, as is apparent in the transcript of the tutoring session that follows, where Ellen tried to fill in the large gaps in Joel's knowledge.

Ellen:	What's this about (pointing the subtitle *Millions of Acres*)?
Joel:	How to make houses in a . . . [**Joel is referring to the next section in the book. He may not understand the word *acres* and be relying on his memory of Ellen's reading the text to him. Ellen tries to see if that is the problem.**]
E:	Well, what are acres?
J:	No response.
E:	*Es una medida de terreno.* It's a unit of land. So, is this about houses?
J:	Houses.
E:	No.
J:	How make a city? [**Joel is referring to another section of the textbook.**]
E:	What do they need first?
J:	To find the land. [**This answer shows that Joel is not completely lost. He understands generally what is involved in settling the plains, and can answer a question based on logic.**]
E:	How did they get it?
J:	Measurements?
E:	But how did they obtain the land? (Ellen points to the relevant sentence in the book.) [***Obtain* is a cognate of Spanish *obtener*. Ellen is trying to make sure Joel understands the question.**]
J:	(Reads) "The government had given the railroad companies ten square miles of land to sell."
E:	(Paraphrasing the next sentence) And the railroad companies advertised for settlers. So, how did the settlers get the land?
J:	No response.

In the end, Joel is unable to understand how ownership of the land was transferred from the government to the settlers, just one concept among many he needed to learn. Ellen commented:

> It made me sad to see how hard Joel was trying and how difficult it was for him. He lacks the background knowledge and the linguistic knowledge to handle this type of reading. I am hard put to help Joel develop strategies for understanding reading that is this difficult for him. He is interested and enthusiastic—unlike Juan and Eva, actually—and it is tragic that he should be failing because the work is beyond him.

Other tutoring sessions (one of which is quoted in chap. 1) reveal that understanding the American history text is beyond Joel's ZPD because he lacks knowledge assumed by the text, including where Europe is located, and what a blizzard is (which is not surprising for a Tucson kid). Like the college student Robbie, discussed in chapter 5, Joel needs to build up a schema of basic facts and relationships about geography and history before he will be ready to do the assignments in Mr. Lorca's class.

Joel's struggle in social studies contrasts with his success when asked to do a task in English that he can handle. Ellen felt that a Language Experience lesson (see chap. 3) would be appropriate for Joel, so she asked him what he did to celebrate his recent birthday and wrote down what he said:

> I went to the park and had a cake and went around the park. We go to the store to buy the presents, like a watch and roller skates. We got home at 6:30 p.m. My Grandpa and my grandma went to my party.

Ellen then asked Joel to read the text once out loud and once silently. Then she dictated the text to him and asked him to write it. He wrote the following:

> I went to tha park and gaf a cake and guent aron the park. Why go to the store to by the presen like kuach and rodo kist. Why got home ant 6:60 p.m. my grapa and my grama gent to my party.

CONCLUSIONS

In summarizing the Cortez children's home situation (and by extension that of many other ELL students at Cholla), we noted both strengths and weaknesses. A major strength is the strong ties within both the nuclear and extended families. This unity is further strengthened by the family's active religious commitment. The church provides many activities that bring the Cortez family together as well as an association with other Hispanic families, and thus an opportunity for *confianza*. On the other hand, the Cortez household does not provide academic support for the children. We observed no books or magazines in the home. The father cannot help the children with schoolwork because he has to work such long hours, and the mother has had little formal schooling and does not speak English.

In regard to the situation at school, this case study shows how different individual students can be in their acquisition of English under very similar circumstances and how this fact creates difficulties for the school. How can the school provide an effective education to students with such different needs as Joel and Eva? We found that generally Cholla provides a good education for monolingual English speakers and for ELL students with high English proficiency. However, for students with low proficiency we observed only partial success. In some classes, all ELL students were able to learn appropriate and meaningful content material, and along with it the conventions of academic discourse. But in other classes these students had to resort to coping strategies: mechanically repeating answers and producing worksheets and exercises that they did not fully understand.

A major obstacle to learning for the Cortez children was that they were not allowed to take books home (and when we mention this fact to parents in more affluent districts, they are shocked). At the same time, the school does have some excellent facilities, as we saw in the description of Mr. Matthews' class. Should the school let students take their books home and spend its money replacing them instead of buying computers? It is difficult to say (and it should be noted that often the money to buy computers and books comes from different pots and cannot be mixed), but it would probably be best to keep buying computers and other high-tech tools since that is a real strength at Cholla, which makes it possible to attract great teachers like Mr. Matthews. However, the problem of providing materials for study at home should be acknowledged and addressed by the school. Perhaps teachers could be encouraged to produce transportable study materials (and supported in this effort by a reduced teaching load) that could be shared in several classes and used for several years.

We have also noted the problems with classroom management and maintaining discipline, and how it limits the possibilities for badly needed individualized instruction. We think this problem is something of a skeleton in the school's closet because for a teacher to admit that discipline is a problem is to admit a shortcoming as a teacher (and, indeed, some teachers like Ms. Palacios do not have major discipline problems). We do not have a proposal for improving discipline at Cholla (or even for dealing with the increasing incivility in our own college classrooms) except to say that the principal must address the problem and that it must be a high priority.

The major challenge to the school is to provide high quality academic instruction at an appropriate level for its ELL students. We saw that Ms. Wirthlin's and Mr. Matthews' classes provided a rich language experience, but both of these were mainstream classes, not specifically designed for ELL students. Mr. Matthews did a good job organizing his projects so that students with very limited English could take part, but this is much easier to do in a science course with its possibilities for hands-on projects than in a language intensive course. We have seen that Joel could not learn the material taught expositorially in his social studies class even with tutorial assistance.

A major strength of the school was the presence of a number of bilingual and bicultural teachers, such as Mr. Lorca and Ms. Palacios. It was clear that these teachers, as well as the Anglo teachers we observed, valued the students' home language and culture and that this attitude had a positive effect on the Cortez children. We note, however, that communication between the school and the Cortez parents was not good, and that ideally bilingual teachers might contact parents who have been out of touch.

Sadly, the BE program at Cholla was not working well, and we have suggested several reasons why this was so. One problem was that the program was haphazard. There was no clear bilingual stream, just a collection of courses that students might or might not take depending on what fit their schedules during a particular semester. A more serious problem was that students of all language abilities were put in the same "bilingual" class. So, Mr. Lorca had monolingual English speakers as well as students like Joel with very poor English. The result was lessons in English at grade level for the better English speakers but beyond Joel's ability. Worse, these lessons were not well-supported by work in Spanish because such lessons would require Spanish above the level of the monolingual English speakers (and, as Mr. Lorca pointed out, he would have to write the lessons himself, an impossible task for an already overworked teacher). Furthermore, there was no consistent method of bilingual teaching, nor direction from the school administration. As we have mentioned, this eclectic approach was probably necessary because of the very different language abilities of the students in the various bilingual classes (and, in fact, the low level of Spanish ability of some of the "bilingual" teachers). Putting students of the same level of Spanish ability in the same class would better allow teachers to offer the kind of rich language experience in Spanish that Eva enjoyed in English.

Mr. Lorca's class illustrated a widespread problem within the school: There was little articulation between the ESL program and the mainstream programs. Eva was doing well despite this lack: She transferred from ESL to the mainstream without serious problems. But Juan and Joel needed some bridge courses, such as a sheltered course where grade-level material (like Joel's social studies lesson) was covered at a slower pace and with a lot of help with background knowledge and academic skills. Even better would be an adjunct course (perhaps taught bilingually) connected to one of the triad courses. Our tutoring sessions provided Juan with support within his ZPD, which allowed him to understand demanding science material, but this support ought to be provided by the school in the form of a course appropriate to his level. However, when we suggested setting up such a course to Dr. Clark and several teachers, they pointed out a serious objection. They observed that a major challenge at Cholla is integrating the Anglo, Chicano, and Mexican immigrant students at school. Other schools in the district have seen tension among these groups that has led to animosity and violence. Thus, the Cholla faculty wants to reduce the isolation of ethnic groups as much as possible, and a sheltered or adjunct course would enroll mostly Mexican immigrants with some Chicanos like Juan and Joel. We believe, nevertheless, that learning should be the main goal of the school, and that some bridge courses are necessary if students are not to fall through the cracks. Perhaps there would be other ways to reduce isolation, such as a dual language program (see chap. 7), where Spanish and non-Spanish speakers met together to learn two languages without the necessity of covering grade-level material (as Mr. Lorca had to do), so that instruction could be geared to the language learning needs of both groups.

We will close this chapter by emphasizing that in our year at Cholla Middle School, we observed and participated in many excellent classes, where we saw a lot of learning taking place. These classes had several things in common. Perhaps most important was the fact that matters of academic substance prevailed over matters of form. Also, in these classes the teacher had a clear agenda of the material to be learned during the semester and during each class session, and the students were often reminded of these objectives. This emphasis on academic goals created an atmosphere of seriousness and engagement and improved classroom discipline. Also, the effective classes we observed featured experiential rather than expository teaching. For example, in Juan's seventh-grade science class (not previously discussed), daily activities always included experiments and demonstrations, in addition to reading and discussion. In one unit, students at each table had to follow instructions to connect circuits in series and parallel and to report on the differences in how these circuits worked. Juan did much better in this class than in Mr. Franco's science class, where he mainly had to read the textbook and answer questions. As we have mentioned, it is easier to teach science than English experientially, but Ms. Wirthlin did a good job by using films, inviting speakers, and giving the students some freedom to choose projects of their own interest. Another feature of the excellent classes we observed was that there was a great deal of small group and individual work. As we saw in Mr. Matthews' class, a well-working group allows individual students to participate according to their own strengths and interests. Finally, we observe that many effective teachers used Spanish with individual students and, to some extent, with the entire class, when it would help to make a meaning clear.

SUGGESTED READING

Agar's (1996) classic, *The Professional Stranger: An Informal Introduction to Ethnographic Research,* is an excellent place to get a feel for doing the kind of research described in this chapter. The ethnography of speaking, with reference to second language acquisition, is discussed in Saville-Troike (2003). The articles in Spindler and Spindler (1987), though dated, provide an overview of the possibilities of school ethnographies in settings throughout the world. A similar collection that focuses on bilingual contexts in the United States is Saravia-Shore and Arvizu (1992). Book-length discussions of research in second language classrooms include Chaudron

(1988), Nunan (1992), and van Lier (1988). Readers who wish to do case studies research, perhaps in their own classes, can profit from a book on descriptive and ethnographic field methods. My favorite is Patton (1990) though Richards (2003) is also excellent and focuses on ESL classrooms. Yin (1984) is a good introduction to case studies research. Johnstone (2000) provides a short general introduction to field methods. Harklau (1994), reprinted in Zamel and Spack (2002), is a good account of how well ESL programs prepare ELL students for mainstream courses. The Zamel and Spack volume, titled *Enriching ESOL Pedagogy: Readings and Activities for Engagement, Reflection, and Inquiry*, is a collection of important articles relating language teaching theory to practice. Adamson's *Academic Competence: Theory and Classroom Practice* (1993) provides more examples of case studies research based on tutoring ELL students in content courses.

APPENDIX: A REVIEW OF THE PERIODIC TABLE OF THE ELEMENTS

The periodic table of the elements is a listing of the 109 known elements arranged according their atomic numbers. The atomic number represents the number of protons in each atom's nucleus. For example, the atomic number of helium is 2 since it has two protons. Protons carry a positive electrical charge. The nucleus of an atom also contains neutrons, which have no charge. The number of neutrons in a nucleus is equal to the number of protons (except for isotopes), so the helium atom contains two neutrons. Electrons are negatively charged particles that orbit around the nucleus. An atom usually has the same number of electrons as protons, so helium has two electrons.

The periodic table also gives the chemical symbol of each element: The symbol for helium is He, the symbol for boron is B, and so on. In addition, the table tells the atomic mass of each element. Protons and neutrons each have an atomic mass of 1, so the atomic mass of helium (with 2 protons and 2 neutrons) is approximately 4. However, as the section of the table displayed shows, the exact atomic mass of helium is 4.003, slightly higher than 4. The reason is that there exist isotopes of helium. An isotope is a rare helium atom that does not contain four particles in the nucleus, but may contain 2 protons and 3 neutrons, so that it has an atomic mass of 5. All elements have isotopes with higher atomic masses than the standard atom, and the atomic masses of these isotopes are averaged in when the atomic mass for the element as a whole is calculated. Thus, all atomic masses are fractionally higher than the figure produced by adding the atomic weights of the protons and neutrons in the standard atom. One point that Ellen is trying to make in her lesson with Juan is that the atomic mass of any element is approximately double its atomic number.

Section of the Periodic Table of Elements

13 IIIA	14 IVA	15 VA	16 VIA	17 VIIA	18 VIIIA
					2 **He** Helium 4.003
5 **B** Boron 10.811	6 **C** Carbon 12.011	7 **N** Nitrogen 14.007	8 **O** Oxygen 15.999	9 **F** Fluorine 18.998	10 **Ne** Neon 20.18
13 **Al** Aluminum 26.982	14 **Si** Silicon 28.066	15 **P** Phosphorus 30.974	16 **S** Sulfur 32.066	17 **Cl** Chlorine 35.453	18 **Ar** Argon 39.948
31 **Ga** Gallium 69.723	32 **Ge** Germanium 72.61	33 **As** Arsenic 74.922	34 **Se** Selenium 78.96	35 **Br** Bromine 79.904	36 **Kr** Krypton 83.80

12
IIB

30
Zn
Zinc
65.38

7

Bilingual Education

INTRODUCTION

Bilingual education (BE) is probably the most controversial educational program in the United States. Whereas New York and Texas are trying to attract bilingual teachers and expand programs, California, Arizona, and Massachusetts have banned BE unless it is specifically requested by parents, and anti-BE proposals have been introduced in other states.

One way to think about BE is to imagine that a large number of American families were forced by economic circumstances to move to Germany. What kind of schooling would we want for the children or our expatriate men and women? Certainly we would want them to become fully fluent and literate in German. But we wouldn't want them to forget English. It is a language of great cultural riches, a valuable professional asset and, of course, the language of their family and heritage. Nor would we want these children to fall behind in learning science, mathematics, geography, and other subjects, as they would if they were placed in German as a second language classes for a year or two or, worse, put in regular classes, where they could not understand the teacher or read the textbooks. It would seem reasonable to continue a part of the children's education in English while they were learning German. This is essentially the position of BE advocates who couch their argument along the following lines: (1) BE helps to ease the home–school transition. (2) BE allows students to learn the background knowledge and study skills necessary for academic work in any language. (3) BE allows students (and their new country) to preserve a valuable resource, that is, fluency in a second language (L2).

However, if American expatriates were to propose that the German government set up a program in English for their children, we might expect some objections, and they might sound like those of journalist Noel Epstein (1977), which were quoted in chapter 1:

> Is the *national government* responsible for financing and promoting attachments to ethnic languages and cultures? Would federal intervention result in more harmony or more discord in American society? Would it lead to better or worse relations between groups? . . . Greater separation or integration? (p. 70).

To gain more of an international perspective on the BE debate, let us take a look at how some other countries educate their language minority students.

BILINGUAL EDUCATION ABROAD

The Netherlands

Frisian is a Germanic language spoken by about 850,000 people in the Friesland Province of the Netherlands. It is closely related to English, and studying Frisian can give English speakers a taste of what it is like to study a foreign language similar to their own, as when Catalans study Spanish or Swedes study Danish. A book of Frisian phrases yields the following examples:

1. Do kinst hjir wol ite.
    You can here well eat.
    [You can eat well here.]
2. Wolst do suker yn 'e tee?
    Want you sugar in the tea?
    [Do you want sugar in the tea?]
3. Ja, it hus is fol.
    Yes, the house is full (Kramer, 2001).

Like many language minority speakers, Frisians grow up exposed to the national language, in this case Dutch, in the schools and the community and become bilingual at an early age. Also like many language minority speakers, they wish to preserve their language and promote its use in public venues within Friesland. To this end, a Frisian language academy was established in 1938 and charged with standardizing Frisian grammar and spelling and producing a dictionary, and since 1980, the study of Frisian has been obligatory.

In the early 1920s, an experiment was conducted to test the educational advantage of using Frisian as the language of instruction in the first years of school (Fasold, 1984). Three groups of students were studied: Group 1 used mostly Frisian in kindergarten and both Frisian and Dutch in Grades 1–3 (in the United States, this would be called *early exit transitional BE*). Group 2 studied predominantly in Frisian in kindergarten but switched to Dutch thereafter (this is very early exit transitional BE). Group 3 used some Frisian but mostly Dutch in kindergarten and only Dutch thereafter (this is one version of *structured immersion*, the method required by law in California and Arizona, where the student is immersed in the L2 but allowed limited use of the first language [L1]). The study also included a control group of native Dutch-speaking students who learned only in Dutch.

Each group was tested annually in Dutch on reading, composition, oral proficiency, grammar, and arithmetic. After one year, the students in Group 1 had the lowest scores; however, by the end of the third year there was no difference in the scores of the three groups. Thus, L1 instruction initially slowed acquisition of the L2, but over time this effect disappeared. Later in the chapter, we will see the same effect in some U.S. bilingual programs, where after 6 years, the bilingually educated students caught up with and, in fact, surpassed the native English speakers on standardized tests in English.

The circumstances of the Frisian bilingual program are unusual. Perhaps because the Frisian-speaking community is so small, all Frisian speakers become bilingual, with or without the aid of BE. Furthermore (and this is unusual for a small speech community), Frisian is not in danger of disappearing, and though Frisians view the central government of Holland as heavy-handed and overbearing, there is no active independence movement, as there is among language minority speakers in many countries, such as Canada and Spain.

Sweden

Sweden is the site of much research on BE that has been referred to in debates in the United States. Sweden differs from some European countries (and resembles the United States) in that it does not have guest workers. By contrast, Germany has hundreds of thousands of foreign workers, mainly from Turkey, Italy, and Spain, who are permanent residents but cannot easily become citizens of Germany.

Sweden officially encourages immigration for the same reason as most industrial countries: It needs workers. (The United States, e.g., has lifted visa restrictions on foreign workers in high-tech industries, a move that was opposed by American labor unions). Official Swedish immigration policy is progressive. Its goals are to create equality, partnership, and freedom of choice for immigrants, and bilingualism is a national educational goal. To reach this goal, Sweden provides for three types of educational programs for immigrant children (Fasold, 1984):

1. Mainstreaming, the most common type, where children are placed in courses with Swedish native speakers. Sometimes instruction is provided in Swedish as a second language, and tutoring in the native language or in Swedish is provided for content subjects.
2. Transitional BE, where content subjects are offered in the mother tongue.
3. Maintenance BE, the least common type, where full bilingual support is provided throughout all or most of the grades.

The largest group of immigrants to Sweden are Finns, and in some border areas many Finnish speakers are native-born: Their ancestors became Swedish citizens when the border between Sweden and Finland was redrawn. This ethnic minority is comparable to the Chicanos of the American Southwest, whose ancestral homeland was annexed by the United States in 1848 following the Mexican War. Another similarity between the two groups is that in both cases, there is considerable movement back and forth across the international border, causing disruption in the education of language minority children.

Despite the official policy, there is prejudice against Finnish and other immigrants in Sweden. For example, the City Council of Haparanda, a town near the Finnish border, forbade the staff in day-care centers to speak Finnish. According to the Swedish-American linguist Christina Bratt Paulston (1994), most Finnish parents desire their children to maintain their native language and culture, but most Swedes desire them to assimilate. As is often the case in these circumstances, the children do assimilate, regardless of the parents' desires. Among ninth graders, over half of immigrant children speak Swedish with their parents always or often (Paulston, 1994, p. 70). This situation is also reminiscent of the American Southwest, where immigrant families typically lose their ability to speak Spanish within three generations, but the language is maintained in the community by the constant influx of new arrivals.

Quebec

French is the official language of Quebec Province, and it is strongly protected. When my wife and I drove to Quebec one summer, we stopped at the tourist information office just over the border to inquire about campgrounds. But the man on duty hardly spoke any English and, though very nice, wasn't much help. I strongly suspect that Quebeckers entering New York State find personnel of comparable bilingual skills in the American information office, and that this is the point the Quebec office is making. When visiting Montreal, I was curious to see how public places like department stores handled both English- and French-speaking customers. I found that the signs were almost all in French, with a few English translations. Walking around the store, I heard conversations between salespeople and customers in both French and English. Some counters seemed to specialize in one of the languages, and I could easily get help by approaching a clerk whom I heard speaking English. (This is pretty much how it works in south Tucson with English and Spanish. My own informal survey revealed that the clerks direct customers who need help in Spanish to the best Spanish speaker on duty.)

In Quebec Province, Canadian children who began their education in English in another province, or whose parents attended English schools in Quebec, can attend an English school, a French school, or a bilingual immersion school (bilingual immersion will be described later). All other immigrants to Quebec, whether from other Canadian provinces or from abroad, must enroll in French schools, as must non-French-speaking Quebec natives, including speakers of Native American languages. These schools do not provide BE. English and other foreign languages are introduced in the fourth grade.

In the city of Montreal, there are two separate school systems that receive public funds: the Catholic system and the Protestant system. The Protestant School System of Great Montreal (PSSGM) offers a good bilingual immersion education program for English-speaking children. In 1995, 32% of the school population was enrolled in the program (Schauber, 1995). There has been a problem finding qualified bilingual teachers, and the PSSGM recruits from as far away as North Africa. The textbooks, however, are not imported from other Francophone areas, but are written specifically for Quebec. The bilingual immersion education program employs the structured immersion method of teaching. Students are immersed in French from the first day of kindergarten until the end of the second grade, though teachers are allowed to use some English on an individual basis to facilitate understanding, and students are allowed to respond to questions in English. To encourage students to use French among themselves, some areas of the school are designated as "French only" zones, and students caught using English there can be fined. The method of teaching in French is similar to the Natural Way and the whole language approach, with a focus on presenting understandable and interesting input in French. Typical activities include reading stories (well-illustrated or acted out), group writing projects, and field trips. French grammar is not emphasized, and accuracy is not insisted on at first. An important element of the program is that parents are contacted often and involved in motivating and helping their children. English is gradually incorporated into the program after Grade 2: 40% in

Grade 3, 60% in Grades 4–6, and 80% (just one class in French) through Grade 11, the final year of high school.

Graduates of the French immersion program do as well or better on standardized tests in English than their peers in other parts of Canada who study only in English (Lyster, 1994). They also speak, read and write good French although they are not completely bilingual. Tested in content areas in French, they do not do as well as children of French-speaking parents schooled in French. In fact, there is evidence of the development of a kind of classroom pidgin French, adequate for everyday conversing and for talking informally about academic subjects, but lacking the grammatical precision and academic style necessary for full professional use. Studies also show that immersion students don't read and write English as well as their English-schooled peers in the early grades (that they read and write English at all is amazing, as they are taught to read and write only French). However, as in the Friesland study, this gap disappears after a few years.

Critics of BE in the United States sometimes ask: If English speakers in Quebec can be immersed in French for 2 years with no academic damage, why can't Spanish speakers in the United States be immersed in English? The two situations are different for several reasons. First, the Quebec immersion students are not mixed in with native French speakers. (Recall from chap. 6 that Mr. Lorca's bilingual social studies class contained monolingual English speakers and monolingual Spanish speakers, as well as the bilingual students.) Second, the Quebec students are overwhelmingly from middle-class families, and their educated parents (who choose to enroll their children in the BE program) are actively involved in helping their children with their studies. Third, the class size is small, no more than 20. But even with all of these advantages, the fact is that many students do not succeed and end up transferring to all-English schools. One group of bilingual educators notes:

> Dismayed parents charge that this has created an inequitable system. Students who are academically unable to persevere in the immersion model may suffer linguistic and economic consequences because they are not acquiring French as intensively. This has led to the charge that only an elite group of students are being properly served and effectively prepared to contribute to the future of Quebec society (Schauber, 1995, p. 534).

Another problem is that even graduates of the immersion schools retain an instrumental rather than an integrative stance toward French. That is, they use French professionally but remain socially isolated from French speakers, many of whom are not rushing to mingle with English speakers, either. Quebec remains a divided society (Laponce, 1992). The solution may require the unthinkable for a Canadian: the willingness to look to the

United States for a model. Here, a number of school districts have instituted two-way bilingual programs where, for example, French-speaking and English-speaking children are schooled together bilingually. These promising programs will be discussed later in this chapter.

BILINGUAL EDUCATION IN THE UNITED STATES

The public discussion of BE in the United States often involves anecdotes of individual learners. Letters to the editor and op-ed pieces relate stories of immigrants who did not receive BE, yet learned English and became leading citizens. Such stories don't prove much because, as we saw in chapter 6, even members of the same family can differ greatly in their success as language learners. Nevertheless, anecdotes are useful as case studies because they help us understand the range of contexts and outcomes in language acquisition. Let me, then, relate three stories of BE in the United States: two of individual students and one of a bilingual school.

Richard Rodriguez

Historically, the most common way of schooling English language learning children is the submersion, or "sink or swim" method, where the student is put in a class with English-speaking children and expected to pick up the language. In his moving autobiography *Hunger of Memory*, Rodriguez (1982) describes his experience as a submersion student. When he entered the first grade in the Sacramento schools in the 1950s, he spoke only about 50 words of English. At home his name was "Ricardo," but at school he heard it pronounced in a strange way: "Rich-heard." He recalls:

> It would have pleased me to hear my teachers address me in Spanish when I entered the classroom. I would have felt much less afraid. I would have trusted them and responded with ease. But I would have delayed—for how long postponed?—having to learn the language of public society (1982, p. 19).

Rodriguez, like many L2 learners (and all L1 learners) went through a silent period for half a year. The nuns ("unsmiling, ever watchful") noted his silence and visited his parents, advising them to speak only English in the home, which they did, to the child's dismay.

> Again and again in the days following, increasingly angry, I was obliged to hear my mother and father: "Speak to us *en inglés.*" (*Speak.*) Only then did I determine to learn classroom English. Weeks after, it happened: One day in school I raised my hand to volunteer an answer. I spoke out in a loud voice.

And I did not think it remarkable when the entire class understood. That day, I moved very far from the disadvantaged child I had been only days earlier. The belief, the calming assurance that I belonged in public, had at last taken hold (1982, p. 22).

As I mentioned in chapter 1, Rodriguez calls himself a "scholarship boy," a term suggesting a privileged colonial child, singled out by British administrators to attend school in a provincial capital. There, the scholarship boy traded his village language and culture for the language and culture of Britain, and his future was assured. This is more or less what happened to Rodriguez. He lost his ability to speak Spanish and was laughed at and called *pocho* by his Mexican relatives. But he went on to earn a PhD in English at Berkeley and is now one of the outstanding writers and social commentators in the English language. He recognizes that he paid a high price for his success, but nonetheless celebrates his achievements and unhesitatingly recommends that others follow in his footsteps. He is a strong critic of BE.

It should be clear from the discussion in chapter 6 that Rodriguez's path to success could not have been followed by the Cortez children. English could not be the exclusive language of their home because Señora Beatriz did not speak English. But even if English were used more at home, it would have been neither desirable nor possible for them to forget Spanish because that language played a vital role in their lives. It served as the means of communication not only among members of their close-knit extended family, but also among members of the religious and social groups to which they belonged. The Cortez children have expanded the boundaries of their parents' lives, and I have no doubt that their children will follow the immigrant pattern and move almost completely into English-speaking society. But for the present generation, the Spanish language is of first importance.

Nuria

To balance Richard Rodriguez's sink-or-swim philosophy, I offer the story of one of my own students, who, like Rodriguez, attended school in California. Nuria was born and raised in a middle-class family in Hermosillo, Mexico. When she was 16, her parents sent her to Los Angeles as an exchange student, and she was placed in a bilingual program. She hated it. Her main complaint echoed the concern of the Cholla teachers: Separating the kids who spoke Spanish from the kids who spoke English and other languages created a Mexican ghetto and stigmatized Nuria as a slow learner. She felt trapped because she desired to join mainstream classes but was not allowed to do so. Nuria's problem was solved violently. She was assaulted by another student, and her parents insisted that she move to another school, which had no BE program, and there she excelled in English and other subjects. But that is not the end of the story.

After her unhappy year in Los Angeles, Nuria returned to Mexico, where she finished high school and college, and then came to the United States for graduate study. She eventually enrolled in the PhD Program in Second Language Acquisition and Teaching at the University of Arizona, where she became my student. When I first discussed BE with Nuria, she said that she opposed it and recounted her negative experience. Nevertheless, she decided to take some BE classes because she realized that she was in a superb position to become an expert in BE, whether critic or advocate. Nuria became an advocate. As a scholar, she found that the underlying theory and rationale for BE, as well as the research on its effectiveness, were convincing.

Nuria's present position on BE is similar to that of Dr. Lily Wong Fillmore, a professor of education at the University of California, Berkeley, who specializes in hands-on, classroom-oriented research. She says:

> Bilingual education done well gives excellent results. Bilingual education done badly gives poor results, just as one would expect. . . . Sad to say, the bad [programs] outnumber the good. . . . The problem has been a lack of commitment on the part of the schools to make it work (L. W. Fillmore, 1992, p. 367).

Coral Way Elementary School

BE advocates suggest that Richard Rodriguez speaks only from his own experience, which may be very different from the experience of others, and that he is not familiar with any good BE programs. One such program is at Coral Way Elementary School near Miami. During the 1960s, large numbers of refugees migrated from Cuba to Dade County, Florida. These refugees, unlike many immigrant groups, were welcomed to the United States because they had fled a communist country, and their presence here represented a strong anticommunist statement. Also, these immigrants were middle class and included engineers, doctors, and journalists. School officials and politicians, both conservative and liberal, wanted to help the Cuban refugees get on in the United States, especially in the schools, but nobody was sure how. So, Dade County asked the Ford Foundation to support an experimental educational program. Ford provided money to hire Pauline Rojas, a disciple of audio-lingual method creator Charles Fries and Director of the English Language Center at the University of Puerto Rico. Rojas set up a bilingual elementary school similar to the American schools that had been established in Guatemala and Ecuador to educate the children of U.S. diplomats and wealthy Guatemalans and Ecuadorians. These schools mixed English- and Spanish-speaking students, teaching all subjects in both languages, a method called two-way BE. A distinguishing feature of this kind of program is that each language is viewed as a resource, not as a liability, and all the children are called on to contribute to the school by helping their peers in the other language group. Coral Way Elementary School has become a model for BE and, as I suggested earlier, Quebec schools might profitably adopt its system.

TYPES OF BILINGUAL EDUCATION PROGRAMS

There are three basic types of BE programs. From most to least common they are transitional, maintenance, and two-way (also called dual) BE.

Transitional Bilingual Education

The goal of transitional BE is to prepare English language learners for mainstream courses by teaching content subjects in the native language, along with English as a second language (ESL) instruction (including sheltered courses), until the students are ready to take all of their courses with native English speakers. In elementary schools, students are usually taught by the same bilingual teacher throughout the day although some programs pull children out of mainstream classrooms for bilingual instruction, especially in the upper elementary grades. In early exit programs, the teacher might use the native language 95% in kindergarten, 75% in first grade, 50% in second grade, and 25% in third grade, after which the children are placed in mainstream classes. In late exit programs, the native language might be used 95% in kindergarten, 75% by third grade, and 50% by sixth grade.

At the secondary level, with less time available before the students must graduate, the transition to English is usually more rapid. Also, because students move around from room to room for different subjects, more complicated programs are possible. A typical transitional program is shown in Table 7.1. The BE program at Cholla fits the model in Table 7.1 with a few rough edges. For one thing, at Cholla monolingual Spanish students often had to take at least one mainstream content course because not enough BE classes were available. Another problem was that the bilingual offerings varied from semester to semester depending on the number of bilingual teachers and students available. Thus, the smooth transition implied by Table 7.1 is an idealization and, no doubt, many programs deviate from it to some extent. Notice also that the ideal transitional BE program is similar to the ESL program in Fairview County, described in chapter 3, in an important way. In both plans, beginning ELL students are mainstreamed in non-language intensive classes, like physical education and music. At the intermediate level, they are placed in classes that do not demand a great deal of culture-specific knowledge, like mathematics and science, and at the ad-

TABLE 7.1
A Typical Transitional BE Program

Level	Mainstream	ESL/Sheltered	L1/Bilingual
Low	art, music, PE	ESL	all core subjects
Intermediate	art, music, PE	ESL, math, science	language arts, social studies
Advanced	art, music, PE, math, science	ESL, social studies, language arts	L1 for native speakers
Mainstream	all subjects		

vanced level they are placed in classes that require more background knowledge of American culture, such as history and literature.

Maintenance Bilingual Education

The goal of maintenance programs is to teach students English and to maintain and enhance their skills in their native language. At the elementary level, the transition to English is usually similar to that in a late exit transitional program, with English and the native language being used equally by the sixth grade. For students who enter at the secondary level, the use of English would increase more quickly. The program shown in Table 7.1 could be changed into a maintenance program by continuing at least one native language class until graduation. Most BE scholars favor maintenance programs, and their reasons can be seen in the case of the Cortez family. Although Eva appears to have a chance for academic success, Juan and Joel are having real problems. Like the ELL students in Fairview County studied by Collier and Thomas (1989), the boys can handle many academic assignments in English, but (especially in the case of Joel) not at the level of their native English-speaking peers. It is doubtful that they will be qualified, on the basis of their English skills alone, for admission to a college or a white-collar job by the end of high school. But with just a few additional Spanish literacy classes, by the end of high school they could possess an asset that is valued in both the academic and professional worlds: fluency and literacy in English and Spanish. It is obviously in these students' best interest for schools to develop this asset.

Two-Way Bilingual Education

The Coral Way Elementary School program, discussed earlier in this chapter, is an example of two-way BE, in which students from two L1 groups meet together so that each can help the other learn the new language. The goal of two-way programs is for both groups to become fluent and literate in both languages and to learn to appreciate each other's language and culture (Christian, 1994). There are about 200 two-way programs in the United States involving Chinese, French, Japanese, Korean, Navajo, Portuguese, Russian, and Spanish languages (Faltis & Hudelson, 1998). Some programs use each language equally in the primary grades; others use the minority language 90% at first with a gradual transition to parity by sixth grade.

METHODS OF BILINGUAL TEACHING

Many different models exist for teaching bilingually. A common method (and the one used most at Cholla) is concurrent translation, with instruction being provided in one language and then translated into the other. Most educators advise against this approach if it allows students to rely solely on one language. One alternative (also widely practiced at Cholla) is to require that some activities be completed in each language. But, as we saw in Mr. Lorca's class, this can be tricky. The reading for the unit "Settling the West" was entirely in English and was appropriate for many of the students in the class, but was too difficult for Joel, who needed more support activities either in Spanish or easier English to give him the background knowledge needed to understand the unit.

Another alternative is to teach certain subjects in only one language throughout the year. An additional possibility is to use the same language on alternate days, or one language in the morning, the other in the afternoon. However, linguists have pointed out that in bilingual communities an all-Spanish day followed by an all-English day is unnatural because speakers in the community switch from one language to another depending on whom they are talking to and what they are talking about. A good compromise is the preview–review technique where, for example, the teacher gives a 5-minute preview of the lesson in one language, then teaches for 20 minutes in the other language, then sums up in the original language. This technique facilitates the psycholinguistic guessing game involved in language comprehension that was discussed in chapter 3.

Bilingual structured immersion is still another possibility. As we have seen, this is the method used in Quebec, where English speakers are taught in French by bilingual teachers who use English only on an individual basis to make a meaning clear or to counsel a student. In bilingual structured immersion courses, students are allowed to ask questions in their L1, but the teacher normally responds in the L2. Another feature of this kind of instruction is that lessons center around content material, not the grammar of the L2. Bilingual structured immersion was also the method we used in Operation SER, described in chapter 1, although we didn't have a fancy name for it.

Structured immersion, without the word *bilingual,* is the method mandated by the English Only laws in California and Arizona. The California law says that languages other than English can be used as long as instruction is "overwhelmingly" in English. This vague description has been interpreted to mean everything from 52% to 98% English (Crawford, 2000), but in any case, in California, structured immersion includes the possibility of some L1 instruction. In Arizona, there is much confusion over what structured immersion means, in part because the Department of Education guidelines use the term interchangeably with sheltered immersion, which as we saw in chapter 3, is a different concept. In a sheltered course, content material is taught to ELL students in understandable English, but because the students may come from different language backgrounds, there is no L1 component. Arizona has tended to interpret structured/sheltered immersion as allowing very little use of the students' L1. This policy has reduced some classes to absurdity. For example, Arizona law also requires that foreign languages be taught in elementary school. So, before a teacher begins a Spanish lesson, all the ELL students who speak Spanish must leave the room. For them to hear a Spanish lesson at school would violate the law. Because of this strict interpretation, structured immersion in Arizona should not be considered a bilingual program, but an ESL program.

However it is provided, BE has a long history of court battles and conflicting legal interpretations, to which we now turn.

LEGISLATIVE AND LEGAL HISTORY

Philosophy of Education

Court decisions and legislation involving BE have been influenced by theories of how best to educate underachieving students who come from minority and working-class groups. Prior to the 1940s, the predominant theory among both educators and laymen was racist. It was believed that immigrants from Southern Europe and Asia were genetically inferior to Northern Europeans and incapable of comparable academic achievement (Stein, 1986). Following the dissemination of research into differences between cultures by anthropologists like Franz Boas and Margaret Mead, the genetic inferiority theory was replaced by the cultural deprivation theory, which persists to this day. This theory was widely accepted during the 1960s when the first BE legislation and court decisions were made. It was backed by psychologists like Judith Krugman of the New York City Schools, who presented the theory in an influential speech to the American Psychological Association in 1955 (Stein, 1986) and by Oscar Lewis, whose book *La Vida*

(1966), portrayed Puerto Rican immigrant families as trapped in a culture of poverty.

The cultural deprivation theory held that what was inferior was not blood but ethnic culture. A complex of factors in minority and working-class communities was believed to block academic performance, including lack of verbal stimulation, lack of reading materials in the home, lack of stable, two-parent families, and the use of a language or language variety other than Standard English (Clark, 1972, p. 5). As a member of the Jets in *West Side Story* told Officer Krupke, "I'm depraved on account of I'm deprived." The cultural deprivation theory lost favor because it lacked a solid research base and because it seemed to offer a counsel of despair. It implied that despite the best efforts of educators, underprivileged children could seldom succeed and, furthermore, that their failure was the fault of the cultures from which they came rather than of the educational system.

In response to these criticisms, a new theory gained popularity. The cultural mismatch theory proposed that the reason for school failure was not that minority cultures were inferior but that they were different. Thus, the blame for academic failure lay at least partly with the schools because they did not accommodate the skills, knowledge, and abilities of all their students.

Many studies have delineated the differences between mainstream and minority cultures. A good example is Heath's (1983) study of storytelling in the European-American community of Roadville and the African-American community of Trackton, which was reviewed in chapter 2. According to Heath, the notion of what makes a good story is so different in the two communities that "for Roadville, Trackton's stories would be lies; for Trackton, Roadville's stories would not even count as stories" (p. 189).

The cultural mismatch theory has also fallen out of favor among some scholars, who view it as simplistic (Vasquez, Pease-Alvarez, & Shannon, 1994). Recently, researchers have proposed a multidimensional perspective, observing that most people participate to varying degrees in several cultures. Minority children are not totally isolated from mainstream culture, which they encounter at school, in the workplace, in the homes of friends, and on television. Of course, the extent to which minority children accommodate to mainstream culture can vary greatly, even within members of the same family, as with the Cortez children. Advocates of the multidimensional perspective also emphasize that students and teachers actively create a classroom culture that is distinct from that of the home. Nevertheless, the multidimensional perspective acknowledges that middle-class Standard English-speaking students are better served by educational institutions than working-class language minority students. Mehan (1991, p. 8) puts it this way:

The cultur[e] . . . of different status groups is related differently to the culture of the school. The language and socialization practices employed at home by middle- and upper-class families are reinforced by the discourse and social organization of classrooms, whereas the language and socialization practices of low-income and linguistic minority families do not match those found in the classroom (quoted in Vasquez et al., 1994, p. 11).

In chapter 6, we also noted material differences between the Cortez family and middle-class families, suggesting that financial deprivation is an important dimension in a multidimensional perspective. The Cortez home lacked books, newspapers, and magazines in Spanish or English and thus did not provide the opportunities for exposure to literacy commonly found in middle-class homes.

Bilingual Education Legislation

Against this philosophical background, legislators and judges have tried to improve educational opportunities for language minority students. These efforts have taken place along two parallel tracks: legislative and legal. The most important piece of legislation was the Bilingual Education Act of 1968, one of many pieces of social legislation passed during the War on Poverty. The Act created the Office of Bilingual Education (OBE), which was empowered to give grants to school districts to fund experimental programs. It was hoped that these experiments would serve as models that would eventually be taken over and funded by local districts. This "throw mud on the wall and see what sticks" approach was very much in the spirit of Great Society programs, many of which included innovative ideas but lacked central guidance and coordination. Under the OBE, many projects were carried out, but they were so different and, in some cases, so badly run, that it was impossible to compare them and to build up a research base of program evaluation that would guide educators and lawmakers in setting up subsequent projects (August & Hakuta, 1997).

In California, public policy is often set not by legislation but by amendments to the state's constitution. Recently, three amendments have affected language minorities. Proposition 187, subsequently thrown out by the courts, prohibited undocumented workers and their children from receiving social services, including schooling. Proposition 209, which is now in effect, forbids those affirmative action programs that involve racial preferences. Proposition 227, passed in 1998, prohibits BE unless parents specifically request it. The amendment also contains a little-discussed provision that may have even greater consequences because it affects all ELL students, not just the 30% or so enrolled in BE programs. The provision mandates structured immersion as the only legal method of BE/ESL instruction and requires that students exit the structured immersion program after only one year (180 days of instruction). Thus, if strictly applied, the amendment forbids several of the effective ESL methods discussed in chapter 3, from Total Physical Response for beginning students to adjunct courses for advanced students. Even worse, students without a waiver are prohibited from entering the mainstream gradually, as in the model in Table 7.1. This is close to a return to the sink-or-swim system that was so disastrous in the past. The amendment is, as widely charged during the campaign, a meat ax approach.

The politics behind Proposition 227, and its twin, Proposition 203 in Arizona, are fascinating. These propositions were conceived and financed by Ron Unz, a Silicon Valley multimillionaire who unsuccessfully sought the Republican nomination for Governor of California in 1994, losing to conservative Pete Wilson. Wilson had successfully appealed to antiminority sentiment in California by backing propositions 187 and 209. Unz, a neoconservative, opposed 187 and attacked Wilson for exploiting nativism for temporary political gain. He no doubt understood that running against ethnic minorities in California is ultimately political suicide as Latinos alone will likely comprise 40% of voters by 2025. Unz named his proposition "English for the Children," and built his campaign on sound bites and anecdotal evidence, not the evidence of systematic research. He also solicited endorsements from minority group members, including Jaime Escalante, the charismatic mathematics teacher portrayed in the movie *Stand and Deliver.*

The campaign for 227 rested on some intuitive but simplistic premises:

1. BE, which in California is basically English–Spanish education, is a failure because the dropout rate of Hispanics is high. This is simplistic because less than 30% of California's ELL students were enrolled in bilingual programs. The dropout rate could more logically be attributed to a lack of bilingual programs.
2. Time spent studying in Spanish is time lost for learning English. But as we saw in Joel's case, trying to learn difficult material in English without the requisite background knowledge is counterproductive, and this knowledge is often best learned in the L1.

English for the Children television spots featured anecdotes of bad bilingual programs. Prominent among these was the Ninth Street Elementary School in Los Angeles, where Latino parents pulled their children out of school to support their demand for all-English instruction. The response from BE advocates was slow in coming, largely because educators are too busy to do much but teach and prepare classes, but eventually the Citizens for an Educated America, largely founded by teachers organizations, was formed to organize a campaign, and proceeded to hire media consultants. The consultants' strategy was, unfortunately, not to argue the merits of BE but to attack Proposition 227. For example, pro-BE ads appealed to voters' distaste for lawsuits by highlighting 227's provision that individual teachers who continued to use a language other than English could be sued. A second issue, emphasized just before the election when 227 looked likely to pass, was the initiative's provision that $50 million a year be spent to teach English to adults who agreed to tutor children. Opposing this idea to serve the greater good of defeating 227 was bitter medicine for many bilingual teachers, who had long supported adult literacy programs, and the strategy made BE advocates look hypocritical.

Proposition 227 passed by a margin of 61% to 39%, with 37% of Latinos and 57% of Asians voting for the initiative. English for the Children was soon exported to Arizona in the form of Proposition 203, which passed by a two-to-one margin.

Bilingual Education Legal History

Lau v. Nichols

The court battle over BE was joined in 1974 when the parents of a Chinese-speaking student named Lau filed a class action suit against the superintendent of the San Francisco Unified School District, named Nichols. Lau, who had not received any kind of special language instruction, had not learned English, but had been socially promoted through the grades and was awarded a high school diploma. In Lau v. Nichols, Lau claimed that he had been denied his constitutional rights, citing the Fourteenth Amendment's prohibition against depriving citizens of property (education being a kind of property) without due process of law.

The Federal District Court judge ruled against Lau, who appealed the case until it reached the U.S. Supreme Court, which ruled in Lau's favor. Justice William O. Douglas noted, "There is no equality of treatment merely by providing students with the same facilities, textbooks, teachers and curriculum; for students who do not understand English are effectively foreclosed from any meaningful education." (Lau v. Nichols, 1974, quoted in Stein, 1986, p. 37). The Court did not base its decision on constitutional grounds, but on the 1965 Civil Rights Act, which forbids discrimination based on national origin. The Court did not mandate BE as a remedy to discrimination, but said that it was one option among others, including ESL.

When a federal court mandates policies for school districts, the enforcement of the ruling is the responsibility of the Department of Education's Office for Civil Rights (OCR), which at that time was housed in the Department of Health, Education, and Welfare. The OCR drew up guidelines for school districts to comply with the Lau decision. In writing the guidelines, the OCR looked not only at the Lau ruling, but also at other court decisions involving language minority students, some of which mandated BE. For example, in U.S. v. Texas (1971) (cited in Brisk, 1998, p. 9) the Federal Court for the U.S. Eastern District of Texas held that districts must provide BE to ELL students. The court also required that the school curriculum value the culture of Mexican-American students by providing bilingual counseling, cultural awareness programs, and ethnic studies courses, rulings that went considerably beyond Lau v. Nichols. In the end, the OCR required only bilingual, not bicultural, education.

Lau Remedies

The OCR's guidelines, called *Lau Remedies,* required several actions on the part of school districts. First, they had to identify language minority children by determining "the language most often spoken in the student's home, regardless of the language spoken by the student . . . and the language spoken by the student in social settings." Second, districts had to provide bilingual instruction until students were ready to participate in mainstream classrooms. The Remedies did not allow a district to employ only ESL instruction unless it could demonstrate that it was as effective as bilingual instruction. Because even today no research exists proving that any method is universally better than any other, this was an impossible requirement. Based on these guidelines, the OCR conducted more than 600 compliance reviews between 1975 and 1980 and negotiated compliance plans with 359 school districts (Stein, 1986). The weapon that OCR could use to force compliance was cutting off federal funding to a district. In fact, OCR never cut off any federal funds, but just the threat of losing federal money, which paid for everything from computers to hot lunches, antagonized many educators, who dragged their feet, complained to their elected representatives, and, in some cases, openly defied the OCR rules.

The Lau Remedies had the technical status of guidelines rather than regulations because they had never been formally proposed and submitted to public comment, but by 1980, it was clear that they had to be proposed as formalized regulations because there was so much dissatisfaction among local school districts. Many educators looked forward to a liberalized proposal, which would give districts more leeway. However, it was an election year, and President Carter badly needed a heavy turnout among Hispanic voters in crucial states like Texas, California, and New York. Partly for this reason, the new Lau Regulations proposed by the Department of Education were even more burdensome than the Remedies. They required that districts provide BE in all schools with 20 or more students from the same L1 group. In addition, districts had to assess the language dominance (not just the English proficiency) of all students. A storm of protest arose from local school districts, who characterized the Regulations as an unfunded mandate. Asked how much the Regulations would cost, Secretary of Education Shirley Hufstuddler estimated somewhere between $29 and $239 million (Stein, 1986, p. 43).

Many members of Congress opposed the Regulations, and their implementation was postponed until after the Reagan administration took over, when they were summarily dumped. The new Secretary of Education, Terrell Bell, characterized them as "harsh, inflexible, burdensome, unworkable, and incredibly costly . . . an intrusion on state and local responsibility" (quoted in Crawford, 1985, p. 53).

With the demise of the Lau Regulations, enforcement of the civil rights of English language learners fell back on other court decisions. One that has become prominent is Castaneda v. Pickard (Fifth Circuit Court, 1981) (cited in Brisk, 1998, p. 11), in which the court required that a program for ELL students must meet three criteria: (1) It must be informed by some recognized educational theory. (2) It must actually implement the theory. (3) It must produce results indicating that it is effective. Thus, districts have considerable flexibility in choosing a program, and they need not choose BE.

The requirement for L1 instruction under the Bilingual Education Act was also weakened during the Reagan Administration. The 1984 reauthorization of the Act provided that 4% of the funding could be used to set up programs that did not use the L1, such as ESL or sheltered instruction.

ARGUMENTS FOR AND AGAINST BILINGUAL EDUCATION

The debate over BE has been conducted in town meetings, newspaper editorials, talk shows, magazine articles, academic journals, and the Internet. Four kinds of arguments are usually made in these discussions:

- Arguments based on BE theory.
- Arguments based on evaluations of BE programs.
- Arguments based on political considerations.
- Arguments based on personal experiences with BE programs.

We will consider all of these in turn.

Bilingual Education Theory

A continuing controversy in BE is the question of how to define language proficiency. Language proficiency has many dimensions and in this book we have discussed a number of them. In fact, the organization of the book reflects a way of thinking about the different components of what it means to know a language. Chapter 2 began with a discussion of the most basic components of linguistic knowledge: sounds, units of meaning, words, and sentence patterns (i.e., phonology, morphology, lexicon, and syntax). The second part of chapter 2 discussed social/cultural aspects of language use, such as style shifting and performing speech acts. Most linguists agree that a speaker must control these aspects of language, as well, to be considered proficient.

Reading and writing skills are, of course, necessary for academic success, yet it seems odd to say that someone must be able to read and write to be proficient in a language. Thus, when the question of school success enters the picture, the notion of language proficiency seems to be a bit different from the everyday notion because school success involves literacy. We might distinguish, then, between *basic language proficiency*, which includes only oral skills, and *academic language proficiency*, which also includes literacy skills. In addition, recall from the discussion of registers in chapter 5 that academic language differs from everyday language and that a successful student must be competent in both. Therefore, academic language proficiency should also include knowledge of academic registers. In chapter 5, we saw that students must also possess other kinds of knowledge and skills to succeed at school. They must have background knowledge in academic subjects as well as effective strategies for learning and working with difficult material. But, background knowledge and academic strategies should not be included in the notion of academic language proficiency. Clearly, strategies like notetaking and using the library are not primarily linguistic in nature. Background knowledge, on the other hand, is partly linguistic because it involves vocabulary; however, it involves a great deal more, namely, the network of schemas in which vocabulary words are embedded. Thus, background knowledge is only partly language specific: One can be an expert on the Panama Canal without knowing English. Academic language proficiency, then, consists of the knowledge of phonology, morphology, syntax, and general vocabulary, plus pragmatic knowledge, plus knowledge of academic registers, plus literacy skills. The broader term *academic competence* includes academic language proficiency, effective academic skills, and the background knowledge necessary for dealing with the mainstream subjects taught in American schools.

BE theorist Jim Cummins (1980; Baker & Hornberger, 2001) has developed these considerations into a theoretical rationale for BE, which contains two related theories. The first theory develops the difference between everyday and academic language, distinguishing between what Cummins calls Basic Interpersonal Communicative Skills (BICS) and Cognitive Academic Language Proficiency (CALP). BICS consists of what I have called basic language proficiency and also communicative strategies like using body language and facial expressions to get a message across. CALP consists of what I have called academic language proficiency plus a dimension of cognitive difficulty. In other words, CALP is the ability to use academic language to express ideas that are cognitively challenging to the student. But Cummins never makes clear what cognitive difficulty means. Is a cognitively difficult text one that is within the Zone of Proximal Development? If so, the notion will differ for each individual, and so is not useful as a general measure of proficiency. Or, perhaps cognitive difficulty is based on a theory of cognitive development like that of Piaget. Thus, a science lesson on the laws of flotation would be cognitively difficult for a learner who has not reached the stage of formal operations. But under this interpretation, CALP is, in part, a measure of cognitive development, not just language proficiency. Perhaps because of these kinds of problems, Cummins has quit using the terms BICS and CALP. Nevertheless, the distinction between proficiency in everyday language and proficiency in academic language remains useful.

Cummins' (1980) second theory related to BE develops the notion that a lot of academic competence can be developed in the L1. A student who knows how to use a dictionary, study for a test, take notes, and so forth in one language can, to a large extent, transfer these skills to an L2 and, as mentioned earlier, background knowledge of a particular subject can be learned in any language. To describe this situation, Cummins proposes the Common Underlying Proficiency (CUP) model, which he illustrates using the metaphor of an iceberg with two peaks sticking up above the water. At first glance, it appears that the peaks are separate icebergs, but actually they share a large common base. Similarly, it appears that academic competence in English is entirely different from academic competence in say Korean, but in fact the two share a great deal, namely the CUP.

The relevance of the CUP theory to BE is obvious. ELL students can develop some aspects of academic competence in their L1 while they are learning English. They need not fall behind in background knowledge of content areas during their first years in the United States if they study these subjects in their L1, and they can develop academic skills that will be useful in mainstream classes, as well. So, although it is counterintuitive, the L1 component of a BE program is important for developing the L2 component. The CUP model provides an explanation for a counterintuitive finding of BE research that we will review: ELL students who have had several years of elementary school in their home countries before coming to the

United States do better on achievement tests administered at the end of elementary school than ELL students who have been schooled entirely in the United States (Thomas & Collier, 1997). If academic competence were entirely language specific, those students who had the most exposure to English should be the best achievers. The only explanation for why those with less exposure to English eventually do better is that they have developed important areas of academic competence in their L1.

I would, however, like to add a caveat to the CUP model that is not explicitly discussed by Cummins: Not everything transfers. Highly developed reading skills in an L1 are a great help in learning to read an L2, but they are obviously not enough. The ELL student has a limited English vocabulary and is not secure in many syntactic and rhetorical patterns. Thus, the student needs to develop effective strategies for dealing with difficult and partially understood material, such as using a dictionary effectively and skimming a text to identify which sections are particularly important in order to concentrate on those. As we saw in chapter 5, not all ELL students have these skills. For example, some overuse the dictionary, looking up every word. Effective dictionary use in an L2 must, to some extent, be learned in the L2 context. The same applies to notetaking. As we also saw in chapter 5, effective L2 notetakers have learned to vary their strategies according to the difficulty of the material, and a lecture in the L2 is obviously a lot more difficult than a lecture in the L1.

In sum, BE theory needs to emphasize more the critical importance of the English component of the program. The content material in English must be appropriate for ELL students, and they must be taught strategies for dealing with the material that are somewhat different from the strategies they employ in the L1.

Program Evaluations

Large-Scale Evaluations

This section reviews four large-scale evaluations of BE programs. We will not, however, be able to draw firm conclusions about the effectiveness of BE because individual learners and schools vary greatly, so that it is impossible to make generalizations that apply to all of them. Nevertheless, it is instructive to review these studies to get the flavor of the highly politicized interpretations of educational research in this area.

The AIR study. The American Institutes for Research (AIR) conducted a study in 1978 that compared students in Spanish–English programs with students in English-only programs (August & Hakuta, 1997). Twice during the school year, 8,200 children were tested in English reading and oral comprehension, Spanish reading and oral comprehension, and mathematics. The researchers looked to see whether the students' scores had improved on the second test. They had, but the improvement was about the same for both groups, so the researchers concluded that the BE programs were no more effective than the English-only programs.

The AIR study came in for a lot of criticism (August & Hakuta, 1997; Krashen, 1996). For one thing, in conducting this kind of study, it is important not to compare apples and oranges or, in educational jargon, to control for all of the relevant variables. If a study compared working-class students from Guatemala taught bilingually to middle-class students from Cuba taught only in English, it would tell us little. We would expect that the Cuban students would learn a lot under any circumstances because they come from an academic background, are highly motivated to succeed in school, and can get help with homework from their educated parents and siblings. The AIR study controlled for the students' ethnicity and social class, but it did not control for other factors, which seriously compromised its validity. Krashen (1996) points out, for example, that about two thirds of the students in the "English only" group were *graduates* of bilingual programs. Furthermore, the study measured test score gains over only a few months, too short a time to expect significant differences.

Baker and deKanter's study. Baker and deKanter (1981) reviewed existing studies of BE programs asking: Is there sufficient research to say that BE is more effective than alternative programs? They looked at 150 studies and eliminated all that they thought were inadequate, leaving 28 to be analyzed. These studies, they claimed, supported the following conclusions:

1. The case for the effectiveness of transitional bilingual education is so weak that exclusive reliance on this method is clearly not justified.
2. There is no justification for assuming that it is necessary to teach in the child's native tongue in order for the child to make satisfactory progress in school.

The report also noted that structured immersion showed promise and should be given more attention.

BE advocates were quick to challenge the Baker/deKanter report. Cummins (1989) charged that the researchers skewed their classification of programs as either bilingual or ESL so that effective programs that used the L1 were classified as structured immersion rather than BE, and that they did so in order to justify the Reagan Administration's policy of using money authorized under the Bilingual Education Act to fund ESL programs.

Willig's study.   Willig (1985) reanalyzed Baker and deKanter's data, focusing on a different research question and drawing very different conclusions. The difference in the research questions addressed in the original study and the questions addressed in Willig's reanalysis illustrates the different political orientations of the researchers. Baker and deKanter had asked, "Does BE work *better* than alternative programs?" a question that implies that if it does not, BE is not justified. Willig asked, "Does BE work well?" a question that implies that if it does, BE ought to be used even if other methods work just as well. Willig threw out several of the studies included in Baker and deKanter's review because either the programs were outside the United States, the instruction took place outside of school, or the study contained insufficient data. Analyzing the remaining studies, Willig concluded that BE works very well, finding "positive effects for bilingual programs . . . for all major academic areas" (p. 297). The National Research Council agreed with this conclusion, noting, "Based on Willig (1985) . . . the Committee accepts the conclusion of the previous National Research Council panel. The panel still supports the theory underlying native language instruction" (quoted in August & Hakuta, 1997, p. 147).

The Council also noted, however, that there is limited value in large-scale studies like Baker and deKanter's and Willig's because circumstances in individual districts, schools, and classrooms can vary greatly. It is more helpful to look at individual programs to see what makes them succeed or fail, and this tactic has been adopted by BE advocates in the wake of the anti-BE propositions. Thus, the debate has come full circle. During the 1980s, BE opponents, who were faced with mandatory BE, argued that it was not appropriate in all circumstances. Now BE proponents, faced with mandatory English-only instruction, argue that it is not appropriate in all circumstances. After 20 years of bitter debate, perhaps both sides can agree on at least this principle: no form of instruction is best in all situations.

Thomas and Collier's study.   An impressive study of English language learners' school success was made in 1997 by Thomas and Collier, who looked at BE programs and English-only programs that were likely to be successful because they were well-established and staffed by trained teachers. The study was massive. From five urban and suburban school districts, Thomas and Collier examined the records of 42,317 students. Recall from chapter 5 that in an earlier study, these researchers had found that in Fairview County, a large suburban school district without BE, ELL students scored at about the 45th percentile on standardized reading tests in 8th grade, but by 11th grade had dropped to the 35th percentile. The lower scores did not mean that the students were becoming worse readers but that they were not keeping up with the gains made by their native English-speaking peers. In the 1997 study, Thomas and Collier asked whether any kind of language education program would allow ELL students to catch up with native speakers in reading test scores. They compared six kinds of programs, all at the elementary school level:

- Two-way developmental BE (i.e., L1 support throughout elementary school).
- One-way developmental BE.
- Transitional BE, including ESL taught through academic content.
- Transitional BE, including ESL, both taught traditionally.
- ESL taught through academic content using current approaches.
- ESL pullout, traditionally taught.

As shown in Figure 7.1, the most successful kind of program was two-way developmental BE. Students in these programs made steady progress, reaching the national average reading score in Grade 6. Even more impressively, in the middle and secondary school grades, these students pulled ahead of native English speakers, reaching the 61st percentile on the 11th-grade reading test. The second most effective program type was one-way developmental BE plus content ESL. Students in these programs reached

Program 1: Two-way developmental bilingual education (BE)
Program 2: One-way developmental BE, including ESL taught through academic content
Program 3: Transitional BE, including ESL taught through academic content
Program 4: Transitional BE, including ESL, both taught traditionally
Program 5: ESL taught through academic content using current approaches
Program 6: ESL pullout, taught traditionally

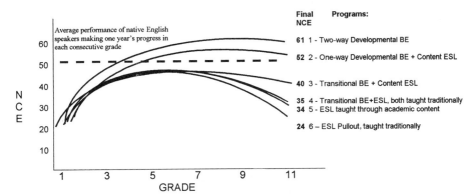

Note. Normal curve equivalents (NCEs) are similar to percentile scores.

FIG. 7.1.   English language learners' long term achievement on standardized tests in English reading compared across six programs.

the national average test score by Grade 7 and maintained that level. The least effective program was ESL pullout traditionally taught, where students made gains toward the national average through Grade 4 but then digressed, falling to the 24th percentile on the Grade 11 test.

The six kinds of programs shown in Figure 7.1 can be grouped into two types: those that enabled students to reach national test norms and those that did not. Those that did share one characteristic: They used the students' L1 throughout elementary school (this is the definition of "developmental"). The other four programs are all transitional, so that students are completely mainstreamed before the end of elementary school. It would be interesting to know how long language support, either BE or ESL, is continued in all six programs. It might be, for example, that the leveling off of scores observed in Grades 3 and 4 in the four less successful programs coincides with the students' being submerged in mainstream classes, where, like Joel, they encountered material that was well beyond their ability.

A second telling comparison in Thomas and Collier's study is between content ESL and transitional BE plus content ESL. The only difference in the outcomes of these programs is the L1 component in the latter. Although neither program enabled students to reach national norms by 11th grade, the BE students scored six points (15%) higher than the English-only students.

Yet, even Thomas and Collier's massive study is of limited use for formulating a general language education policy because the districts they studied provided better than average programs, so the conclusions cannot be generalized to weaker programs, as the authors themselves note. Indeed, as Hornberger, Harsch, and Evans (1999) state, "We lack sufficient school-based data to examine on a national scale the educational achievements of [ELL] students" (p. 28).

Evaluations of Individual Programs

The National Research Council's conclusions on large-scale comparisons between BE and English-only programs remains valid: These studies are not as helpful as had been hoped because circumstances differ greatly between schools and districts. It is better to look at individual programs that have worked well or not so well and generalize the findings only to schools that have similar needs, populations, and resources. Let us look at some studies of specific BE programs, starting with those that are cited by BE critics.

Porter's critique. Rosalee Porter, a veteran teacher and administrator, criticizes BE in her book *Forked Tongue: The Politics of Bilingual Education* (1990). Although her critique is a personal perspective rather than a systematic study, I include it here because it is often cited in BE debates. Porter entered the American public schools at age 6 in Newark, New Jersey, and, like Richard Rodriguez, she did not speak English. Unlike Rodriguez, Porter's native language was Italian. Porter learned Spanish, became a BE teacher and, at first, a BE advocate. Her break with orthodoxy came when she was put in charge of teaching in Spanish to Puerto Rican kindergarten children. She discovered that many of these kids were more fluent in English than in Spanish, and that her attempts to get them to speak in Spanish were not very effective.

> "Juan, ¿qué color es este?" I would ask pointing to a green box. "Green" . . . would be Juan's reply. So, I would correct him, "Verde," and he would say again, "green." In the early years I followed the curriculum and taught all subjects in Spanish, but I came to feel that I was going about things the wrong way around, as if I were deliberately holding back the learning of English (p. 21).

Porter's underlying priority was to prepare the students for success in mainstream classes. Theory aside, she believed that if teaching in Spanish furthered that goal, she would use Spanish, but if Spanish was an obstacle, she would use English.

Porter's practical, as opposed to cultural, orientation is evident in her criticism of teacher hiring practices. She believed that administrators hired BE teachers on the basis of their ethnicity rather than on the basis of their abilities as teachers or as speakers of English and Spanish. For example, two candidates who were not Puerto Rican were turned down for teaching positions. "They were told that the bilingual teachers had to be from the same cultural group as the students in order to be effective" (p. 27).

Gerston and Woodward's study. Gerston and Woodward's (1995) study is cited by BE opponents because it does not support the finding of Thomas and Collier (1997) that more L1 instruction eventually results in higher academic achievement. Gerston and Woodward looked at a transitional BE program and a bilingual structured immersion program in El Paso, Texas. The transitional program exited students by the fifth or sixth grade and the bilingual structured immersion program exited students by the third or fourth grade. The researchers gathered data from teacher questionnaires, student interviews, and scores on the Iowa Tests of Basic Skills, a test given in English.

The students selected for the study had almost no English proficiency on entering the programs in the first grade, but by the fourth grade, the bilingual structured immersion students showed significantly better test scores than the transitional students in all areas. This short-term gain stands to reason because, as we have seen, bilingual structured immersion uses more English than transitional bilingual education. However, by the seventh grade, after both groups had been mainstreamed, the test scores of the two groups were about the same, contra Thomas and Collier (1997).

The researchers concluded that neither program prepared the students well for standardized tests in English because both groups ended up with lower than average scores on reading and vocabulary. Moreover, according to the interviews, students from both programs were more comfortable speaking Spanish than English, found reading in English very difficult, and preferred classes in math to classes in language arts and social studies. Thus, the students were not comfortable in classes requiring them to produce and comprehend academic English. The teachers, however, perceived the bilingual immersion program to be more beneficial, possibly because they saw achievement in areas that written tests cannot measure.

Gerston and Woodward (1995) concluded that there is no certain answer to the question of which type of program was more beneficial to the language minority students. They encourage school districts and teachers to experiment with various programs and instructional methods and conduct classroom research to determine their effectiveness.

The Rock Point study.   BE advocates have a wealth of studies with which to argue their position. One of the best is the Rock Point study (Rosier & Holm, 1980; Vorih & Rosier, 1978), which compared the achievement (as tested in English) of Navajo children who had been schooled bilingually with Navajo children who had been schooled in ESL programs. After 6 years of schooling, the bilingual group was above grade level in reading, whereas the ESL group was below grade level and had been falling behind since the fourth year. As shown in Figure 7.2, at first, children in the bilingual programs fell behind the children in ESL programs, but then the bilingual group caught up and moved ahead. The English reading scores of the Rock Point BE group fell from Grade 2 to Grade 3, but then soared at Grade 4. The scores of the ESL group rose from Grade 2 to Grade 3, but then fell off dramatically. As Troike and Park (2001) point out, the striking increase in the scores of the BE group at Grade 4 suggest that bilingual instruction has a cumulative effect, which is lost if BE is ended after Grade 3, as is the case in many early exit BE programs.

Krashen and Biber's study.   In their book *On Course: Bilingual Education's Successes in California* (1988), Stephen Krashen and Douglas Biber describe seven bilingual programs that they consider successful on the basis of students' standardized test scores. One of the studies looked at the Baldwin Park Unified School District, located in a suburb of Los Angeles, where

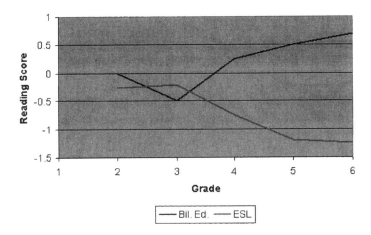

FIG. 7.2.   Effectiveness of BE versus ESL instruction in the Rock Point study.

40% of the kindergarten students are Spanish speaking. These students received instruction in Spanish, math, and other subjects when Spanish-speaking teachers were available. When they were not available, the students were tutored in these subjects by aides and older Spanish-speaking students. Reading instruction in English began in Grade 3. In Grade 5, 115 students who had followed this program took the California Test of Basic Skills, and their scores were compared to those of 492 students who had learned entirely in English, 92% of whom were native English speakers or considered "fluent English speakers." The bilingually educated group did as well or slightly better than the English-only group on tests of reading, language, and math.

In addition, a longitudinal study was made of Baldwin Park students, tracing their scores in Grades 1 through 5. A look at the reading scores is particularly instructive because it shows how students who started out knowing little English brought their scores up to the national average within 4 years. The scores are as follows: Grade 1, 19th percentile; Grade 2, 41st percentile; Grade 3, 44th percentile; Grade 4, 52nd percentile.

A study of 80 eighth graders in the district compared the scores of BE graduates with those of English-only graduates (mostly native speakers). The BE group outscored the English-only group in math (53rd percentile to 43rd percentile) and language arts (56th percentile to 47th percentile). The English-only group, however, did better in reading, outscoring the BE group (45th percentile to 38th percentile).

It is interesting that in some of the districts discussed by Krashen and Biber, bilingually educated students did not do as well on the tests as English-only students. The San Jose Unified School District is one example. Here, the researchers compared a bilingual group to an ESL group, which is more revealing than comparing a bilingual group to a native speaker group, as in the Baldwin Park study, because it addresses the question of whether the bilingual program or the ESL program is more effective for preparing students for success in English. In this case, the ESL learners outscored the BE learners on all of the tests. The scores were as follows:

	Reading	Language	Mathematics
BE	56	59	54
ESL	60	64	64

The differences here are not great and may be due to chance (Krashen and Biber do not provide statistical tests).

The fact that Krashen and Biber, BE advocates, included these figures in their argument for BE underscores the different philosophies of BE advocates and opponents. Recall that the El Paso study cited by many BE opponents also found little difference between the transitional BE group and the structured immersion group. But BE opponents are usually interested only in the students' achievements in English, which, they say, is consistent with the legal motivation of BE. So, if BE students do worse than English-only students on tests in English, the BE program should go. But BE advocates see great benefit in fostering dual language proficiency for the reasons I have mentioned. So, if BE students perform well on tests in English, though perhaps not quite as well as ESL students, then BE should stay.

California Update

We end our review of bilingual programs with a look at what happened in California in the years after the passage of Proposition 227, which required mainstreaming ELL students after only one year of "structured English immersion," defined as teaching "overwhelmingly in English." Native language instruction was allowed if parents requested a special waiver and the school district agreed to grant the waiver. The actual effect of the proposition was not great because there are a number of ways that districts that wanted to offer BE could still do so. One way was to encourage parents to sign waivers and, predictably, schools that had large BE programs strongly encouraged waivers, whereas schools without BE programs did not. A second possibility lay in interpreting what "overwhelmingly in English" meant. As we have seen, structured immersion allows some use of the native language, and districts could interpret "overwhelmingly in English" to mean as little as 52% English (Crawford, 2000). The percentage of official bilingual programs in the state declined from 29% in 1998 to 12% in 1999, but bilingual teachers could continue to teach bilingually, for a year at least.

Ron Unz and his followers were quick to publicize the results of standardized tests after Proposition 227 had been in effect for a year. The scores for ELL students were up. But Unz's press releases didn't mention that the scores for ELL students in BE programs were also up, as were the scores for native English speakers. The higher test scores across the board probably resulted from the state's renewed emphasis on standardized testing, enforced with a strict system of rewards and sanctions. The effect of "teaching to the test" can also be seen in comparing the math test scores of ELL students and native English-speaking students. Recall that in chapter 3 we observed that the national emphasis on testing has caused reading scores to go up across the country, but with a greater rise in the scores of non-minority students, creating a larger gap in the reading levels of minority and majority students. The same effect was observed in the math scores of the ELL and native English-speaking students in California. In 2000, 59% of the native English-speaking students scored above the 50th percentile, an improvement of 9 percentage points in 2 years. But only 26% of the ELL students scored above the 50th percentile, and the group improved only 7.5% from 1998 (Crawford, 2000).

During the 1998 California election, many BE advocates predicted that passing Proposition 227 would result in catastrophe, and this hasn't happened so far. But it is still early for an educational program. I mentioned that the greatest effect of the proposition may be its requiring ELL students to be mainstreamed after only one year. The research by Cummins (1989) and Collier and Thomas (1997) shows that this is far too little time to learn enough English to profit from mainstream classes, and, as stressed in chapters 5 and 6, ELL students require extra help with both language and academic skills from ESL or bilingual teachers after they have joined the mainstream. That help is now denied by law.

CONCLUSIONS

Research shows that well-run BE programs are effective. Research also shows that some BE programs are not as effective as they should be, and in chapter 6 we saw an example of a program, which (for reasons largely beyond the control of the teachers) was not well-run. It should be recalled, however, that the same can be said of ESL-only programs, as Valdez's (2001) research, reviewed in chapter 5, has shown.

So, should schools pay their money and take their chances with an ESL-only program or a bilingual program? I have suggested that there is no blanket answer because conditions vary so much from school to school. Comparing different programs is often comparing apples and oranges: Some programs have trained teachers, good materials, and community support, but others don't. Conclusions about the effectiveness of a BE program can only be generalized to other programs that have similar resources and students. It follows, then, that decisions about how to educate ELL students should be made by districts, not states, with plenty of input from individual schools.

If both BE and ESL-only are feasible, however, BE is clearly the way to go for several reasons. First, a BE program provides a voice in the school for the students' home culture, and helps to ease the transition from home to school. Second, many ELL students can learn the background knowledge and skills necessary for academic work in their mother tongue. Though it is still necessary to provide bridge courses (sheltered or adjunct) in English, where students can learn to apply their academic skills in the new language, L1 instruction forms a solid base for transfer to English. The third reason is so obvious that even Epstein (1977) and Bell (1988) agree with it. If American students can become bilingual without jeopardizing their academic success in English (and we know that this is possible), we would be foolish not to enable them to do so. This last argument can be put in more personal terms. As we have seen, school is not easy for language minority children like Juan, Eva, and Joel for many reasons. The Cortez children do, however, possess a cultural resource that can be of great value in the academic and professional worlds: competence in two languages. American schools would be remiss to deny them this resource.

SUGGESTED READING

Stein (1986) traces the history of BE legislation in the context of legal and cultural theories, as do the articles in Crawford (1992), which also discusses the debate over official English policies. Crawford (2000) comments on the recent politics of BE, especially California's Proposition 227. Three good books for those who wish to learn more about methods of BE as well as how different kinds of BE programs can work in schools are Faltis and Hudelson (1998), Brisk (1998), and Lemberger (1997). This last book contains personal narratives of bilingual teachers. August and Hakuta (1997) provide an overview of BE research that is fairly neutral politically. Schauber (1995) discusses BE in Quebec. Thomas and Collier (1997) reviews the authors' important research in light of theoretical issues. The case against BE, based partly on the author's personal experience, is presented in Porter (1990). Rossell and Baker (1996) review research supporting the anti-BE position. Krashen (1996) rebuts Porter, Rossell and Baker, and others. Baker and Hornberger (2001) is a compendium of articles by BE theoretician Jim Cummins, an articulate BE advocate.

References

Adamson, H. D. (1989). Does the bioprogram affect second language acquisition: English article acquisition in American children and Korean adults. In M. Eisenstein (Ed.), *Variation in second language acquisition: Empirical approaches* (pp. 33–47). New York: Plenum.

Adamson, H. D. (1992). Social and processing constraints on relative clauses. *American Speech, 67*(2), 123–133.

Adamson, H. D. (1993). *Academic competence: Theory and classroom practice: Preparing students for content courses.* New York: Longman.

Adamson, H. D., & Kovac, C. (1981). Variation theory and second language acquisition. In D. Sankoff & H. Cedergren (Eds.), *Variation omnibus* (pp. 215–255). Carbondale, IL: Linguistic Research.

Adamson, H. D., & Regan, V. M. (1991). The acquisition of community speech norms by Asian immigrants learning English as a second language: A preliminary study. *Studies in Second Language Acquisition, 13*(1), 1–22.

Agar, M. (1996). *The professional stranger: An informal introduction to ethnographic research* (2nd ed.). San Diego: Academic Press.

Andersen, R. (1981). Two perspectives on pidginization as second language acquisition. In R. Andersen (Ed.), *New dimensions in second language acquisition research* (pp. 165–196). Rowley, MA: Newbury House.

Andersen, R. (1983). *Pidginization and creolization as language acquisition.* Rowley, MA: Newbury House.

Anderson, J. R. (1980). *Cognitive psychology and its implications.* San Francisco: Freeman.

Anderson, J. R. (1983). *The architecture of cognition.* Cambridge, MA: Harvard University Press.

Aukerman, R. (1971). *Approaches to beginning reading.* New York: Wiley.

August, D., & Hakuta, K. (Eds.). (1997). *Educating language-minority children.* Washington, DC: National Academy Press.

Austin, J. (1962). *How to do things with words.* Oxford, UK: Clarendon.

Bachman, L. F. (1990). *Fundamental considerations in language testing.* Oxford, UK: Oxford University Press.

Baker, C., & Hornberger, N. (2001). *An introductory reader to the writings of Jim Cummins.* Avedon, UK: Multilingual Matters.

Baker, K. A., & deKanter, A. A. (1981). *Effectiveness of bilingual education: A review of the literature.* Washington, DC: Office of Planning and Budget, U.S. Department of Education.

Baker, K. A., & deKanter, A. A. (1983). Federal policy and the effectiveness of bilingual education. In K. Baker & A. deKanter (Eds.), *Bilingual education* (pp. 33–85). Lexington, MA: Heath.

Baratz, J. C., & Shuy, R. W. (1969). *Teaching black children to read.* Washington, DC: Center for Applied Linguistics.

Barrio, R. (1971). *The plum plum pickers.* Binghamton, NY: Bilingual Press.

Barry, D. (2001, April 23). Go figure. *Arizona Daily Star,* p. B-2.

Battista, M. T. (1999). The mathematical miseducation of America's youth: Ignoring research and scientific study in education. *Phi Delta Kappan, 80*(6), 425–433.

Baugh, J. (1999). *Out of the mouths of slaves.* Austin, TX: University of Texas Press.

Bayley, R., & Preston, D. (Eds.). (1996). *Second language acquisition and linguistic variation.* Amsterdam: John Benjamins.

Bell, T. (1988). *The thirteenth man: A Reagan cabinet memoir.* New York: The Free Press.

Bialystok, E., & Hakuta, K. (1994). *In other words: The science and psychology of second language acquisition.* New York: Basic Books.

Biber, D. (1988). *Variation across speech and writing.* Cambridge, UK: Cambridge University Press.

Biber, D. (1995). *Dimensions of register variation: A cross linguistic comparison.* Cambridge, UK: Cambridge University Press.

Biber, D., Conrad, S., & Reppen, R. (1998). *Corpus linguistics: Investigating language structure and use.* Cambridge, UK: Cambridge University Press.

Bickerton, D. (1981). *Roots of language.* Ann Arbor, MI: Karoma.

Bickerton, D. (1984). The language bioprogram hypothesis. *Behavioral & Brain Sciences, 7*(2), 173–221.

Biesenbach-Lucas, S. (1989). The use of relative markers in modern American English. In K. M. Denning, S. Inkelas, F. C. McNair-Knox, & J. R. Rickford (Eds.), *Variation in language: NWAV-XV at Stanford* (pp. 13–21). Stanford, CA: Department of Linguistics, Stanford University.

Birch, B. (2002). *English L2 reading: Getting to the bottom.* Mahwah, NJ: Lawrence Erlbaum Associates.

Blair, R. W. (1982). *Innovative approaches to language teaching.* Rowley, MA: Newbury House.

Bley-Vroman, R. (1989). What is the logical problem of foreign language learning? In S. Gass & J. Schacter (Eds.), *Linguistic perspectives on second language acquisition* (pp. 41–68). Cambridge, UK: Cambridge University Press.

Bley-Vroman, R. (1990). The logical problem of foreign language learning. *Linguistic Analysis, 20,* 3–49.

Bloom, P. (1993). *Language acquisition: Core readings.* Cambridge, MA: MIT Press.

Blum-Kulka, S. (1991). Interlanguage pragmatics: The case of requests. In R. Phillipson, E. Kellerman, L. Selinker, M. Sharwood-Smith, & M. Swain (Eds.), *Foreign/second language pedagogy research* (pp. 255–272). Clevedon, UK: Multilingual Matters.

Bolinger, D. (1980). *Language: The loaded weapon.* London: Longman.

Braidi, S. (1999). *The acquisition of second-language syntax.* New York: Oxford University Press and Arnold.

Braine, M. D. S. (1971). On two types of models of the internalization of grammars. In D. I. Slobin (Ed.), *The ontogenesis of grammar: A theoretical symposium* (pp. 153–186). New York: Academic Press.

Brinton, D. M., & Master, P. (Eds.). (1997). *New ways in content-based instruction.* Alexandria, VA: TESOL.

Brinton, D. M., Snow, M. A., & Wesche, M. B. (1989). *Content-based second language instruction.* New York: Harper/Newbury.

Brisk, M. E. (1998). *Bilingual education: From compensatory to quality schooling.* Mahwah, NJ: Lawrence Erlbaum Associates.

Brooks, B. (1960). *Language and language learning.* New York: Harcourt, Brace & World.

Brown, R. (1973). *A first language: The early stages.* Cambridge, MA: Harvard University Press.

Bruffee, K. (1984). Collaborative learning and the "conversation of mankind." *College English, 46*(7), 635–652.

Bruffee, K. (1986). Social constructionism, language, and the authority of knowledge: A bibliographical essay. *College English, 48*(8), 773–790.

Canale, M., & Swain, M. (1980). Theoretical bases of communicative approaches to second language teaching and testing. *Applied Linguistics, 1,* 1–47.

Celce-Murcia, M. (2001). *Teaching English as a second or foreign language* (3rd ed.). Boston: Heinle & Heinle.

Chaudron, C. (1988). *Second language classrooms: Research on teaching and learning.* New York: Cambridge University Press.

Chomsky, N. (1957). *Syntactic structures.* The Hague, Netherlands: Mouton.

Chomsky, N. (1959). Review of B. F. Skinner's *Verbal Behavior. Language, 35,* 26–58.

Christian, D. (1994). *Two-way bilingual education: Students learning through two languages.* Education Practice Report No. 12. Santa Cruz, CA and Washington, DC: National Center for Research on Cultural Diversity and Second Language Learning.

Clark, H. H., & Clark, E. V. (1977). *Psychology and language: An introduction to psycholinguistics.* New York: Harcourt, Brace, Jovanovich.

Clark, K. B. (1972). *The educationally deprived: The potential for change.* New York: Metropolitan Applied Research Center.

Clive, J., & Pinney, T. (Eds.). (1972). *Thomas Babington Mccauley: Selected writings.* Chicago: University of Chicago Press.

Cofer, T. (1972). *Linguistic variability in a Philadelphia speech community.* Unpublished doctoral dissertation, University of Pennsylvania, Philadelphia.

Coles, G. (2000). *Misreading reading: The bad science that hurts children.* Portsmouth, NH: Heinemann.

Collier, V. (1989). A synthesis of research on academic achievement in a second language. *TESOL Quarterly, 23*(3), 509–531.

Collier, V., & Thomas, W. (1989). How quickly can immigrants become proficient in school English? *Journal of Educational Issues of Language Minority Students, 5,* 26–38.

Collins, J. (1997, October 27). How Johnny should read. *Time, 64,* 78–81.

Cook, V. (2001). *Second language learning and language teaching* (3rd ed.). London: Arnold.

Cook, V., & Newson, M. (1996). *Chomsky's Universal Grammar* (2nd ed.). Cambridge, MA: Blackwell.

Crain, S., & Lillo-Martin, D. (1999). *An introduction to linguistic theory and language acquisition.* Oxford, UK: Blackwell.

Crain, S., & McKee, C. (1986). Acquisition of structural restrictions on anaphora. In S. Berman, J.-W. Choe, & J. McDonough (Eds.), *Proceedings of the North Eastern Linguistic Society, 16* (pp. 94–110). Amherst, MA: GLSA.

Crawford, J. (1992). *Language loyalties: A source book on the official English controversy.* Chicago: University of Chicago Press.

Crawford, J. (2000). *At war with diversity: US language policy in an age of anxiety.* Clevedon, UK: Multilingual Matters.

Cubberly, E. P. (1919). *Public education in the United States: A study and interpretation of American history.* Boston: Houghton Mifflin.

Cummins, J. (1980). The entry and exit fallacy in bilingual education. *NABE Journal, 4,* 25–60.

Cummins, J. (1989). *Empowering minority students.* Sacramento, CA: California Association for Bilingual Education.

Cummins, J., & Swain, M. (1983). Analysis by rhetoric: Reading the text or the reader's own projections? A reply to Edelsky et al. *Applied Linguistics, 4*(1), 23–39.

Curran, C. A. (1976). *Counseling—Learning in second language.* Apple River, IL: Apple River Press.

Cziko, G. A. (1986). Testing the language bioprogram hypothesis: A review of children's acquisition of articles. *Language, 62*(4), 878–898.

deSauze, F. (1920; rev. ed. 1959). *The Cleveland plan for the teaching of modern languages with special reference to French.* Philadelphia: Winston.

Dewey, J. (1916). *Democracy and education.* New York: Macmillan.

Diller, K. C. (1978). *The language teaching controversy.* Rowley, MA: Newbury House.

Doman, G. (1964). *How to teach your baby to read.* New York: Random House.

Doughty, C. (1991). Second language instruction does make a difference: Evidence from an empirical study of SL relativization. *Studies in Second Language Acquisition, 13*(4), 431–469.

Doughty, C., & Williams, J. (1998). *Focus on form in second language acquisition.* New York: Cambridge University Press.

Eckert, P. (1991). Social polarization and the choice of linguistic variants. In P. Eckert (Ed.), *New ways of analyzing sound change* (pp. 213–232). San Diego: Academic Press.

Eckert, P. (2000). *Linguistic variation as social practice: The construction of identity in Belton High.* Malden, MA: Blackwell.

Ellis, R. (1994). *The study of second language acquisition.* Oxford, UK: Oxford University Press.

English standards. (1997, January 6). [Editorial]. *USA Today,* p. A-8.

Epstein, N. (1977). *Language, ethnicity, and the schools: Policy alternatives for bilingual-bicultural education.* Washington, DC: Institute for Educational Leadership, George Washington University.

Epstein, S. D., Flynn, S., & Martohardjono, G. (1996). Second language acquisition: Theoretical and experimental issues in contemporary research. *Brain and Behavior Sciences, 19*(4), 677–758.

Faltis, C., & Hudelson, S. (1998). *Bilingual education in elementary and secondary school communities: Toward understanding and caring.* Boston: Allyn & Bacon.

Fasold, R. W. (1983). *Variation in the form and use of language: A sociolinguistics reader.* Washington, DC: Georgetown University Press.

Fasold, R. (1984). *The sociolinguistics of society.* Oxford: Basil Blackwell.

Feagin, C. (1979). *Variation and change in Alabama English: A sociolinguistic Study of the White community.* Washington, DC: Georgetown University Press.

Feynman, R. P. (1998). *The meaning of it all: Thoughts of a citizen scientist.* Reading, MA: Addison-Wesley.

Fillmore, C. (1997). *A linguist looks at the Ebonics debate.* Posted on the Center for Applied Linguistics website. http://www.cal.org

Fillmore, L. W. (1992). Against our best interest: The attempt to sabotage bilingual education. In J. Crawford (Ed.), *Language loyalties* (pp. 367–376). Chicago: University of Chicago Press.

Frawley, W. (1997). *Vygotsky and cognitive science.* Cambridge, MA: Harvard University Press.

Freire, P. (1970). *Pedagogy of the oppressed.* New York: Seabury.

Gardner, R. C., & Lambert, W. E. (1972). *The role of attitudes and motivation in second language learning.* Rowley, MA: Newbury House.

Gee, J. P. (1986). Units in the production of discourse. *Discourse Processes, 9,* 391–422.

Gee, J. P. (1996). *Social linguistics and literacies: Ideology and discourses* (2nd ed.). Bristol, PA: Taylor & Francis.

Geertz, C. (1983). *Local knowledge: Further essays in interpretive anthropology.* New York: Basic Books.

Gerston, R., & Woodward, J. (1995). A longitudinal study of transitional and immersion bilingual education programs in one district. *Elementary School Journal, 95*(1), 223–239.

Ghawi, M. (1995). *Developing second language proficiency and academic competence: A case study of a modified literature course.* Unpublished doctoral dissertation, University of Arizona, Tucson.

Goodman, K. S. (1968). *The psycholinguistic nature of the reading process.* Detroit, MI: Wayne State University Press.

Grabe, W. (1998). *Annual review of applied linguistics* (Vol. 18). New York: Cambridge University Press.

Graves, R. (1957). *Goodbye to all that* (Rev. ed.). Garden City, NY: Anchor Doubleday.

Graves, R., & Hodge, A. (1943). *The reader over your shoulder: A handbook for writers of English prose.* New York: Macmillan.

Green, P. S., & Hecht, K. (1993). Language awareness of German pupils. *Language Awareness, 2*(3), 125–142.

Gregg, K. (1996). The logical and developmental problems of second language acquisition. In W. C. Ritchie & T. K. Bhatia (Eds.), *Handbook of second language acquisition* (pp. 49–81). San Diego: Academic Press.

Grice, H. P. (1975). Logic and conversation. In P. Cole & J. L. Morgan (Eds.), *Syntax and semantics: Vol. 3. Speech acts* (pp. 41–58). New York: Academic Press.

Grice, H. P. (1978). Further notes on logic and conversation. In P. Cole (Ed.), *Syntax and semantics: Vol. 9. Pragmatics* (pp. 113–127). New York: Academic Press.

Grice, P. (1989). *Studies in the way of words.* Cambridge, MA: Harvard University Press.

Harklau, L. (1994). ESL versus mainstream classes: Contrasting L2 learning environments. *TESOL Quarterly, 28*(2), 241–272.

Heath, S. B. (1980). Standard English: Biography of a symbol. In T. Shopen & J. M. Williams (Eds.), *Standards and dialects in English* (pp. 3–32). Cambridge, MA: Winthrop.

Heath, S. B. (1983). *Ways with words: Language, life, and work in communities and classrooms.* Cambridge, UK: Cambridge University Press.

Hill, J. (2000, March 9). Ebonics lessons. Chicago Tribune on the USA Today website. Retrieved March 20, 2000 from http://www.pqarchiver.com/USAToday.

Hilton, J. (1934). *Good-bye Mr. Chips.* New York: Little, Brown.

Hinkel, E., & Fotos, S. (2002). *New perspectives on grammar teaching in second language classrooms.* Mahwah, NJ: Lawrence Erlbaum Associates.

Holborow, M. (1999). *The politics of English.* London: Sage.

Hornberger, N., Harsch, L., & Evans, B. (1999). *Working papers in educational linguistics: Special edition: The six nation research project: The United States: A country report: Language education of language minority students in the United States.* Philadelphia: University of Pennsylvania Press.

Hughes-Hallett, D., Gleason, A. M., et al. (1994). *Calculus.* New York: Wiley.

Hunter, B., & McBain, E. (2001). *Candyland.* New York: Simon & Schuster.

Hymes, D. (1972). Models of the interaction of language and social life. In J. Gumperz & D. Hymes (Eds.), *Directions in sociolinguistics: The ethnography of communication* (pp. 35–71). New York: Holt, Rinehart & Winston.

Ivins, M. (1998). No shit Sherlock! Why the government shut down. In M. Ivins, *You got to dance with them what brung you* (pp. 145–147). New York: Random House.

James, W. (1890). *The principles of psychology* (Vol. 1). New York: Holt.

Johnson, J. S., & Newport, E. L. (1989). Critical period effects in second language learning: The influence of maturational state on the acquisition of English as a second language. *Cognitive Psychology, 21*(1), 60–99.

Johnson, M. (1987). *The body in the mind.* Chicago: University of Chicago Press.

Johnstone, B. (2000). *Qualitative methods in sociolinguistics.* New York: Oxford University Press.

Kasper, G., & Blum-Kulka, S. (Eds.). (1993). *Interlanguage pragmatics.* Oxford: Oxford University Press.

Kasper, G., & Rose, K. (2001). *Pragmatics and language teaching.* Cambridge, UK: Cambridge University Press.

Keenan, E. L., & Comrie, B. (1977). Noun phrase accessibility and universal grammar. *Linguistic Inquiry, 8*, 63–99.

Kelly, L. (1969). *Twenty-five centuries of language teaching.* Rowley, MA: Newbury House.

Kintsch, W. (1988). The role of knowledge in discourse processing: A construction-integration model. *Psychological Review, 95,* 163–182.

Kovac, C., & Adamson, H. D. (1981). Variation theory and first language acquisition. In D. Sankoff & H. Cedergren (Eds.), *Variation omnibus* (pp. 403–410). Carbondale, IL: Linguistic Research.

Kramer, P. (2001). *Frisian course* [On-line]. Available: http://mitglied.lycos.de/seelt/ kurs.htm. (January 15, 2001).

Krashen, S. (1981). *Second language acquisition and second language learning.* Oxford, UK: Pergamon.

Krashen, S. (1996). *Under attack: The case against bilingual education.* Culver City, CA: Language Education Associates.

Krashen, S. (1999). *Three arguments against whole language and why they are wrong.* Portsmouth, NH: Heinemann.

Krashen, S., & Biber, D. (1988). *On course: Bilingual education's successes in California.* Sacramento, CA: California Association for Bilingual Education.

Krashen, S., & Terrell, T. (1983). *The natural approach: Language acquisition in the classroom.* Oxford, UK: Pergamon.

Kuhn, T. (1973). *The structure of scientific revolutions* (2nd ed.). Chicago: Chicago University Press.

Kuhn, T. (1977). *The essential tension.* Chicago: University of Chicago Press.

Labov, W. (1972a). Is the Black English vernacular a separate system? In W. Labov (Ed.), *Language in the inner city: Studies in the Black English vernacular* (pp. 36–64). Philadelphia: University of Pennsylvania Press.

Labov, W. (1972b). *Language in the inner city: Studies in the Black English vernacular.* Philadelphia: University of Pennsylvania Press.

Labov, W. (1972c). *Sociolinguistic patterns.* Philadelphia: University of Pennsylvania Press.

Labov, W. (1978). *The study of nonstandard English.* Champaign, IL: National Council of Teachers of English.

Labov, W. (1994). *Principles of linguistic change: Vol. 1. Internal factors.* Oxford, UK: Blackwell.

Laffey, J. L., & Shuy, R. (1973). *Language differences: Do they interfere?* Newark, DE: International Reading Association.

Lakoff, G. (1987). *Women, fire, and dangerous things: What categories reveal about the mind.* Chicago: University of Chicago Press.

Lakoff, G. (1987). *Women, fire, and dangerous things.* Chicago: University of Chicago Press.

Lakoff, R. T. (2000). *The language war.* Berkeley, CA: University of California Press.

Lantolf, J., & Appel, G. (1994). *Vygotskian approaches to second language research.* Norwood, NJ: Ablex.

Laponce, J. A. (1992). Reducing the tensions resulting from language contacts: Personal or territorial solutions? In D. Bonin (Ed.), *Reconciliation? The language issue in Canada in the 1990* (pp. 125–132). Kingston, Ontario: Queens University Press.

Larsen-Freeman, D. (2000). *Techniques and principles in language teaching* (2nd ed.). New York: Oxford University Press.

Leaverton, L. (1973). Dialectal readers: Rational, use and value. In J. Laffey & R. Shuy (Eds.), *Language differences: Do they interfere?* (pp. 114–126). Newark, DE: International Reading Association.

Lemberger, N. (1997). *Bilingual education: Teachers' narratives.* Mahwah, NJ: Lawrence Erlbaum Associates.

Lewis, O. (1966). *La vida: A Puerto Rican family in the culture of poverty—San Juan and New York.* New York: Random House.

Linguistics Society of America. (1997). Linguistics Society of America Resolution on Ebonics. In T. Perry & L. Delpit (Eds.), *The real Ebonics debate* (pp. 160–161). Boston: Beacon Press.

Long, M. (1990). The least a second language acquisition theory needs to explain. *TESOL Quarterly, 24,* 251–285.

Luria, A. (1976). *Cognitive development.* Cambridge, MA: Harvard University Press.

Macaulay, T. B. (1972). Minute on Indian education. In J. Clive & T. Pinney (Eds.), *Thomas Babington Macaulay: Selected writings* (pp. 73–84). Chicago: University of Chicago Press. (Original work published 1835)

Masgoret, A., Bernaus, M., & Gardner, R. C. (2000). A study of cross-cultural adaptation by English-speaking sojourners in Spain. *Foreign Language Annals, 33,* 548–558.

Mason, M. K. (1942). Learning to speak after six and one-half years. *Journal of Speech Disorders, 7,* 295–304.

McCrum, R., Cran, W., & MacNeil, R. (1986). *The story of English.* New York: Viking.

McDaniel, D., McKee, C., & Cairns, H. S. (1996). *Methods for assessing children's syntax.* Cambridge, MA: MIT Press.

McLaughlin, B. (1980). Theory and research in second language learning: An emerging paradigm. *Language Learning, 30,* 331–350.

McLaughlin, B. (1987). *Theories of second language learning.* London: Edward Arnold.

McNeill, D. (1966). Developmental psycholinguistics. In F. Smith & G. A. Miller (Eds.), *The genesis of language: A psycholinguistic approach* (pp. 15–84). Cambridge, MA: MIT Press.

McWhorter, J. (1998). *Word on the street: Debunking the myth of a "pure" Standard English.* Cambridge, MA: Perseus.

Mehan, H. (1991). *Sociological foundations supporting the study of cultural diversity.* Report No. R117G10022. Santa Cruz, CA and Washington, DC: National Center for Research on Cultural Diversity and Second Language Learning.

Mitchell, R., & Myles, F. (1998). *Second language learning theories.* New York: Arnold.

Moll, L. (1990). *Vygotsky and education.* Cambridge: Cambridge University Press.

Moll, L., & Greenberg, J. B. (1990). Creating zones of possibilities. In L. Moll (Ed.), *Vygotsky and education* (pp. 319–348). Cambridge, UK: Cambridge University Press.

Murphy, M. F. (1979). *The vicar of Christ.* Toronto, Ontario: Random House.

National Research Council. (1998). *Preventing reading difficulties in young children.* Washington, DC: National Academy Press.

Newman, F., & Holzman, L. (1993). *Lev Vygotsky: Revolutionary scientist.* London: Routledge.

Nolan, P. S. (1972). Reading nonstandard dialect materials: A study of grades two and four. *Child Development, 43,* 1092–1097.

Nunan, D. (1992). *Research methods in language learning.* Cambridge, UK: Cambridge University Press.

Oakland School Board. (1996). Resolution of the Board of Education adopting the report and recommendations of the African-American Task Force. In T. Perry & L. Delpit (Eds.), *The real Ebonics debate* (pp. 143–144). Boston: Beacon Press.

O'Brien, T. C. (1999). Parrot math. *Phi Delta Kappan, 30*(6), 444–450.

O'Reilly, B. (2000). The parents factor. In B. O'Reilly, *The O'Reilly Factor: The good, bad and completely ridiculous in American life* (pp. 85–96). New York: Broadway Books.

Osherson, D., & Smith, E. (1982). Gradedness and conceptual combination. *Cognition, 27,* 422–452.

Palermo, D. (1978). *Psychology of language.* Glenview, IL: Scott, Foresman.

Panofsky, C. P., John-Steiner, V., & Blackwell, P. J. (1990). The development of scientific concepts and discourse. In L. Moll (Ed.), *Vygotsky and education* (pp. 251–267). Cambridge, UK: Cambridge University Press.

Patton, M. (1990). *Qualitative evaluation and research methods.* Beverly Hills, CA: Sage.

Paulston, C. B. (1980). *Bilingual education: Theory and research.* Rowley, MA: Newbury House.

Paulston, C. B. (1994). *Linguistic minorities in multilingual settings.* Amsterdam: John Benjamins.

Paulston, C. B., & Bruder, M. N. (1976). *Teaching English as a second language: Techniques and procedures.* Cambridge, MA: Winthrop.

Pavesi, M. (1984). The acquisition of relative clauses in a formal and an informal setting: Further evidence in support of the markedness hypothesis. In D. Singleton & D. Little (Eds.), *Language learning in formal and informal contexts* (pp. 151–153). Dublin: IRAAL.

Pennycook, A. (1994). *The cultural politics of English as an international language.* London: Longman.

Pennycook, A. (1998). *English and the discourses of colonialism.* New York: Routledge.

Perfetti, C. A., Britt, M. A., & Georgi, M. C. (1995). *Text-based learning and reasoning: Studies in history.* Hillsdale, NJ: Lawrence Erlbaum Associates.

Piaget, J. (1972). *The child and reality.* New York: Wiley.

Pinker, S. (1994). *The language instinct: How the mind creates language.* New York: Harper.

Porter, R. P. (1990). *Forked tongue: The politics of bilingual education.* New York: Basic Books.

Preston, D. (1989). *Sociolinguistics and second language acquisition.* Oxford: Blackwell.

Preston, D. (1996). Variationist perspectives on second language acquisition. In R. Bayley & D. Preston (Eds.), *Second language acquisition and linguistic variation* (pp. 1–95). Amsterdam: John Benjamins.

Prideaux, G. D., & Baker, W. J. (1986). *Strategies and structure: The processing of relative clauses.* Philadelphia: John Benjamins.

Quan, J. (1996). [Interview]. Cited in Lakoff, R. (2000). *The language war* (p. 234). Berkeley: University of California Press.

Ravitch, D. (2000). *Left back.* New York: Simon & Schuster.

Richards, J. C., & Rodgers, T. S. (2001). *Approaches and methods in language teaching.* Cambridge, UK: Cambridge University Press.

Richards, K. (2003). *Qualitative inquiry in TESOL.* New York: Palgrave Macmillan.

Rickford, A. E. (1999). *I can fly.* Lanham, MD: University Press of America.

Rickford, A. E., & Rickford, J. R. (1995). Dialect readers revisited. *Linguistics and Education, 7,* 107–128.

Rodriguez, R. (1982). *Hunger of memory: The education of Richard Rodriguez.* Boston: Godine.

Rodriguez, R. (1992). The romantic trap of bilingual education. In J. Crawford (Ed.), *Language loyalties: A source book on the official English controversy* (pp. 351–354). Chicago: University of Chicago Press.

Romaine, S. (1994). *Language in society: An introduction to sociolinguistics.* Oxford, UK: Oxford University Press.

Rorty, R. (1979). *Philosophy and the mirror of nature.* Princeton, NJ: Princeton University Press.

Rorty, R. (1989). *Contingency, irony, and solidarity.* Cambridge, UK: Cambridge University Press.

Rosier, P., & Holm, W. (1980). *The Rock Point experience: A longitudinal study of a Navajo school program.* (Bilingual Education Series No. 8). Washington, DC: Center for Applied Linguistics.

Roskos, K. (1999). Play as story. In D. Nestor & W. Linek (Eds.), *Practical classroom applications of language experience* (pp. 42–49). Boston: Allyn & Bacon.

Rossell, C. H., & Baker, K. A. (1996). The educational effectiveness of bilingual education. *Research in the Teaching of English, 30,* 7–74.

Rumelhardt, D. E. (1975). Notes on a schema for stories. In D. G. Bobrow & A. Colling (Eds.), *Representation and understanding: Studies in cognitive science* (pp. 211–236). New York: Academic Press.

Said, E. W. (1979). *Orientalism.* New York: Vintage.

Sanguinetti, E. (1971). *McBee's Station.* New York: Holt, Rinehart & Winston.

Saravia-Shore, M., & Arvizu, S. F. (1992). *Cross-cultural literacy: Ethnography of communication in multiethnic classrooms.* New York: Garland.

Saunders, D. (1996, January 12). Why kids can't read in California. *San Francisco Chronicle,* p. A-13.

Saville-Troike, M. (2003). *The ethnography of communication: An introduction* (3rd ed.). Malden, MA: Blackwell.

Schauber, H. (1995). The second language component of primary French immersion programs in Montreal, Quebec, Canada. *Bilingual Research Journal, 19*(3–4), 483–495.

Schumann, J. (1978). *The pidginization hypothesis.* Rowley, MA: Newbury House.

Selinker, L., & Douglas, D. (1989). Research methodology in contextually based second language research. *Second Language Research, 5*, 93–126.

Shaklee, M. (1980). The rise of standard English. In T. Shopen & J. M. Williams (Eds.), *Standards and dialects in English* (pp. 33–62). Cambridge, MA: Winthrop.

Shopen, T., & Williams, J. M. (1980). *Standards and dialects in English.* Cambridge, MA: Winthrop.

Simon, J. (1983). Why good English is good for you. In G. Goshgarian (Ed.), *Exploring Language.* Boston: Little, Brown.

Simpkin, G., & Simpkin, C. (1991). Cross-cultural approach to curriculum development. In G. Smitherman (Ed.), *Black English and the education of Black children and youth: Proceedings of the National Invitational Symposium on the King Decision.* Detroit, MI: Center for Black Studies, Wayne State University.

Skinner, B. F. (1948). *Walden two.* London: Collier Macmillan.

Skinner, B. F. (1957). *Verbal behavior.* New York: Appleton-Century-Crofts.

Slobin, D. (1977). Language change in childhood and in history. In J. McNamara (Ed.), *Language learning and thought* (pp. 67–89). New York: Academic Press.

Smith, E., & Medin, D. (1981). *Categories and concepts.* Cambridge, MA: Harvard University Press.

Smith, F. (1994). *Understanding reading* (5th ed.). Hillsdale, NJ: Lawrence Erlbaum Associates.

Smitherman, G. (1985). "It bees dat way sometime": Sounds and structure of present-day Black English. In V. P. Clark, P. A. Eschholz, & A. F. Rosa (Eds.), *Language* (pp. 552–571). New York: St. Martin's Press.

Snow, C., & Brinton, D. (Ed.). (1997). *The content based classroom: Perspectives on integrating language and content.* White Plains, NY: Longman.

Spindler, G., & Spindler, L. (1987). *Interpretive ethnography of education: At home and abroad.* Hillsdale, NJ: Lawrence Erlbaum Associates.

Stein, C. B. (1986). *Sink or swim: The politics of bilingual education.* New York: Praeger.

Study finds more English learners in schools. (2001, August 4). *Arizona Daily Star*, p. 8.

Swain, M., & Lapkin, S. (1989). Canadian immersion and adult second language teaching: What's the connection? *Modern Language Journal, 73*(2), 150–159.

Taylor, H. (1989). *Standard English, Black English and bidialectalism.* New York: Lang.

Tharp, R., & Gallimore, R. (1988). *Rousing minds to life: Teaching, learning and schooling in social context.* Cambridge, UK: Cambridge University Press.

Tharp, R., & Gallimore, R. (1990). Teaching, schooling, and literate discourse. In L. Moll (Ed.), *Vygotsky and education* (pp. 175–205). Cambridge, UK: Cambridge University Press.

Thomas, W., & Collier, V. (1997). *School effectiveness for language minority students.* Washington DC: NCBE.

Trabasso, T., Secco, T., & van den Broek, P. (1984). Causal cohesion and story coherence. In H. Handl, N. L. Stein, & T. Trabasso (Eds.), *Learning and comprehension of text* (pp. 83–111). Hillsdale, NJ: Lawrence Erlbaum Associates.

Traugott, E. C., & Pratt, M. L. (1980). *Linguistics for students of literature.* New York: Harcourt Brace Jovanovich.

Troike, R., & Park, M.-R. (2001). The challenge of elementary school English education in Korea: Insights from the North American bilingual experience. *The Journal of English Language Teaching, 13*(1), 79–106.

Trudgill, P. (1984). *Language in the British Isles.* Cambridge, UK: Cambridge University Press.

T.S.W. (1970). Hints on pronunciation for foreigners. In D. MacKay (Ed.), *A flock of words* (pp. 73–76). New York: Harcourt.

Turner, M. (1991). *Reading minds: The study of English in the age of cognitive science.* Princeton, NJ: Princeton University Press.

Tyler, A. (1995). The co-construction of cross-cultural miscommunication: Conflicts in perception, negotiation and enactment of participant role and status. *Studies in Second Language Acquisition, 17,* 129–152.

Valdés, G. (2001). *Learning and not learning English: Latino students in American schools.* New York: Teachers College Press.

van Lier, L. (1988). *The classroom and the language learner: Ethnography and second-language classroom research.* New York: Longman.

Vasquez, O., Pease-Alvarez, L., & Shannon, S. (1994). *Pushing boundaries: Language and culture in a Mexicano community.* Cambridge, UK: Cambridge University Press.

Vorih, L., & Rosier, P. (1978). Rock Point Community School: An example of a Navajo-English bilingual elementary school program. *TESOL Quarterly, 12,* 263–271.

Vygotsky, L. (1986). *Thought and language.* Cambridge, MA: MIT Press.

Vygotsky, L. S. (1978). *Mind in society.* Cambridge, MA: Harvard University Press.

Vygotsky, L. S. (1987). *The collected works of L. S. Vygotsky* (Vol. 1). New York: Plenum.

Wardhaugh, R. (1992). *An introduction to sociolinguistics* (2nd ed.). Oxford, UK: Blackwell.

Wells, G. (1986). *The meaning makers: Children learning language and using language to learn.* Portsmouth, NH: Heinemann.

Wertsch, J. (1985). *Vygotsky and the social formation of mind.* Cambridge, MA: Harvard University Press.

Wertsch, J. P., Minick, N., & Arns, B. (1984). The creation of context in joint problem solving. In B. Rogoff & J. Lave (Eds.), *Everyday cognition: Its development in social contexts* (pp. 151–171). Cambridge, MA: Harvard University Press.

Wertsch, J. P., Rio, P. del, & Alvarez, A. (1995). *Sociocultural studies of mind.* New York: Cambridge University Press.

Wildner-Bassett, M. (1984). *Improving pragmatic aspects of learners' interlanguage.* Tubingen, Germany: Narr.

Will, G. F. (1997). The "growth model" and the growth of illiteracy. In G. F. Will (Ed.), *Conservatism and America's fabric* (pp. 138–140). New York: Scribner.

Williams, G. (1992). *Sociolinguistics.* London: Routledge.

Willig, A. (1985). A meta-analysis of selected studies on the effectiveness of bilingual education. *Review of Educational Research, 57,* 363–376.

Wolfram, W., & Fasold, R. (1974). *The study of social dialects in American English.* Englewood Cliffs, NJ: Prentice-Hall.

Wood, D., Bruner, J., & Ross, G. (1976). The role of tutoring in problem solving. *Journal of Child Psychology and Psychiatry, 17,* 89–100.

Yin, R. K. (1984). *Case studies research: Design and methods.* Beverly Hills, CA: Sage.

Zamel, V., & Spack, R. (Eds.). (2002). *Enriching ESOL pedagogy: Readings and activities for engagement, reflection, and inquiry.* Mahwah, NJ: Lawrence Erlbaum Associates.

Index